Spanish Cinema

Inside Film Series

Forthcoming Titles

Contemporary US Cinema	Dr Michael Allen
Film Noir	Dr Andrew Spicer
French Cinema	Lucy Mazdon
Documentary	Alan Marcus
The Horror Film	Dr Peter Hutchings
The Western	David Lusted
Russian Cinema	Dr David Gillespie
Shakespeare on Film	Dr Judith Buchanan
Women and Film	Pamela Church Gibson
Italian Cinema	Dr Mary Wood

More information can be found at:
www.booksites.net/mclean

SPANISH CINEMA

Rob Stone

Longman

An imprint of **Pearson Education**

Harlow, England · London · New York · Reading, Massachusetts · San Francisco
Toronto · Don Mills, Ontario · Sydney · Tokyo · Singapore · Hong Kong · Seoul
Taipei · Cape Town · Madrid · Mexico City · Amsterdam · Munich · Paris · Milan

Para Esther, mi estrella.

Pearson Education Limited
Edinburgh Gate
Harlow
Essex CM20 2JE

and Associated Companies throughout the world

Visit us on the World Wide Web at:
www.pearsoneduc.com

First published 2002

ISBN 0582 43715 6

British Library Cataloguing-in-Publication Data
A catalogue record for this book is available from the British Library

Library of Congress Cataloging-in-Publication Data
Stone, Rob.
    Spanish cinema / Rob Stone.
      p. cm. — (Inside film)
    Includes bibliographical references and index.
    ISBN 0-582-43715-6 (alk. paper)
    1. Motion pictures—Spain—History. I. Title. II. Series.

  PN1993.5.S7 S76 2001
  791.46'0946—dc21   2001036715

10 9 8 7 6 5 4 3 2 1
05 04 03 02

Typeset in 10/13pt Giovanni Book by 35
Printed in China

CONTENTS

ACKNOWLEDGEMENTS

Elías Querejeta told me that the privilege of his life was to have worked with excellent friends on something he loved. The writing of this book was a kindred experience for me and I would like to thank friends and colleagues for their interest and support. My deepest gratitude to Esther Santamaría Iglesias, *por haber compartido las películas, las ideas, los viajes y la vida conmigo.*

Many thanks also to Tom Charity, who edited this manuscript, for his generosity, collaboration and endless consideration. I am also very grateful to my editor Alexander Ballinger of the McLean Press for his enthusiasm and guidance.

Gracias a mi gran amigo Fernando Carricajo Garrido *por su generosidad.*

Thanks also to Jesús Robles and María Silveyro of Madrid's *Ocho y medio* bookstore, Alfredo Santamaría *y* Caridad Iglesias, Carmen Stone, Eric Thau, Robert Havard, Gwynne Edwards and Paul Cooke for all their assistance and encouragement. *Gracias también a* Ana Blázquez Blanco (Aiete/Ariane Films), Alicia Potes (Filmoteca Español), Peio Aldazabal and M. Carmen Ausans (Filmoteca Vasca), Juan Luis Buñuel, Inmaculada Rodríguez (Juan Lebrón Producciones), Paz Sufrategui (El Deseo), Germán Sela (Sogepaq), Pedro Costa, Arturo Marcos, Alfonso Buhigas, and Eva Garrido (Fernando Colomo P.C.).

Finally, I am immensely grateful to Carlos Saura, Imanol Uribe and Elías Querejeta for their time, generosity and good will.

Unless otherwise stated, all translations of Spanish texts and dialogue are the author's own.

LIST OF PHOTOGRAPHS

Leaving the church
1. *Un chien andalou* (Luis Buñuel, 1925) **p.24**
2. *La verbena de la paloma* (Benito Perojo, 1935) **p.30**
3. Imperio Argentina in *Morena Clara* (Florián Rey, 1935) **p.32**

Under Franco
4. 'We were happy, we had no money'. Fernando Fernán Gómez and Elvira Quintillá in *Esa pareja feliz* (Luis García Berlanga and Juan Antonio Bardem, 1951) **p.42**
5. 'He's still alive . . .'. Lucía Bosé and Alberto Closas in *Muerte de un ciclista* (Juan Antonio Bardem, 1955) **p.48**
6. Fernando Rey and Silvia Pinal in *Viridiana* (Luis Buñuel, 1961) **p.53**

Another reality
7. Emilio Gutiérrez Caba, Alfredo Mayo and José María Prada in *La caza* (Carlos Saura, 1965) **p.65**
8. Merche Esmeralda dances a guajira in *Flamenco* (Carlos Saura, 1995) **p.81**

Spirits and secrets
9. 'Soy Ana'. Ana Torrent in *El espíritu de la colmena* (Víctor Erice, 1973) **p.93**
10. Icíar Bollaín as Estrella in *El sur* (Víctor Erice, 1983) **p.97**
11. Like mother, like daughter? Ana Torrent and Geraldine Chaplin in *Cría cuervos* (Carlos Saura, 1975) **p.99**
12. Charo López embraces Andoni Erburu as Javi in *Secretos del corazón* (Montxo Armendáriz, 1997) **p.107**

Over Franco
13. Victoria Abril as the pre-op José María in *Cambio de sexo* (Vicente Aranda, 1976) **p.116**
14. Carmen Maura in *Tigres de papel* (Fernando Colomo, 1977) **p.121**
15. Oscar Ladoire surprised by Paula Molina in *Ópera prima* (Fernando Trueba, 1980) **p.124**

We are grateful to the following for permission to reproduce copyright material:

Stills 1 and 6 courtesy of Juan Luis Buñuel; 2 and 3 courtesy of Alfonso Buhigas, CIFESA; 4 courtesy of Arturo Marcos, Marte Films; 7, 9, 10, 11 and 17 courtesy of Elías Querejeta P.C.; 8 courtesy of Juan Lebrón Producciones, S.A.; 12, 18, 19 and 26 courtesy of Aiete-Ariane Films, S.A.; 14 and 15 courtesy of Fernando Colomo, P.C.; 16, 24 and 27 courtesy of El Deseo, S.A.; 20, 21, 22, 23 and Cover courtesy of Sogecine; 25 courtesy of Pedro Costa, P.C.

Whilst every effort has been made to trace the owners of copyright material, in a few cases this has proved impossible and we take this opportunity to offer our apologies to any copyright holders whose rights we may have unwittingly infringed.

CHAPTER ONE

By way of Elías Querejeta

An overview of Spanish cinema

If there is a common thread through Spanish cinema, and so too this book, its name is Elías Querejeta. Born October 1934 in Hernani, in the Basque province of Guipuzcoa, Querejeta is the producer and sometime screenwriter whose name links the emergence of film as a political medium in the Basque Country with the cinema of resistance under Franco. His is the first credit on the most important films of Carlos Saura, Víctor Erice, Jaime Chávarri, Mañuel Gutiérrez Aragón, Ricardo Franco, Montxo Armendáriz and many others. He was a player in the New Spanish Cinema of the 1960s, a mover behind key films of the transition and a shaker of the increasingly independent nature of contemporary Spanish cinema. Thus, in a warm office on a freezing December evening, Querejeta listened with mock irritation to the outline of this book and surmised that the intent of its author was to work out 'what the hell I'm doing in this world'.[1] His first response was to call the Civil Guard, who were 'to come immediately and chain up this nuisance'. But then he put down the phone – 'You don't mind me making jokes do you?' – and, wine glass in hand, cigarettes at the ready, began to tell his story.

'I have an idyllic vision of the Basque Country,' he says, 'because my childhood was very happy, always. Except for school, which was terrible. It was the only horror that I've ever lived in my life.' An infant during the Spanish Civil War, Querejeta grew up in one of the Basque provinces that had been declared traitors to the crusade of General Franco by the decree of November 1937. The Spain he lived in was subject to the fascist dictatorship that had been established following the defeat of Republican forces in the Spanish Civil War (1936–9). This regime was sanctioned by the Catholic Church and Querejeta's education was typical of the repressive pedagogy that marked a number of Spain's greatest artists, writers and film-makers both before and after the Civil War. 'Maybe I exaggerate a little,' he reflects, 'but in the middle of that Hernani that I knew, with my friends and the wild games we played, going to school split me right down the middle.' Did it destroy him? 'No. Because I resisted. I wouldn't let them destroy me. But it's the worst: a useless, repressive education.' To combat this lack, Querejeta set about his own education at home, where his father, a nationalist, Carlist and Catholic, kept a splendid library and allowed his children to enter and read when they were very young. 'I was just a kid,' he recalls, 'not too aware of the repression, but very aware of the political happenings. I could talk to my father about anything. We kids had permission to talk about anything, to read anything.'

Even so, free speech was to some extent curtailed because the various regional languages of Spain had been outlawed by a dictatorship determined to centralise all government and homogenise all culture. The Basque language of Euskera was declared illegal and Querejeta's formal education was therefore in Castilian Spanish, though Euskera still marks his memories of family life. 'We never spoke Euskera at home, but my mother sang marvellously in Euskera. There was also a problem because the name of our house was in Euskera – Villa Gurutze – meaning cross or crossroads. And one day the Civil Guard came to tell us to take down the name of the house. My father was president of the Guipuzcoan Council (*diputación*) and didn't let it happen. It was the only home to keep its name in Euskera'.[2]

Circles within circles: Querejeta's childhood home is a place full of games and books and songs in a beautiful, forbidden language, surrounded by a country in the grip of a fascist dictatorship where culture, education and even language were controlled. This home is a refuge and a memory that not even the worst years of oppression and deprivation brought on by the Francoist regime can spoil. It is a tangible ideal perhaps, one that energised Querejeta's future as a producer and screenwriter. Inevitably as he grew up the experience of this timeless place was replaced by a sense of lost innocence and an awareness of rural hardship and injustice under the dictatorship, two themes that dominate in most of the films with which he is associated, including *La caza* (The Hunt, 1965), *El espíritu de la colmena* (The Spirit of the Beehive, 1973), *La prima Angélica* (Cousin Angelica, 1973), *Cría cuervos* (Raise Ravens, 1975), *Pascual Duarte* (1975), *A un dios desconocido* (To an Unknown God, 1977), *Dulces horas* (Tender Hours, 1982), *El sur* (The South, 1983), *Tasio* (1984), *27 horas* (27 Hours, 1986), *Historias del Kronen* (Stories from the Kronen, 1995), *Familia* (Family, 1996), *Barrio* (1998) and *La espalda del mundo* (The Back of the World, 2000).

An enthusiastic home-scholar, Querejeta devoured novels and books on chemistry, but found the Spain beyond his front door a disappointment, the militarist regime having conspired with the Catholic Church to forestall any evolution in the country's industry and educational system that had been pending since the end of the nineteenth century. Back then, the filmshow had arrived in Spain offering portals to progress in other countries and glimpses of better lives; but such incentives to social disquiet had been quickly suppressed by Church-backed censorship, while fledgling film companies suffered their share of the harsh indifference that successive governments showed to most manufacturing industries. Pre-Civil War, Spanish cinema had trundled along in fits and starts and sometimes stopped altogether. There had been occasional sparks from the surrealist provocation of Luis Buñuel and the spirited artistry of such directors as Benito Perojo and Florián Rey, whose all-singing, all-dancing wife Imperio Argentina was more than a star: she was a phenomenon. But the Civil War put paid to dissidence and the cinema was now little more than a medium for propaganda, whether it was the imported kind from Germany and Italy or the home-grown variety of folkloric musicals and military epics that celebrated a God-fearing nation of loyal servants to the intertwined precepts of Catholicism and fascism. For six-year old Querejeta, however, his first experience of the cinema came from an older, more wonderful time:

We were in the garden playing at jumping off the swing. We'd put lines on the ground to show who'd jumped the furthest. My father travelled a lot and one day he came home carrying something on his shoulder. He called us and we followed him up to the fourth floor, to our games room. And he put a sheet on the wall and connected something and there was Chaplin.

The gift was a Pathé baby projector that fascinated the young Querejeta and would, in time, distract or perhaps just divert his talent from a promising career with explosives. 'I loved chemistry,' he recalls, 'we did lots of experiments and explosions. My father had books on chemistry and one of them had lots of formulas for explosives. So we experimented and put explosives on the tram rails. One day we increased the amounts, the tram came, there was the most amazing explosion and the tram glowed blue. The driver ran after us screaming, "It was the Querejetas!".' Querejeta claims it was his last experiment, while a growing passion for the cinema led him to an enduring friendship with Antxon Eceiza, with whom he started writing scripts and, aged just seventeen, co-founded the *cine-club* of San Sebastian. At a time when all cultural and most social gatherings in the Basque Country were regulated and often policed, the *cine-clubs* were film societies that allowed for the union of similar-minded folk with a common interest in film. As Querejeta describes: 'We had lots of difficulties because the Francoist censor was atrocious. But the *cine-clubs* had ways of getting films that didn't go through the censor, very carefully mind, and we organised meetings that were more political than filmic. It was an excuse.'

Cine-clubs had served a similar function since before the Civil War, when Luis Buñuel had collaborated on the running of the *Cine-club español* in

Madrid's *Residencia de Estudiantes* that provided a forum for many notable artists and writers of his generation (including Federico García Lorca, Rafael Alberti and Salvador Dalí) to savour and debate the advances and aesthetics of the developing art form. Films chosen by Buñuel and shipped to Madrid from Paris had inspired many of the Spanish avant-garde into appropriating the cinematic aesthetic for their poetry, painting and plays. Surrealism, for example, so naked and proud in Buñuel and Dalí's *Un chien andalou* (An Andalusian Dog, 1928) prompted writers and artists to experiment with philosophy and form in a way that would take them away from inscribed Spanish values towards more instinctive ideas of identity that were provocative and unavoidably profane. Similarly, the reclaimed tradition of the film society created a breeding ground for political dissidence in the Basque Country at a time when unions and most universities were banned, though the organisers, who aspired to a partisan selection of films (Soviet or Weimar films, for example), were not always commensurate with the political leanings of their members. 'Three years later we thought it was too right wing,' says Querejeta of the San Sebastian film society, 'so we formed another – *el cine-club Cantábrico* – which we hoped was more left wing.' Querejeta was smitten with the films of Carl Theodor Dreyer, whose *Ordet* (The Word, 1954), a story of a member of the Danish resistance who is murdered by the Nazis that becomes a meditation on life and faith, possesses many of the qualities that are evident in the films produced and written by Querejeta: a thematic contrast of serenity with brutality, and an aesthetic fusion of austerity and precision. 'Dreyer,' says Querejeta, 'showed us how to contemplate reality.'

This enthusiasm for the cinema caused Querejeta to vacillate about the question of a career. Universities in the traitorous provinces of Spain had been closed down and there was little option for those young Basques who wished to remain in the Basque Country to study anything but practical sciences. Querejeta was close to leaving Spain altogether to study in Paris or London, but for family reasons he stayed in San Sebastian and went to university where he resumed his passion for chemistry. He also played for Real Sociedad, the local football team, and earned himself the abiding nickname *mono-gol* (mono-goal) for his single, fabulous, politically portentous placing of the ball in the back of Real Madrid's net. 'It's true,' he chuckles, 'the whole stadium filled with white handkerchiefs.' Nevertheless, his enthusiasm for football never turned to passion, while his university studies also came to nought. 'I took my exams, but the professor said "Querejeta, you're copying!" I stood up and said, "No, that's not true." He answered back, "You're lying." I said, "The only one who's lying here is you." And I was expelled.' Subsequently he left the Basque Country for Madrid, following Antxon Eceiza who had enrolled in Madrid's Official Film School (Escuela Oficial de Cine, EOC) in 1957.

Querejeta was twenty-four and considered himself too old to study film, but he shared Eceiza's notes and they resumed their collaboration on scripts.

The mid-1950s was an exciting time for film-makers. Led by the example and rhetoric of Juan Antonio Bardem, they had challenged the dominion of the state over independent film-makers and the censor's final word on their alternative views on Spain. Bardem had been one of the first to enrol in the film school that was established in 1947 as part of the Francoist regime's response to economic and political pressure from abroad to soften its fascism and invest in its own culture and industry. Working with Berlanga and UNINCI, Bardem had spearheaded an attempt to inject a conscience and relevance into Spanish cinema by imitating the aesthetic of the Italian neo-realist movement in films that dealt with ordinary people and pressing, social themes. *Esa pareja feliz* (That Happy Couple, 1951) and *Bienvenido Mister Marshall* (Welcome Mister Marshall, 1952) were comedies that poked fun at the pretentions of a society that was, in truth, threadbare and repressive, while celebrating the values of solidarity and class consciousness which had been largely eradicated by the regime. In 1955 Bardem had actually said so in the Salamanca Congress that was organised by the film society of the University of Salamanca. A member of the illegal and clandestine Communist Party, he had followed up a speech in which he attacked the condition of Spanish cinema with a screening of his *Muerte de un ciclista* (Death of a Cyclist, 1955), an example of cinema with a social conscience and a pointedly politicised aesthetic.

'UNINCI was a progressive production company,' avers Querejeta, 'with a lot of connections with the Communist Party, and when I arrived in Madrid it was my first contact.' So was it films or politics first?

Films first. I've never made political cinema. Quite another thing is that there have been political considerations about the films that I've produced. It's a label that I don't like and it's certainly not my intention. To reduce films, novels or books to this is very inconvenient. It's limiting.

Nevertheless, Querejeta's reputation as a political film-maker was immediate and has endured, largely thanks to his long history of battles with Franco's board of film censors that began with the very first short films he wrote and directed in collaboration with Eceiza and Laponia Films, a production company whose major shareholders were all friends and members of the Real Sociedad football team. *A través de San Sebastián* (By Way of San Sebastian, 1960) was a philosophical montage that *Cahiers du cinema* compared to Sergei Eisenstein's *Battleship Potemkin* (1925), but 'because it was so strange [the censor] left it alone,' remembers Querejeta. Not so *A través del fútbol* (By Way of Football, 1961), an 11-minute feature that suffered the excision of a whole four minutes.

A través del fútbol was an impressionist account of Spanish history through the metaphor of football. It included one shot of a goalkeeper lying in the mud like a downed soldier that was accompanied by the voiceover: 'In the year 1936 the typical national competitions were suspended for a period of three years.' This obscure reference to the Spanish Civil War was also accompanied by music from a popular song of the Republican and Communist armies: 'If you want to write to me / you know where you can reach me / On the front line of Gandesa / in the first line of fire'.[3]

'The censor understood it,' recalls Querejeta with begrudging admiration, 'and destroyed it.' These were the years following the scandal of Luis Buñuel's *Viridiana* (1961) and it was the first and most important lesson for Querejeta, that to evade the censor he would have to develop techniques of deceit and subterfuge which would be reflected in the complex, metaphorical nature of many of the films he produced with such collaborative directors as Carlos Saura and Víctor Erice. 'I had a certain ability,' he explains,

> *I always used* usted *[the formal address] with everyone and demanded that everyone used* usted *with me. I was just a kid, but it marked the distances. And I deceived the censor, fundamentally, by telling them the truth. That's how I did it, because they never believed me.*

Querejeta established the production company which bears his name in 1963, but problems persisted and many film projects were derailed, including one he wrote with Bardem that was due to be filmed in San Sebastian when production was stopped by the censor.

More than a footballer, Querejeta resembles a flyweight boxer. Slight and unassuming, he surely packs a powerful punch, though he laughs when asked about the extent of his authority as producer: 'Do I look like a boss to you?' Yet even this physical nature attests to his tendency to be contrary. The popular notion of the film producer in Spain during the 1960s was personified by Samuel Bronston, a Russian Jew, who graduated from making documentaries for the Vatican to producing blockbusters shot in Spain that exploited various loopholes in the arrangements for international financing and the obsequiousness of the dollar-hungry Spanish government to make a virtue of their extravagance. *King of Kings* (1961) and *El Cid* (1961) were shot on purpose-built studios and sets and, in their hagiography of Francoist idols, they received the wholehearted support of a regime that saw in them the reclaimed ideals of the jingoistic cinema of the 1940s and 1950s.[4]

Querejeta, meanwhile, was working at the opposite end of the film-making scale, producing films with limited financing and distribution that were directed by Antxon Eceiza: *El próximo otoño* (Next Autumn, 1963), *De cuerpo presente* (1965) and *Último encuentro* (Last Meeting, 1966).[5] These first incursions into the territory of Francoist cinema were the precursors of the dissident, critical and metaphorical films that would characterise the so-called New Spanish Cinema, but for Querejeta they were simply part of a learning process that allowed him to get to know his censor.

Even after the legislation of 1964 that established a new classification of *interés especial* (special interest) for films that presented an alternative view of Spanish society to that which was propagated in the Francoist films of *interés nacional* (national interest), the system of film censorship continued to oblige film-makers to submit their scripts for revision or a shooting permit would not be granted. Querejeta, however, devised a counter-system of producing two versions of the script:

> *If I hadn't actually collaborated on the script, I calculated where the censor was going to get upset and revised it and that's the one I submitted. Then I filmed the real script. So if I got the script through the censor, the film would get made. It made no difference what the censor said because it was much more difficult for them to censor a finished film than it was the script. I put them in the situation: "The film's finished, what can we do?"*

It was an effective method of subversion that Querejeta would perfect by getting his finished films to foreign festivals before they were submitted to the censor, whereby jurors, critics and audiences in Cannes, Berlin, New York and Venice became an essential support mechanism for dissident film-makers in Spain because their acclaim and prizes, which were often awarded in consideration of the film-makers' resistance to the Francoist regime, took films beyond the reach of the Spanish censor. Wasn't it dangerous? 'Without doubt it was dangerous. Without a shadow of a doubt.' Was it a challenge? 'Without a doubt it was a challenge. I felt that I was resisting the regime, but not just by making films, by going to demonstrations. I was a part of everything.'

Although the films produced by Querejeta were wholly collaborative projects, it is apparent that they share a look and a tone that resulted from his particular style of production. Being both budget-conscious and inclined to take risks, Querejeta favoured rehearsals, single takes and direct sound, while also opting to cast unknowns or those actors who were prepared to play against type. Thereafter his determined entering of films in international festivals kept foreign audiences informed of the situation in Spain. At the same time it obliged the Spanish authorities to grin and bear a public taunt that they could only accommodate by pointing to the success of films produced by Querejeta as an example of their tolerance and openness. In Querejeta's own words: 'It was proven that what I could produce could have international repercussions. That's how I got *La caza* [The Hunt, 1965] to

Berlin in 1966. It has international impact and I get more power. More power . . .' For one long moment, he recoils from the memory and shudders: 'More power . . . power is nothing. It's insignificant.'

La caza is a key film in the history of Spanish cinema for a number of reasons, not the least of which is that it constitutes the first of Querejeta's thirteen collaborations in the space of sixteen years with the director Carlos Saura, Spain's leading film-maker under Franco and a beacon of resistance to both fascist and commercial pressures during the years of the dictatorship and the democracy respectively. 'I met Carlos at a screening of *Los golfos* and *A través de San Sebastián* in the university,' remembers Querejeta. *Los golfos* (The Louts, 1959) was Saura's ground-breaking attempt at a realistic portrait of marginalised characters in Madrid and is one of the few Spanish films that Querejeta considers an influence on his own work. 'Later, Carlos called me and turned up at my house with the script for *La caza*. I read it and we argued. We're still arguing. Our last argument was last night on the phone.'

Notwithstanding the types of argument that Querejeta professes to enjoy with all his collaborators, the tandem Querejeta–Saura earned itself an international reputation on the basis of a series of films that employed a complex system of metaphors in their narratives and invited audiences to reflect upon their meaning: *Peppermint frappé* (1967), *Stress es tres, tres* (1967), *La madriguera* (The Warren, 1969), *El jardín de las delicias* (The Garden of Delights, 1969), *Ana y los lobos* (Ana and The Wolves, 1972), *La prima Angélica* (Cousin Angelica, 1973) and *Cría cuervos* (Raise Ravens, 1975). Their success placed them at the forefront of cultural resistance to the dictatorship and gave rise to the oft-disputed classification of New Spanish Cinema. 'I was completely against it,' says Querejeta, 'I'm against the idea of all labels.' More importantly, these films were also the focus for a team of technicians, writers and actors that became the 'Querejeta family'. 'The family business is an old Guipuzcoan tradition,' he remarks,

> *and I come from that tradition. I've always thought of film-making in this way. The possibility of collaboration was important for what I had in mind. It was our survival plan. It wasn't just my risk. The risk was shared between all of us.*[6]

This extended family of friends and collaborators allowed Querejeta to establish his company as an independent production unit that was largely financed by co-production agreements and distribution arrangements with foreign companies. 'I always knew and understood the external system of financing,' he admits, and it was this skill with people and numbers that took him away from directing his own films towards a more natural vocation as a hands-on film producer. 'I've never helped anyone ever,' he avers,

'I've only ever worked with them. Anyway, I think I don't know how to direct. If one day I find the passion to direct inside me, maybe I will. But I've never felt that passion, only for writing. I've more passion for inventing projects, guiding them.'

It is, he agrees, a lucky sort of privilege to have been able to work with friends – *'excelentísimos amigos'* – in a medium that he loves, even if the risk and repercussions could be grave:

At one time the ministry under Sánchez Bella offered me a pact that required me to speak to them even before the formal presentation of the project. They offered it to me three times. I consulted with a few friends and I didn't accept. And for two years I couldn't set foot in the ministry.

This prohibition effectively outlawed all of Querejeta's projects because, being forbidden from contacting the ministry, he was unable to apply or gain any licences for making films in Spain. His punishment coincided with the revoking of the special interest classification in 1969 and a time of increasing oppression. Querejeta took to working on foreign co-productions that included a conflictive experience with Wim Wenders on his 1973 version of *The Scarlet Letter*.[7] Nevertheless, even the worst of times could be ennobled by the best of friends. 'Carlos [Saura] wouldn't say so, but I'm telling you it's true. He didn't accept a single offer of work until my sentence had passed.'

Víctor Erice was another such friend whom Querejeta had known since his days in the Basque Country. Erice studied alongside Antxon Eceiza and was one of three recent graduates that Querejeta contracted to make the compilation film *Los desafíos* (The Challenges, 1968) when two Americans gave him a load of dollars to produce a film in which they could star.[8] Shortly afterwards Erice and Querejeta discovered in conversation that they both adored the myth of Frankenstein and were equally inspired by a still from James Whale's 1931 film version with Boris Karloff as the monster to transpose the themes of man-made horrors and lost innocence into a tale of life in Spain under the dictatorship that became *El espíritu de la colmena* (1973). Made during the final years of the dictatorship, *El espíritu de la colmena* was a film that reached beyond its time and geographical borders to become an ageless and universal contemplation of human innocence and dread. Yet, as Querejeta recollects, 'when the film was shown in the San Sebastian Film Festival, everyone gave me their condolences. Someone told me, "Elías, your parents are rich, go back home, they'll treat you well. Because this . . . this is impossible." He shrugs. 'I never know which films are likely to be risks or successes.'

Querejeta's anger and frustration with the interminable dictatorship was heightened by his experience of liberalism and knowledge of progress abroad.

The sense of injustice gave rise to a fury and fear which is tangible in *Pascual Duarte* (1975), a film about rural deprivation and spiralling violence that he adapted from the book by Camilo José Cela in collaboration with the film's director Ricardo Franco. Yet the death of Franco in 1975 was followed by the lifting of censorship in 1977 and a new pluralist character for democratic Spain that was founded on the recognition of seventeen autonomous regional communities in 1978. The stability of the transition to democracy surprised most Spaniards and foreign observers and even gave rise to a grudging respect for the policies of Francoism. Querejeta is quick to respond: 'Lately there have been these considerations . . . Absolutely not! It was a horror! Francoism was a horror! A horror without mitigation. Francoism was a horror and I don't want to hear a single word in its favour!' Nevertheless, democracy and the liberalism that came with it did to some extent render the films of Querejeta and his collaborators redundant for their obduracy and now unnecessary metaphors. Films such as Saura's *Dulces horas* (Tender Hours, 1981) and Manuel Gutiérrez Aragón's cryptic *Feroz* (Fierce, 1984) were critical and commercial disasters, while Querejeta was obliged to suspend the filming of Erice's *El sur* (The South, 1983) after only half the script had been filmed.

During the dictatorship Querejeta had relied on a minority audience of responsive intellectuals both at home and abroad; but now that commercial considerations held sway there was little chance for films based on social realism to compete with those that ignored reality and history and imitated the American entertainment model instead. Censorship and the official *Noticias y Documentales Cinematográficos* (NO-DO) newsreel had gone, but so had distribution quotas that obliged cinema owners to screen Spanish films in order to qualify for dubbing and distribution licences for the infinitely more profitable Hollywood product. The modernisation and reform of the film industry was haphazard at best, though victory for the Socialist Worker's Party (PSOE) in the elections of 1982 did attest to the consolidation of democracy. To a large extent the film policy of the ruling PSOE was a copy of that implemented by their French counterparts. It had the support of a group of left-wing, liberal directors and producers and was overseen by the director Pilar Miró, whose *El crimén de Cuenca* (The Cuenca Crime, 1979) had prompted the hardline remnants of Francoism to process her for court martial in 1980. The so-called Miró Law of 1983 allowed film-makers to apply for advance subsidies of up to 50 per cent of their budget; though this generous system of financing was far in excess of that in other European countries and quickly gave rise to accusations of influence-peddling (*amiguismo*) and governmental control of film-making that was every bit as insidious as that which had been propagated by the Francoist authorities during the brief period of openness in the 1960s. Miró resigned in 1985 and since then the policies of her successors have aimed at making Spanish film producers share the risks that, in some cases, would make them self-sufficient and independent. Pre-production subsidies, for example, were linked to the available funds of the producer and box-office returns, while a new sliding scale of government funding was particularly favourable to films made in the various regional languages.[9]

For Querejeta, the period from the mid-1980s is marked by a series of films made in collaboration with Montxo Armendáriz – *Tasio* (1984), *27 horas* (27 Hours, 1986), *Las cartas de Alou* (Alou's Letters, 1990) and the massively successful *Historias del Kronen* (Stories of the Kronen, 1995) – as well as various attempts at nurturing new film-making talent in projects such as *Siete huellas* (Seven Imprints, 1988). This involved the production of seven 30-minute films by debutante writers and directors that included his daughter, Gracia Querejeta, and Julio Medem. 'It was necessary,' he claims, 'in order to find new talent that would provide fresh perspectives on the things happening in Spain.' Indeed, Medem has since become a celebrated *auteur* with a worldwide reputation, while Gracia Querejeta is one of a growing number of talented and committed female directors in Spain that includes Icíar Bollaín, Chus Gutiérrez, Isabel Coixet and Patricia Ferreira. In 1995 the official film school was reopened in Madrid and there was a new home for the Filmoteca Nacional (the Spanish film institute). Despite a series of measures ending film subsidies that were pushed through parliament by José María Aznar's new right of centre government in 1996, financing increased from private television companies and new companies such as Sogecine emerged.[10] Film production in Spain appeared to be booming, with plenty of room alongside indigenous blockbusting comedies such as Juanma Bajo Ulloa's *Airbag* (1996) and Santiago Segura's *Torrente, el brazo tonto de la ley* (1998) for smaller, independent films such as those which Querejeta produced for the director Fernando León de Aranoa: *Familia* (Family, 1996), a melancholic, thoughtful satire on the mechanics of the family unit, and *Barrio* (1998), a keenly observed, grimly funny portrait of slum kids in Madrid.[11]

Elías Querejeta doesn't like modern cinema much:

> *A few months ago some highly placed official said that Spanish cinema is the best in Europe. That's stupid. I remember fifteen years ago someone said Spanish cinema was the best in the world. Stupid. Only in 100-metre races with a chronometer can you ever say who's best.*

Nevertheless he looks forward to a reaction against the vulgarity and mindless evasion of most contemporary cinematic product, when audiences will return to films that are made 'to make them feel emotions, to put them back in touch with reality.' His *La espalda del mundo* (The Back of the World, 2000), which he co-wrote with the directors Javier Corcuera and Fernando León de Aranoa, is a film with which he is particularly satisfied. A triptych of short documentaries on a Peruvian boy who cuts rock to support his family, a Kurdish exile and a black American on death row in Texas, *La espalda del mundo* demonstrates how the perspective that Querejeta once brought to bear on injustice and oppression in Spain has become a universal concern. However, far from propaganda, it is a film that listens to its subjects as they marshal dignity through solidarity and humour in the face of suffering caused by social, racial and moral arrogance. 'Pride is a stupid thing,' he states. 'Vanity is even stupider, it's one of the stupidest things in the world. I'm in favour of modesty – we have to control the potential for arrogance!'

Elías Querejeta is a man who loves football, Carl Dreyer's *Day of Wrath* (1943), the city of Edinburgh, 1950s' melodramas, inclement weather, the Basque Country, film noir and Orson Welles' *Touch of Evil* (1958), who once drank one on one with Welles only to turn down his request to produce his long-term project *The Other Side of the Wind*: 'It would have been impossible. I'm not Metro-Goldwyn-Mayer.' However, for all his own achievements, he claims 'the next project is more important than all the previous ones' and is anxious to return to work in the editing suite on the ground floor of the building that holds his office. Although they are touchstones for the history of Spanish cinema, he modestly disregards the immense value and importance of the films he has produced when he answers a final request to define his life and work: 'Put "a trade", nothing else. Just a trade.' Outside it's dark and raining, the cacophony of horn-blasts that accompanies Madrid's rush-hour has become an urgent, solid thing. Querejeta reconsiders: 'It's all about having a good time, enjoying yourself. I'm still having a good time, even in this interview.' But it's getting late and he's sorry but he has to work. 'Shall I tell you something?' he asks, perhaps not quite satisfied with the way this particular collaboration is ending and willing to try again:

> *You remember I said I was good at jumping off the swing. Well, I wasn't just good – I was the best! I was the most scared, the smallest, the most insignificant of my brothers. But the lines on the ground . . . the first line was always mine. Am I telling you something? You only have to put passion into what you do. You only have to put passion into what you* want *to do. Without passion, there is nothing.*

Notes

1. All quotes are from an interview with Elías Querejeta in Madrid, December 2000.
2. Later, between 1941 and 1945, Querejeta senior was Civil Governor of the southeastern province Murcia.

3. 'Si me quieres escribir / ya sabes mi paradero / en el frente de Gandesa / primera linea de fuego.' I am grateful to Esther Santamaría Iglesias for providing the lyrics to this song.

4. *55 Days in Peking* (1963) and *The Fall of the Roman Empire* (1964) were other of Bronston's projects.

5. Querejeta also co-wrote *De cuerpo presente* (1965) and *Último encuentro* (Last Meeting, 1966).

6. Notable members of this extended, professional family included Pablo del Amo (editor), Luis de Pablo (music), Luis Cuadrado and Teo Escamilla (camera), Maiki Marín (designer) and Primitivo Álvaro (production director).

7. Wenders accused Querejeta of cutting ten minutes from the finished negative, declaring, 'I'd rather work with a fascist who leaves my negatives alone.' But it was a misunderstanding that was later resolved when the two met up in Cannes.

8. The Americans were Dean Selmier, an actor, and Bill Boon, his ex-marine buddy. The other directors were José Luis Egea and Claudio Guerín.

9. These subsidies could then be topped up by regional governments such as that in Catalonia which subsidises the dubbing of films into Catalan as a way of promoting the language.

10. Spanish television companies were obliged to invest 5 per cent of their revenue in the making of films.

11. Querejeta also participated in the co-production of Jeunet and Caro's *The City of Lost Children* (1995).

CHAPTER TWO

Leaving the church

Early Spanish cinema

Those at prayer during midday mass had no way of knowing that immortality awaited them outside. They might not even have noticed as they left, but Eduardo Jimeno Peromarta and son, proprietors of a waxworks museum, had set up their *kinetofonógrafo* on a balcony across the street from the church and were busy making the first Spanish motion picture. *Salida de la misa de doce del Pilar* (Leaving the Midday Mass at the Church of Pilar in Zaragoza, 1896[1]) still exists, having been restored by the Zaragoza Filmoteca in 1996; and in it, scrubbed and sinless in their Sunday best, the faithful can still be seen blinking their way into the midday sun, good-humouredly jostling each other down the steps, towards the camera, celebrity and perpetual life. Indeed the film was so popular that the first Spanish film-makers went back the following week to shoot its remake-cum-sequel, *Salidas y saludos* (Leavings and Greetings); only this time the faithful and not so pious alike were wise to their new roles as film stars and crammed the steps to wave. This enthusiastic welcome for the camera might have seemed an auspicious beginning for Spanish cinema but, in truth, Spain's pre-Civil War film industry was a spluttering non-starter, bedevilled by foreign competition, an indifferent government, a meddling Church and a lack of investment that was symptomatic of the lack of progress in the country as a whole. Consequently the tale of early Spanish cinema is not one of industry but of visionaries, pioneers, craftsmen and rebels.

In May 1896 Eduardo Jimeno Peromarta had been amongst the first to witness Alexander Promio's demonstration of the Lumière brothers' new invention in Madrid's Hotel Rusia. Spotting a business opportunity, he'd headed straight for Paris to buy one for himself; but *les frères* Lumières weren't selling, so he bought a Vernée instead, an expensive but inferior copy that duly failed to work. Undeterred, the resolute Jimeno Peromarta headed for Lyon, where he picked up some French reels and a genuine Lumière projector for 2,500 francs. He was going to charge 30 *céntimos* for entry and show these films as an adjunct to his waxworks museum; and he was well on his way to profit too, when copycat competitors started a scuffle for audiences that implored the growing crowds of cinema-goers to feel the width: 'Thirteen reels over the road: here, fourteen!' screamed the placards. But such calculated one-upmanship failed to peak, investment went up, profits went down, and that was when Jimeno Peromarta decided to film a church in the hope that people would pay to see this flattering record of themselves.

Film-makers in other countries may have trained their cameras on the crowds passing through factory gates, train stations and other such signs of progress into the twentieth century, but, in a largely pre-industrial Spain, Jimeno Peromarta's camera caught Spaniards as they really were, devout and humble, trapped in time and a little blinded by the light. Almost without exception the first films from the regions of Spain were similarly heaven-minded. In Asturias in 1897 *La vista del Campo Valdés tomada a la salida de misa de doce de la iglesia de San Pedro* (The View of Campo Valdés Taken at the Leaving of Midday Mass at the Church of Saint Peter) was filmed; in Cantabria Pradero Antigüedad shot *La salida de misa de doce de la iglesia de Santa Lucía* (Leaving the Midday Mass at the Church of Saint Lucía, 1907), while in Madrid religiosity was at least linked with education when Lumière's delegate, Alexander Promio, filmed *Salida de las alumas del Colegio de San Luis de los Franceses* (Pupils Leaving the College of Saint Luis) on 11 May 1896. And if it wasn't the church it was deified royalty, with Valencia the setting for the 1905 film *Viaje de su majestad a la Albufera* (Voyage of His Majesty to Albufera) and its none too imaginatively titled sequel *Regreso de Su Majestad de la Albufera* (Return of His Majesty from Albufera). Such films reinforced the dominion of the monarchy and the Catholic Church and distracted a largely illiterate population from the political and economic crises that engulfed them.

With little sign of leadership from a corrupt and self-interested government, Spain ended the nineteenth century plagued by several agricultural crises and growing demands for separatism from the regions. Yet the Catholic Church still dominated and thereby maintained a medieval atmosphere of vassalage in collusion with the ruling classes and the military, while the isolation of the mainly rural population meant that most Spaniards were unaware of current affairs both at home and abroad and were therefore ignorant of the social and technological advances elsewhere. But filmshows at least were new, and when travelling showmen (*barracas*) and open-air cinemas appeared their screen-ings of foreign showreels meant that Spaniards were confronted with the twentieth century as it was happening abroad and were thus able to compare their social conditions with those in France, Germany and the United States. And where were all the Spanish trains, ships and factory workers?

A growing awareness of Spain's backwardness and stagnation prompted a process of national self-examination that inspired new claims for autonomy from Catalonia and the Basque Country. Emergent workers' movements butted heads or bonded with fired-up nationalists, while intellectuals (the so-called 'Generation of '98' led by the Basque philosopher and writer Miguel de Unamuno) rallied the populace to campaigns for reform, redirection and regeneration. But it was already too late to avoid the disaster of 1898, when Spain lost Cuba along with its entire navy in a war with the United States. This, on top of the recent Carlist wars, famines, military uprisings, the loss of Puerto Rico and the Philippines, a workers' revolt in the south, bandits in the north and war in North Africa! In addition, 68 per cent of Spaniards were peasants and 50 per cent were illiterate. There were few urban areas and little investment in their construction because it suited the ruling classes to safeguard their privileges by maintaining the dispersion and illiteracy of the rural workforce. Raw materials were exported for quick profits before a manufacturing industry could emerge, so the potential for growth and urbanisation was consequently limited. However, this only led to new problems in such areas as the Basque Country, where a sudden increase in rural emigration from all areas of Spain to the busy port of Bilbao resulted in abject poverty for most and an emergent, potentially violent campaign for Basque separatism. Meanwhile, visiting film-makers filled out showreels with the most spectacular clichés of Spanishness. Alexander Promio, for example, filmed eleven scenes of military pomp and bullfights during his visit in June 1896, though Spain was not itself perceived as a profitable market for this product. Filmshows were just one more novelty in cities that were a novelty in themselves; while cinematography was a personal affair that required vocation and foresight to see its potential as an art form or long-term investment.

One such visionary was Fructuoso Gelabert. Born in 1874 in Barcelona, he was a carpenter and photographer, who constructed his own copy of the Lumière camera in order to record the Spanish royal family's visit to Barcelona in 1898 and sell it to the French Pathé distribution company as a filler for their popular compilation reels. Empowered by profit, Gelabert set to making well-composed footage of similar events that was also snapped up by Pathé. Soon he was making plot-driven features that required substantial experimentation in montage. Indeed, his *Riña en un café* (Brawl in a Café, 1897) was the first Spanish fiction film and thus a telling example of the determined political and creative distinction of Catalonia. While the rest of Spain slept hungry, the Catalans awoke to their possibilities for advancement in the new century and believed this self-knowledge to be yet another argument in favour of their separation from the centralised government that held them back. Showreels of Catalan origin tended to press home the point, with such films as Gelabert's *Salida de los trabajadores de la España industrial* (The Leaving of

Industrial Workers of Spain, 1897) serving to underline the social and industrial ambition of their makers. In Valencia too, the thriving ports allowed
for an emergent middle class that trumpeted its own wealth by sponsoring
films that showed their trains and ships in rapid turnaround.

Gelabert continued to develop new techniques in the production and
projection of films and in 1903 was named technical director of the Diorama
company. He also worked for Films Barcelona, pioneering the fusion of
sound with moving pictures by standing his actors behind the screen to dub
their voices to the action during the screening and, when that proved
unfeasible, introducing intertitles with *Baño imprevisto* (Unexpected Bath) in
1909. Films Barcelona was only one of the many emergent Catalan production companies for which Gelabert oversaw technical matters while delegat-
ing the direction of actors to others. His *Guzmán el bueno* (1909) provided the
first cinematic role for Margarita Xirgu, patron and friend of Federico García
Lorca and the greatest theatrical actress of her day. When a print of a film such
as *Guzmán el bueno* did the rounds of rural Spain it was welcomed as all but a
tour by Xirgu herself, but Gelabert's technical innovations (including an
attempt at filming in 3-D) were ignored by a public that clamoured for comic
features and filmed *zarzuelas* (light, folksy operettas) with an accompanying
band or record, or melodramas in the company of *un explica* (an explainer)
who narrated from beside the screen.[2] In filming one-act farces, melodramas
and scenes from popular *zarzuelas*, film-makers hoped to duplicate the success
of tried and tested theatrical traditions. A good *zarzuela* was a vigorous light
operetta, combining knockabout comedy and romantic melodrama with a
background of folk traditions and anthemic songs for each type of character
or scene: the mournful ballad, the comic melody and the rousing singalong.
The *zarzuelas* presented Spain as a rural Arcadia that was maintained by true
love, country-style common sense and integrity. Or, if set in the new cities,
they focused on an emigrant group's maintenance of its previously rural
customs. Sumptuous and direct, they connected with an audience that
recognised just enough of themselves in the characters and settings to be
strung along by onscreen presumptions of their bliss.

Another consequence of the filming of theatrical works was that stage actors
were transformed into film stars, ripe to be idolised and desired in the new
film magazines that served a spellbound public. The future of Spanish cinema
seemed to lay firmly in its stars; and, when the glut of filmed *zarzuelas* resulted
in the genre becoming so hackneyed that public appetite for the filmshow
waned, film-makers turned to the *sainete* (comic playlets featuring recognisable types and social archetypes) in their search for the next popular genre.
However, unlike the singing stars of the *zarzuela*, who had been taken aback
by the success of the new medium, comic actors were already wise to their
pulling power and demanded commensurate wages and billing. An all-star

cast was thus expensive and within a few years film-makers were obliged to reduce their output in the light of an inevitable reduction in profits.[3] Actors priced themselves beyond film-makers' budgets and scurried back to the theatre. The novelty of the cinema had faded and film-making became a risky business both financially and literally, as the highly flammable film stock was the cause of numerous fires in production houses and theatres. Investment and innovation dried up and filmshows were reduced to the indignity of fillers between boxing matches and sing-songs in the ragbag theatrical variety shows that film-makers had once dreamt of replacing.

Due to the sideshow origins of Spanish cinema money was rarely reinvested and it was not until 1905 that Catalan film-makers began to plough back the profits from newsreels sold abroad in the hope of establishing some sort of functional film industry. This profitable export of documentary shorts prompted many film-makers to specialise in particular fields of their production and distribution, thereby laying the foundations for an indigenous film industry. Ricardo de Baños, for example, a Catalan who had studied at the Gaumont studios in Paris, began experimenting with the synchronised projection of *zarzuelas* in both their cinematic and audio formats and soon joined with Alberto Marro, a travelling salesman with access to his mother's fortune, to establish Hispano Films in 1907. This company made newsreels and ambitious fictions that included an adaptation of José de Zorrilla's *Don Juan Tenorio* in 1908 – a success which allowed them to construct their own film studio and develop a line of comic and dramatic films that successfully tested the attention span of their audiences to the point at which their films might be considered the first full-length Spanish features.[4] These signs of industry attracted the major French companies of Pathé, Méliès and Gaumont, which established their own bases in Barcelona and, with their innovation and healthy sense of competition, inspired rather than defeated Catalan film-makers, who rose to the challenge by collaborating on a variety of projects.

Segundo de Chomón, an engineer from Teruel, was another pioneer who, like Ricardo be Baños, had served his apprenticeship in the thriving French film industry. Chomón was in Paris, romancing the actress Julienne Mathieu, when he saw his first motion picture. Destiny was postponed, however, when he was conscripted to fight in the war for Cuba and obliged to abandon Mathieu and their child. When he returned to Paris in 1899 Mathieu was working to support herself in the laboratory of the film pioneer Georges Méliès, whose footage she coloured by hand. Chomón found an opening there too and soon delighted Méliès with his invention of a stencil that facilitated the rapid and precise colouring of filmstrips. In 1902 Chomón returned to Barcelona with a plan to introduce his tinting process and revolutionise the Spanish film industry but, finding it as yet non-existent, he decided to make films as well. He opened his own colouring laboratory, built his own camera and set about experimenting with frame-by-frame filming that allowed for the first stop-motion cinematography. *Choque de trenes* (Train Crash, 1902) was the self-explanatory result of his early work with models, while *Pulgarcito* (Tom Thumb, 1903) and *Guliver en el país de los gigantes* (Gulliver in the Land of the Giants, 1905) were fairy tales that displayed good humour, imaginative intertitles and technical genius in their realisation of fantastic worlds. Just as his innovations in the processing and colouring of films had become an internationally recognised standard, so too did these short features reveal not just the potential of Spanish film-making, but of cinema itself.

United in their vision of a viable and competitive film industry, Chomón joined Ricardo de Baños and Alberto Marro in Hispano Films. Chomón had the camera and production expertise, while Baños and Marro took charge of distribution on a selection of *vistas panorámicas* (scenic views) designed to be sold abroad and raise capital, but whose quality also brought them substantial fame and frequent commissions from companies such as Pathé. Ever more adventurous, Chomón was the first film-maker to actually move the camera during filming and thus the travelling shot may be claimed as a verifiably Catalan invention. The quality of his films meant that Chomón was soon recalled to Paris, where he designed and implemented special effects and trick photography for a variety of companies as he worked up to his masterpiece, *El hotel eléctrico* (The Electric Hotel) in 1905. Shot frame-by-frame by progressively turning the camera's crank handle (*paso de manivela*), *El hotel eléctrico* owes a debt to the trickery of Chomón's previous employer, Georges Méliès, but it's a debt that it repays with interest. Like a delighted poltergeist, Chomón orchestrated the possession of a hotel by all kinds of previously inanimate objects (including the camera itself) and so helped establish the cinema as a unique and separate art form. By 1909, however, the French film industry was also in crisis. Méliès' studio had been absorbed by Pathé and public appetite for escapism favoured the more spectacular American product over the quaint and respectable features from their national studios. Chomón lost his livelihood and returned to Barcelona to work with Joan Fuster Gari, a theatrical entrepeneur. As with Hispano Films before them, Chomón and Fuster established their own film studios and set to the production of thirty-seven features with an eye to raising capital, but only two of them were purchased by Pathé, while neither the Spanish distribution companies nor the cinema-going public could cope with such a surfeit. Despite approximating the status of a national film studio, Chomón and Fuster were effectively operating in a vacuum and, fearing bankruptcy, Fuster split from Chomón, who was left without a studio or production facilities.[5]

Despite the best efforts of pioneers such as Gelabert and Chomón a Spanish film industry did not emerge until the First World War, when the benefits of

19

isolation became apparent as the flood of foreign films dried up and a gap in the market appeared. By then, Spanish film-makers could work fast in the production of newsreel and the week's bullfights became a staple of the cinema programme. Short adventure films and comic episodes added variety to a visit to the cinema, as well as documentary footage of the war in Europe and, for the more discerning clientele in the gentleman's clubs, an occasional nudist film or bawdy short feature. Spanish cinema might at last have flowered, were it not for the reaction of the Catholic Church and the hastily established censor. The appeal of filming churchgoers had long since waned and where, the Church demanded to know, was the moral instruction in all this entertainment? In 1913 the alarm of the clergy roused the indifferent government of a self-serving King Alfonso XIII into ruling that all films had to be screened for the police and representatives of the Church, who had the power to demand cuts or confiscate that which they deemed immoral or liable to corrupt. Film-makers duly responded with a few biblical features and a number of literary adaptations that made a new claim for respectability. The Catalan company Barcinógrafo, for example, set about the filming of works by Cervantes, Calderón de la Barca and Tolstoy and, in 1915, a series of self-consciously honourable star vehicles for the great stage actress Margarita Xirgu. Nevertheless, the Church's perception of films as an influence on social misbehaviour convinced the supreme court to brand the cinema 'a school of criminality' and in 1920 a law was passed forbidding men and women from sitting next to each other in cinemas.

Ever the separatists, Catalan film-makers moved away from feature films into the production of filmed serials that transposed the American model to the streets and studios of Barcelona. Joan María Codina's *El signo de la tribu* (The Sign of the Tribe, 1915) for Condal Films was the first, but Hispano Films' *Los misterios de Barcelona* (The Barcelona Mysteries, 1915) was better. Its eight episodes grew increasingly popular as audiences warmed to its piece-meal tale of types and characters from Catalan society; so popular in fact that a six-episode sequel called *El testamento de Diego Rocafort* appeared in 1917. The many film series favoured popular themes and stories drawn from the headlines and streetlife as much as from the worlds of the *zarzuela* and the bullfight, but they also offered a glimpse of social realism in their calculated appeal to the working classes by depicting their society and culture.[6] Nevertheless the First World War ended too soon for Spanish film-makers to make headway in the international market. A revived Hollywood already sensed profit and was busy mass-producing exportable melodramas, westerns and historical epics that, with no language barrier beyond the splicing of alternative intertitles, soon drove the inferior Spanish product from the national screens. Ironically, this was partly because the Hollywood studios had headhunted many of the best Spanish technicians to produce Spanishified versions of features with an eye to capturing the burgeoning South American markets and, as an opportunist afterthought, that of Spain. When the Hispano Films studio was destroyed by fire in June 1918 it seemed a particularly symbolic funeral pyre for the hopes of an independent Spanish cinema.

Indeed what was left of a Spanish film industry retreated into the safest of genres, making and remaking *zarzuelas*. Perennially popular and theatrically proven, the filmed *zarzuela* became the *genre nacional*, with its own star system of bullfighters and singers, who were obliged to romance each other onscreen and off for the benefit of a glamour-hungry public.[7] Production companies such as Atlántida pretty much churned them out: José Buchs' 1921 version of *La verbena de la paloma* (The Fair of the Dove), for example, was filmed in August and in the cinema by December of that year. Moreover there was no end to the queue of businessmen and aristocrats ready to invest some of their fortunes in the glamorous world of the *zarzuela*, until, in 1923, more than 50 per cent of all Spanish features belonged to this hackneyed genre. This creative stagnancy was but a symptom of a greater malaise, however, as Spain found itself increasingly unable to cope in a rebuilt, newly progressive and competitive Europe. Tentative moves towards liberalism were required but, rather than much-needed reform of industry and agriculture, the first response was the 1923 military coup of Miguel Primo de Rivera, a staunch traditionalist who failed to install much of a political structure and simply prolonged the agony of Spain's backwardness until the desperate recession of 1930, when he walked away from all responsibility and left the country.

A new Republican movement swung the municipal elections of 1931, but film-makers were unable to celebrate in kind. The dictatorship of Primo de Rivera had established such strict control of all forms of culture the cinema had been marginalised to the extent that when the world's first sound film, *The Jazz Singer* (1927), reached Spain it could only be screened in silent form. It would take many years for Spain to catch up with the rest of the world in terms of film production and technique – a situation that was hopelessly exacerbated by the exodus of out-of-work Spanish technicians and actors to the United States. Between 1930 and 1935 only eighteen films were made in Spain, while one hundred and sixty Spanish language films were made in Hollywood, including a reputedly superior version of Tod Browning's original *Dracula* (1931) that was shot at night on the same sets using a line-by-line translation of Browning's script and a Mexican and South American cast.[8] Meanwhile film-makers in Spain fought a losing battle to be taken seriously by the state, which only responded with censorship. The arrival of sound film was the final nail in the coffin of a prematurely deceased national cinema.

Nevertheless the dream of Spanish cinema was kept alive, not by film-makers but by the intellectuals of the time. The 'Generation of 1927' included Rafael Alberti, Federico García Lorca, Salvador Dalí and Luis Buñuel. Most came from bourgeois backgrounds, but their heightened sensibilities had inevitably estranged them from the ignorant self-interest and arrogant Catholicism of their class. In poetry and art they sought to free themselves of the mind-set, fears and inhibitions that had resulted from their own religious education, and they relished cinema for its ability to create alternative worlds, to put flesh on poetic possibilities. In addition, their celebration of the cinema was a self-conscious sign of their progressiveness and, even if they had little intention of working in the medium themselves, their literature was suffused with the aesthetic glow and movement of the motion picture. Most of all they liked the American comedians. Especially Buster Keaton.

'I was born – respect me! – with the cinema' wrote Rafael Alberti in his poem *Carta abierta* (Open Letter) from the collection *Cal y canto* (1926–27). Lorca too found the cinema a source of inspiration, writing in 1929 during his visit to New York that he had become a fan of sound cinema, 'of which I am a fervent supporter because one can create wonders. In sound cinema one can hear the sighs, the wind, all the noises, however little they might be, with a precise sensibility' (1994, VI:1092). More than involvement with the narrative or identification with the protagonists, Lorca loved films because they allowed for the cultivation of the incongruous. However, Lorca was typical of the generation of 1927 in that he aimed not to make films but to appropriate their aesthetic as a framework for his own poetic sensibility.[9]

Thus the key figure in this group is clearly Luis Buñuel, the sportsman and intellectual from Aragon, who renounced Catholicism at the age of sixteen while an intern at a Marist boarding school. Nevertheless, coming from a wealthy family, Buñuel went to university in Madrid and stayed at the exclusive *Residencia de Estudiantes*, which is where he met Dalí and Lorca.[10] The *Residencia* was a boisterous kind of Spanish Oxbridge, where the students received lectures from such as H.G. Wells, George Bernard Shaw and Einstein, and where newly translated works by the likes of Freud were devoured and debated without end. For Buñuel, who was without faith in the most devout of countries, the confluence of sin, sex and death in the writings of Freud seemed to justify his waywardness, providing a reason for his anti-clericalism, a validation of his imagination and a sign that he belonged in Paris, where Andre Bretón's Surrealist group was similarly enthused by Freud and, wrote Buñuel, 'already practising instinctive forms of irrational expression' (1983, p.103). To Paris then, in January 1925, ostensibly to work as unpaid assistant for the Spanish representative of the Society for Intellectual Co-operation, but really to live on a monthly cheque from his mother as he searched for an entry into Bretón's group. Buñuel spent his days in the cinema, where Eisenstein's *Battleship Potemkin* (1925) and especially the work of Fritz Lang revealed to him the vocation that he subsequently sought to realise by working as assistant to the director Jean Epstein. Soon he was ready to make his own film and invited his old friend Dalí, who was longing for an excuse to visit Paris and maybe meet his hero Picasso, to join him in the venture. Their twenty-minute feature *Un chien andalou* (An Andalusian Dog, 1928) was written in six days and shot in fifteen on a 25,000-peseta budget from Buñuel's mother. It would revive Surrealism and redefine cinema.

It begins, as do all fairy tales, with the legend *'Il était une fois...'* (Once upon a time...) and then skips from Brothers Grimm to de Sade in the slitting of an eye. Seemingly inspired by a cloud's slide across the moon, Buñuel sharpens a razor and slices through the cornea of a young woman (another timely cut means it's actually that of a dead horse), thereby creating a portal into the subconscious through which the rest of this film's imagery, like the eye's thick jelly, pours. *Un chien andalou* is a phantasmagoria of free association, in which images quarrel for space in the frame and disparate ideas butt against each other with all the belligerence and sudden senti-mentality of a perturbed drunkard. 'Eight years later' reads one intertitle, then 'Sixteen years earlier' says another, and in between the audience struggles to join the dots in a puzzle that is designed to mislead. Indeed, the script was concocted by Buñuel and Dalí (who also appears in the film as one of two startled Marists being dragged behind a pair of grand pianos upon which lie the carcasses of rotting mules) by interspersing images from their nightly dreams and rejecting any juxtapositions that made sense. Much has been made of the film's dreamlike disavowal of logic and disturbing imagery, but this is film as vivisection and the subject being dissected is the audience: the only valid response is that of each individual viewer, who would be well advised to keep their interpretations to themselves, for such diagnoses reveal nothing more than a singular subconscious response to such stimuli.[11] Buñuel made *Un chien andalou* with Dalí in order to gain entry to the Surrealist clique of André Bretón, but the film's artistry, wit and influence far exceeds its initial purpose. Buñuel was fond of recalling that he had stood behind the screen at the film's first showing with his pockets full of stones ready to defend himself; but long before the final shot of spring and sprouting humans *Un chien andalou* had revealed the potential of film as a surrealist medium and was duly championed by Bretón *et al.* as the saviour of a movement that was already showing signs of having lost its youthful fervour.

Buñuel and Dalí were in; though shortly thereafter called to account by Bretón who obliged them to denounce the continuing success of their film in the Parisian cinema, its *succès de scandale* having assured its popularity amongst the same bourgeois society that the Surrealists had vowed to destroy, even though most of them came from good families and, as Buñuel described them, were 'bourgeois revolting against the bourgeoisie' (1983, p.107). Indeed, most Surrealist artists and writers relied on rich patrons for their livelihood even as they pretended that their ultimate aim was to rid them of

Un chien andalou (Luis Buñuel, 1925)

their privileges. One such patron was Vicomte Charles de Noailles who, along with his wife Marie Laure (a descendant of the Marquis de Sade), liked to sponsor the artists of the moment. His commission for Buñuel to make another 20-minute film resulted in the hour-long *L'Âge d'or* (The Golden Age, 1930). However, at the time Buñuel received the news of de Noailles' patronage, his relationship with Dalí was turning sour over the latter's relationship with the possessive Gala Eluard and an undoubtedly related dispute over the authorship of *Un chien andalou*.[12] Moreover, Buñuel's enthusiasm for Surrealism was being subsumed into the even more libertarian doctrine that he had discovered in a copy of the Marquis de Sade's *120 Days of Sodom*, which recounts the abuse and degradation inflicted on selected young women by a quartet of degenerate noblemen. Here was sin, celebrated and exercised as the essence of freedom, as a potent antidote to the centuries of Catholic repression and indoctrination against which the schoolboy Buñuel had once rebelled. To sin by accident or uncontrollable instinct required repentance that earned forgiveness – but to sin on purpose! This was the means by which man became superior to bourgeois morality, religious doctrine and God, while any remnants of guilt only added to the delicious, erotic frisson. Buñuel's Catholic education had exposed him to a terrifying awareness of divine retribution, but now this only heightened the pleasure that came from knowing his art was a defiant and public sin. His films were the cinematic embodiment of the Spanish curse *'me cago en Dios'* (I shit on

God). His subconscious, once liberated, could not be controlled, not even by priests or generals. Sin was synonymous with freedom; atheism was both a comfort and a thrill: 'Still an atheist, thank God' was Buñuel's oft-quoted bon mot.

L'Âge d'or may have come in at an hour but it was still under budget. Its sequential narrative of sorts concerns a lustful couple (he a foul-tempered, animal-hating madman; she a twee though sexually voracious young madam), who are repeatedly prised apart by priests, policemen and dinner guests at a well-to-do chateau.[13] For Buñuel it was 'a film about passion, *l'amour fou*, the irresistible force that thrusts two people together, and about the impossibility of their ever becoming one' (1983, p.117). More laboured in its subversion than the ever-youthful *Un chien andalou*, *L'Âge d'or* is a farce about military, clerical and bourgeois characters on an excursion to see fossilised bishops, that begins as a zoological essay on the scorpion and ends with its own sting in the tail: a brief, elliptical re-enactment of *120 Days of Sodom* in which Christ emerges as the leader of de Sade's dedicatedly sinful 'sadists'. Meanwhile, in the narrative gaps and lurches appear leftover characters from *Un chien andalou*: a gentleman with a rock on his head, a puppy-like cow on the heroine's bed, and a bishop flung from a castle window followed closely by a giraffe and a flaming tree. Scatological and surprisingly erotic (especially in the prolonged sequence of the heroine sucking on the toes of a statue), the film duplicated the scandal of its predecessor. Cinemas where it was playing were attacked, the French police banned it and Vicomte de Noailles was expelled from the Jockey Club.[14]

After the Parisian triumph of *Un chien andalou*, Buñuel had returned to Spain to show off his newly acclaimed masterpiece in the *Cine-club español*. This was a film society that had been set up in 1928 by the intellectuals who contributed and subscribed to *La gaceta literaria*, a literary journal that also featured Buñuel's occasional writings on the cinema and was run by Ernesto Giménez Caballero. The meetings of the *cine-club* involved not only the screening of a few films (most of which were chosen by Buñuel and sent to Spain from Paris) but also lectures, recitals of work in progress by assorted poets and authors, and spirited *tertulias* (debates) on art and politics. At its first session the group treated itself to Stroheim's *Greed* (1923) and Murnau's *Tartüff* (1925), while the second, in January 1929, featured a showing of *The Jazz Singer* at which there was no soundtrack but a hired band which was commissioned to keep up and play along with the Jewish music and jazz that it could truthfully only imagine.[15]

The *Cine-club español* raised awareness of film amongst the intelligentsia and literati and prompted their revaluation of the silent era. It also brought Russian and Chinese cinema to Spain along with the surrealist work of their prodigal son, Buñuel.[16] Having fostered this consciousness from afar, Buñuel returned to Spain hoping to lead a cinematic renaissance, but discovered that he had misjudged the actual desire of these intellectuals, most of whom preferred to admire the cinema and transpose its aesthetic into their preferred media of art or poetry rather than make films themselves.[17]

To his dismay, Buñuel found that Spain was still the indifferent host of a hopelessly inadequate film industry. Worse, at a time of convulsions surrounding the birth of the Second Republic, the *cine-clubs* and journals had begun to reflect the polarisation of society in their choice of films and the possibility of nurturing a collaborative infrastructure seemed unlikely. *Cine-clubs* declared their political affiliations by programming German expressionist films or Soviet features, but the revolution of sound film remained resolutely elsewhere, a distant phenomenon that Spaniards could only read about until 1931, when Spain's first sound motion picture, Adelqui Millar's *Toda una vida* (A Whole Life), reached Spanish cinemas. Nonetheless filmmakers failed to explore the possibilities of the new technology, preferring to plunder an already ransacked cultural heritage by remaking silent films with sound, thereby occasioning yet another surge of *zarzuelas*. The cinema-going public, however, was so excited by the quality of American sound films that it could only be roundly disappointed by the comparative quality of the Spanish. Theirs was a retrograde, simplistic and subservient national cinema, lacking ambition and therefore without evolution: when the *zarzuelas* dried up a second time Spanish film-makers merely took to remaking American films in Spanish, promoting home-grown versions of Chaplin and Keaton that were little more than blatant counterfeits of the originals. Of the five hundred films released to Spanish cinemas in 1931 only three were Spanish. In 1932 it was the same ratio, with one of the three being Edgar Neville's tellingly titled *Yo quiero que me lleven a Hollywood* (I Want Them to Take Me to Hollywood).

Undeterred, Buñuel resolved to continue in his independent ways by making a short film with the 20,000 pesetas that his friend Ramón Acín had won on the national lottery.[18] *Tierra sin pan* (Land Without Bread, aka *Las hurdes*, 1932) would be Buñuel's first Spanish film and, as might be expected, was a virulent attack on the selfishness of society and on man's inhumanity in general. After borrowing a camera and buying an old Fiat, Buñuel headed into the mountains between Caceres and Salamanca with friends Eli Lotar and Pierre Unik. They were seeking an isolated area known as Las Hurdes, which had been a place of refuge for Jews during the period of the Spanish Inquisition (sixteenth to seventeenth centuries) and had been isolated from Spain and the rest of the world ever since. The eight thousand inhabitants had no knowledge of bread, and were ravaged by disease, inbreeding and malnutrition. Buñuel filmed in a calculatedly objective manner, most often tilting his camera down on them like a scientist peering through a microscope;[19]

but he also strayed purposefully into didactics by staging such scenes as a live goat falling from a mountain ledge to illustrate the hazardous terrain, a mule stung to death by the bees whose hives it was transporting, a row of smiling cretins posing ignorantly for his camera, and a tiny, dead girl, whose mother – 'La mere' – sits impassively in Buñuel's frame, for all the world like an abject madonna. All of this Buñuel edited together on his kitchen table using a magnifying glass. It had its first screening (in silent form) at Madrid's Prensa cinema, with the director delivering the commentary through a microphone. Was this a humanist documentary or another surrealist plaything, crueller than before but no less cynical in its presumption of the guilt and complacency of its audience? Certainly Doctor Gregorio Marañón, the president of a benefit organisation for the region, was sufficiently incensed to procure the film's prohibition in Spain.

Tierra sin pan is both repellent and fascinating; like Goya's sketches of paupers, Buñuel's subjects exist at the frayed edges of the human race, but in their helplessness they also reside at its very heart. The toothless, grinning faces of the inbred children project a forceful diatribe against man's inhumanity to man and a more specific criticism of Spain. Buñuel is manipulative in his film-making, arrogant in his mere presence and infuriating in his passivity: but purposefully so. An audience is hardly likely to forgive Buñuel his close-up of the dead little girl, or even the sacrifice of the goat, but his rhetoric is underplayed, even absent at moments when compassion is required: images of diseased peasants are cut with shots of a textbook, for example, in which the mosquito is identified as the culprit in place of a stagnant society and its lack of compassion. Consequently, the surrealist effect of this film is perhaps even more insidious than that of *Un chien andalou*, for these images cannot be dismissed as the result of febrile minds, but must be confronted as the detritus of a collective subconscious. Like the Mexican street kids in Buñuel's *Los olvidados* (The Forgotten Ones, 1950) the infants of Las Hurdes had been conveniently 'forgotten' by society, but Buñuel still conspired to stir suppressed memories of them into tormenting the psyche of his audience.

Buñuel was a film-maker whose obsessions, conflicts and enmities were to develop into a singularly persuasive example of *auteurist* cinema; but what is often overlooked is that he was also a pragmatist who, in the tumultuous pre-Civil War years, exercised a politicised commitment to the future of Spanish film-making when he started to work for Ricardo María Urgoiti's Filmófono distribution company. Under Buñuel's supervision Filmófono produced a series of low-budget films (150,000 pesetas each) with the aim of nurturing new writing, directing and technical talent that would eventually constitute some sort of infrastructure for a reborn Spanish cinema. On films such as *La hija de Juan Simón* (Juan Simón's Daughter, 1935) Buñuel gave new film-makers such as Nemesio Sobrevila, whom he sacked for filming too slowly, and José Luis Sáenz de Heredia their first shot at directing new performing talent such as the flamenco dancer Carmen Amaya (though Buñuel may well have come to rue the opportunity given to Sáenz de Heredia, who would become a primary exponent of the *cine cruzada* (crusade cinema) of the dictatorship). Buñuel's work for Filmófono therefore presents itself as a prime example of how Spanish cinema was resuscitated as a result of two factors: first, the return of apprenticed Spanish film-makers from abroad, and second, the movement of profitable distribution companies into the field of film production. Indeed, an even greater example was that of the confluence of the film-makers Florián Rey and Benito Perojo with the Valencian distribution company CIFESA.

In time the *Compania Industrial del Film Español, S.A.* (CIFESA) would become the prime exponent of Francoist cinema, but it was set up by the Casanovas family in 1932 to distribute the films of Columbia Pictures in Spain. After the massive success of Frank Capra's *It Happened One Night* (1934), CIFESA was now looking to move into film production in collaboration with Rafael Salgado, the manager of *Cinematográfica Española Americana* (CEA). CEA was a studio complex on the outskirts of Madrid that had been built with an investment of four million pesetas raised on the agreement of a group of authors and composers to cede the rights to film adaptations of their work in return for eventual profits.[20] Their first collaboration, *El agua en el suelo* (Water on the Ground, 1934, directed by E. Fernández-Ardavín), had been made by CEA and distributed by CIFESA, but *La hermana San Sulpicio* (Sister San Sulpicio, 1934) was CIFESA's first attempt at production. This romance with a background of Catholicism and folklore was Florián Rey's remake of his same-titled film of 1927. Then, it had marked the sensational debut of Imperio Argentina, an actress whom Rey would marry: now she was one of the greatest Spanish film stars and their 1934 version with sound was a calculated success.

Rey had previously been an actor, appearing in José Buchs' aforementioned 1921 version of *La verbena de la paloma* before setting up his own company, Goya Films, with close friend, fellow actor and director Juan de Orduña. For his own and other production companies Rey had filmed a variety of *zarzuelas* before achieving fame and critical respect with *La aldea maldita* (The Cursed Village, 1930). *La aldea maldita* was a poignant melodrama that tracked three generations in a Segovian village and featured shocking representations of poverty in an agile narrative about a woman who is forced into prostitution after the jailing of her husband. In its theme, bleakness, and considered, intelligent framing, *La aldea maldita* achieved both social realism and an evolution in film grammar. But the crisis in Spanish cinema obliged Rey to complete the film's post-production in Paris, where he would remain until being recalled by CIFESA for directing duties on *La hermana San Sulpicio*, the success of which allowed CIFESA under Vicente Casanovas to widen its roster of star directors and performers by also contracting Benito Perojo.

Perojo was born in 1894, the illegitimate son of a philosopher and government minister (*diputado liberal*), and was sent to boarding school in Hastings, England, until his father's death in 1908. Upon finishing his education in Madrid he set about directing and acting in short comic films with his brother José as cameraman. His character, Peladilla, was a cheeky imitation of Chaplin which proved to have such popular appeal that the brothers established a production company, Patria Films, with their profits. However, the crisis in Spanish cinema obliged Perojo to seek work as an actor in the more thriving film industries of Germany and France, from where he collaborated with the writer Jacinto Benavente on adaptations of works by Blasco Ibáñez and Benavente himself. Scenes shot in Parisian studios were intercut with Spanish exteriors and by 1930 Perojo had become a reknowned Spanish film-maker in all but Spain, where critics rejected the diluted Spanishness that resulted from the artificiality of the interior scenes and what they jealously derided as his cosmopolitan lifestyle. In 1931, moreover, Perojo was called to Hollywood to make *Mamá* (1931), one of many films written expressly for the South American market instead of the more usual tactic of remaking second-hand English language scripts, and it was only the appearance of sound film technology in Spain that tempted him back. When he returned to Spain it was not just experience and technical innovations that he brought with him, but a unique global perspective on both the business and artistry of the cinema. His first Spanish sound film was *El hombre que se reía del amor* (The Man Who Laughed at Love, 1933) while his *Se ha fugado un preso* (A Prisoner Has Escaped, 1933) was the first Spanish feature to be invited to the Venice Film Festival. Perojo's knowledge and skill with the technical and popular aspects of film-making made him a vital player in the plans of the CIFESA studios. Here was a would-be mini Hollywood and an already-was Hollywood director. The virtue of their collaboration was rapidly confirmed by three films in quick succession, beginning with *Rumbo al Cairo* (Cairo Bound, 1935) and *Es Mi Hombre* (It's My Man, 1935). Both were critical and commercial triumphs that proved the promise of a Spanish star system and the benefit of keeping directors such as Rey and Perojo under contract, but Perojo's masterpiece was that same year's *La verbena de la paloma* (1935).

La verbena de la paloma is impossible to watch without imagining the laughter, shrieks and sing-along of the audience it was intended to flatter. Its warm-hearted burlesque of life in Madrid in 1893 bursts with affectionate caricatures and spirited renditions of classic songs. Julián (Roberto Rey), a dapper printer's apprentice, loves Susana (Raquel Rodrigo), a dainty, wilful dressmaker, who's too busy stringing along Don Hilarión (Miguel Ligero), a

La verbena de la paloma (Benito Perojo, 1935)

decrepit but wealthy pharmacist, to return Julián's affections; until, that is, what seems like the entire population of Madrid gets involved in the romantic shenanigans that climax at the annual open-air fair to celebrate the eve of the Virgin of the Dove. In reflecting the stereotype of the urban community in Madrid – *los chulapos* – the film's tone is arrogant and witty, its dialogue is colloquial to the point of incomprehension and the romance is frothy but determinedly seductive. Susana is a surprisingly independent young miss, who knows how to keep men at arm's length while taking them for all they're worth, which isn't much. Indeed, in its gender politics, this version of *La verbena de la paloma* is at least equal to Capra's *It Happened One Night*, though here the final kiss is blatantly forestalled in compliance with the censor: Susana and Julián draw close but don't quite touch. The songs are anthemic and varied and include a sing-along on a horse-drawn carriage, Julián's romantic lament, Don Hilarión's rhyming discourse on the pleasures of young women and, in the film's most delightful scene, a passed-along song that moves from balconies to open windows over the roofs of houses on a hot *madrileña* night. Here, as in Julián's final Marx Brothers-like chase of Don Hilarión, Perojo's film-making is sprightly and innovative, incorporating cranes and energetic travelling shots, wipes, fades, dissolves and an often empathetic movement of the camera alongside his performers. The detail is also superb, with the studio recreation of late nineteenth-century Madrid sporting barrel organs, boys on penny-farthings and a parodic interlude in a *café flamenco*, where a portly madam dances with restraint to an incongruous pianola. Most spectacular of all is the recreation of the fairground, with big dipper, roundabout, carousel and a cast of hundreds, all in traditional dress and munching on freshly-made *churros*. Indeed, *La verbena de la paloma* presents such a loving and boisterous portrait of life in Madrid that even the characters' bursting into song seems enviable and natural.

In the brief Republican spring of 1935 CIFESA made full use of its studios, national network of distributors and worldwide representatives to host the filming and commercial triumph of *La verbena de la paloma*. However, at a time of increasing fragmentation in Spanish society, CIFESA also nurtured projects that were purposefully conservative, determinedly escapist and commercially assured, thanks largely to the glamorous and prolific Florián Rey and Imperio Argentina. Argentina was the Argentina-born daughter of a Gibraltarian guitarist and an actress from Malaga. She was boisterous and blessed with the most dazzling smile, and since her debut in Rey's 1927 version of *La hermana San Sulpicio* she had become the darling of the musical comedy and had even shared billing (and a unique duet) with Carlos Gardel in *Melodía de Arrabal* (Melody of Arrabal, 1933). In Rey's *Morena Clara* she plays Trini, an archetypically prepossessing Spanish Gypsy, a flirty motor-mouth with a knack for ingratiating herself with the wealthy Andalusians, partly because she is of mixed Gypsy and 'white' or *paya* blood.[21] The illiterate Trini and her brother Regalito (Miguel Ligero) first appear misreading the 15 km milestone on the road to Seville: 'Fifteen millimetres!' declares Regalito. In a spontaneous attempt at easing their passage, they trick the owner of a local tavern into buying back the legs of ham that they've only just stolen from him, but are rapidly apprehended by the Civil Guard and marched away for trial; and there, despite Trini's best attempts at amusing the court with her mock indignation, she comes up against Enrique (Manuel Luna), the prosecutor whose view of Gypsies is that, 'their wit, verbiage and ignorant naivety are nothing more than a flowery tapestry that hides the hurtful intention of these eternal enemies of society.'

Nevertheless, thanks to Trini's verbal and physical charms (and the strikingly incongruous presence of her female defence attorney, who claims that the trial should really be against the industries that exploit the poor and Gypsies of Andalusia), Trini is released, only to wangle her way back into the house of the prosecutor by flattering his parents so much that they adopt her as a kind of pet Gypsy. Complications ensue, there's a rousing Busby Berkeley-style set piece of flamenco dancers on an Andalusian patio, and Argentina sings both *Échale guindas al pavo* (Put Cherries on the Turkey) and *La farsa monea* (The Counterfeit Coin) with, respectively, gusto and great poignancy: 'I'm the counterfeit coin / passed from hand to hand / and never kept by anyone.' The story, such as it is, comes and goes without bothering the star, who flounces through disjointed scenes of palm-reading, slapstick and vampish sparring with a confidence that comes from knowing the film, as a star vehicle, is far too small for her.[22] She, Rey and CIFESA are all out to entertain and, although there is a glimpse of social criticism in the trial, the film resolutely avoids the anarchy of Reñoir's *Boudo Saved From Drowning* (1932), preferring to flatter all instead. Released just before the outbreak of the Civil War, *Morena Clara* was such an optimistic view of conciliation between men and women, rich and poor, 'whites' and Gypsies, that it was sufficiently devoid of controversy to remain playing in cinemas in both Republican and Nationalist zones several months after the beginning of the Civil War.

The time between 1935 and 1936 was the briefest of golden ages. Despite growing competition from foreign films, which had only intensified when Spanish distributors switched from subtitling to dubbing with a grateful response from a largely illiterate audience, it was a moment when Spanish cinema came close to being a thriving industry. Nevertheless, films like *La verbena de la paloma* and *Morena Clara* were in a sense still routine: despite the best efforts of Perojo and Rey to establish a cinema of national characteristics most film-makers continued to rehash previously filmed theatrical works.

Imperio Argentina in *Morena Clara* (Florián Rey, 1935)

Indeed, it was only in the months preceding the insurrection of 1936 that film-makers grew ambitious, encouraged by the appearance of a film-making infrastructure and by new ideas of film as propaganda that brought about politically charged versions of the literary classics *Fortunata y Jacinta*, *Tirano Banderas* and *Wuthering Heights*, which would have been directed by Luis Buñuel had he not fallen so dramatically from favour following *Tierra sin pan*.[23] But, by then, right-wing groups such as José Antonio Primo de Rivera's Falange had already abandoned hope of regaining power by democratic means and were conspiring to overthrow violently the troubled democracy of Manuel Azaña's Republic.[24] With support from disgruntled generals, who agreed with the Church's diagnosis of an increasing degeneracy caused by liberalism, Franco took upon himself the cause of righting Spain and by his actions became a rallying point for traditionalists, the wealthy, the religious and those peasants and workers who could be persuaded to fall for his romanticised brand of fascism.

The initial uprising in Morocco was scrappy, but salvaged and redirected by the intervention of both Hitler and Mussolini, who answered Franco's calls for assistance with the loan of their airforces. By the end of September 1936 the already polarised country had become geographically fragmented into Republican and Nationalist zones. The recent innovation of sound film made it an ideal medium for agitprop and both sides set to the making of documentary films and newsreels. In November 1936 Franco established a Department of Press and Propaganda and charged General Millán Astray, the one-eyed, one-armed founder of the Spanish Foreign Legion (where Franco had received most of his military training and nationalist fervour) with its running. A borderline psychopath, Millán Astray adored his protégé-turned-patron and took to his role as Franco's image-maker with deadly seriousness, including shouting down the intellectual Miguel de Unamuno in the University of Salamanca with the deathless heckle: '¡Muera la inteligencia!' (Death to intelligence!). In addition, the sympathies of Vicente Casanovas drove CIFESA into the service of increasingly fascist propaganda, such as the three films that Perojo made under contract for CIFESA in Berlin, each featuring Estrellita Castro and a hyperbolic sense of Spanish folklore which merged with Francoist doctrine to celebrate Spanishness as defined by the future dictator and the Church. Florián Rey spent the beginning of the Civil War in Cuba, before receiving an offer from Hispano-Film-Produktion to make *Carmen, la de Triana* (Carmen, The one from Triana, 1938) with Imperio Argentina in Berlin under the aegis of Adolf Hitler. The *Führer* had dreamt of remaking *Lola Montes* with Nazi soldiers in place of the original work's students, but Rey twisted his commission into a version of *Carmen* in which José, Carmen's lover and killer in the original, here dies in the course of patriotic duty and Carmen (Imperio Argentina) becomes the bearer of his torch. Remaining in Berlin, Rey and his wife also made *La canción de Aixa* (Aixa's Song, 1939) but would divorce shortly after, following rumours of Argentina's affair with Hitler.[25]

Meanwhile, most of the film companies and studios, being located in the cities, remained in Republican hands.[26] In Barcelona, the Republican ideal of collectivisation was implemented by the CNT union (*Confederación Nacional del Trabajo*), which created a Department of Information and Propaganda and nationalised one hundred and sixteen of the city's cinemas. In addition, the co-operative *Film Popular* (People's Film) produced a weekly newsreel entitled *España al día* (Spain Today), that, following its fifth episode, shared its footage with the Catalan production company Laya Films for them to make a Catalan-language version entitled *Espanya al día* alongside their own documentaries and distribution of Soviet propaganda. In Madrid too the film industry union, the *Co-operativa Obrera Cinematográfica*, commandeered the city's cinemas as outlets for Soviet films that delivered a propagandist call to arms. Individual film-makers were also drafted into the conflict, with Rafael Gil at work on short information films such as *Ametralladoras* (Machine Guns, 1939) and Buñuel busy editing several documentaries in Paris, which is when the Spanish embassy even paid him to dub *Tierra sin pan* into French and English (and add music by Brahms) so that it could be used as propaganda.[27]

The end of the Civil War brought victory to Franco, whose dictatorship held absolute sway over a decimated country. In what would become a familiar tactic of oppression the state censor wielded powers by which all film material was screened and classified and, if necessary, burnt. Thus, of all the films made between the years 1897 and 1931, only one hundred and thirty-seven films survived both the conflagration of war and that of the Fascist furnace. And of these only thirty-five were complete films; the rest were merely fragments. Worse still, all of this material was housed in a dedicated archive in Madrid, which was destroyed by fire in August 1945. The few pieces left were moved to the new *Filmoteca Nacional* (National Film Institute) in 1953. Film had barely emerged as an art form or industry before the Civil War, having suffered from a lack of investment and indifference on the part of the ruling classes that was characteristic of their treatment of society as a whole. Consequently the exodus of film-makers to foreign studios eroded the foundations of any potential film industry and left the Spanish market open to exploitation by the American studios. Only the style and wit of Perojo, Rey and Imperio Argentina, along with the impudence and commitment of Luis Buñuel, managed to spark the pre-Civil War history of Spanish cinema. And it is here that we may find a clue to the origins of the conflict to come; for the pathetic wretches of Buñuel's *Tierra sin pan* and the joyful frolickers of Perojo's *La verbena de la paloma* are both the ancestors of Spanish cinema and the ghosts of pre-Civil War Spain.

Notes

1. The exact date has been disputed by the historian Luis Seguin.
2. Fructuoso Gelabert formed his own studio, Boreal Films, but this failed and he was forced to sell his equipment. In 1952 he remade *Riña en un café*.
3. Perhaps the evolution of Spanish cinema would have been different had some of these stars been more closely involved in directing/producing their films, as did Chaplin, Keaton and Harold Lloyd.
4. They weren't above the occasional *zarzuela* either, as even their *Amor andaluz* (Andalusian Love, 1911) was a cut above the usual dross. Later, with Royal Films, Baños would specialise in profitable episodic serials such as *Fuerza y nobleza* (Strength and Nobility, 1917).
5. Thereafter, Chomón was briefly employed by Pathé as a waged film-maker for their subsidiary Ibérico Films, for whom he produced eleven short features, but he was soon forced to seek work as a jobbing cameraman. Nevertheless he continued experimenting, bringing travelling shots indoors and developing a series of editing techniques, such as jump cuts. In 1912 he took a job with Itala Films in Turin, where he continued to experiment in the use of electric lighting for interior filming and worked on Giovanni Pastrone's epic *Cabiria* (1914). In 1925 he returned to Paris to work on Abel Gance's epic version of *Napoleon*, but would never return to Spain, dying in 1929 from a disease that he had contracted while filming in Morocco the previous year. At the time of his death he was busy with the development and use of colour film.
6. The novelist Blasco Ibáñez even part-financed and co-directed a film version of his own bullfighting melodrama *Sangre y arena* (Blood and Sand) with the Frenchman Max André in 1916.
7. The rather more contemptuous term for the *zarzuela* was *españoladas* (best described as folksy musicals with an Andalusian setting).
8. This version, directed by George Melford, was discovered by film historian David J. Skal in Cuba in 1989 and released in American cinemas in 1992. Many critics and fans claim that this version is superior to Browning's original, being more atmospheric and considerably more erotic.
9. Lorca's theatrical sketch *El paseo de Buster Keaton* (Buster Keaton's Bicycle Ride) was a meditation on the comedian as a vehicle for Lorca's usual concerns, while his filmscript *Viaje a la luna* (Trip to the Moon) juxtaposed seemingly arbitrary images in imitation of cinematography but was never meant to be filmed, although a version was filmed during the Lorca centenary celebrations of 1998.
10. The *Residencia de Estudiantes* was established in 1910 by Don Alberto Jiménez Fraud, who modelled it on his experience of England's Oxbridge system as a student residence and a centre for intellectual thought.
11. Nevertheless it is possible to detect a schoolboy-cruel satire of Lorca in the film, which so enraged the poet that he referred to the feature as 'a little shit of a film.' The aforementioned first image, for example, carries an echo of Lorca's *Romance sonámbulo* (Sleepwalking Ballad), while glimpses of the fey, cross-dressing protagonist suggests a nasty dig at the homosexuality that Lorca always struggled to hide. The title itself – *An Andalusian Dog* – might also be intended as an insult.
12. The argument over the authorship of both *Un chien andalou* and then *L'Âge d'or* continued between Buñuel and Dalí, but would eventually be resolved by Dalí's self-serving disavowal of all creative input when accused of anti-clericalism by

the Francoist regime that took power in Spain at the end of the Civil War. Dalí's denial effectively branded Buñuel a communist in the eyes of the United States, a fact that undoubtedly contributed to his seeking exile in Mexico City.

13.   The sequences at the chateau are interspersed with scenes of guests at an actual dinner party hosted by the Vicomte.

14.   The cinemas were attacked by that which Ruth Brandon describes as 'a commando group of the Anti-Jewish League and the League of Patriots' (2000, p.354).

15.   Other sessions of the *Cine-club español* featured such films as Pudovkin's *Storm Over Asia* and Weine's *The Cabinet of Dr Caligari*.

16.   In Barcelona, meanwhile, the equivalent journal *Mirador* celebrated Soviet film-making at a time when most were unavailable in Spain, but still managed to screen Eisenstein's *Battleship Potemkin* in 1931.

17.   One exception was Ramón Gómez de la Serna, one of Buñuel's favourite authors, who collaborated with him on a script for a film that was never made about a man who reads a newspaper and sees the headlines enacted as vignettes.

18.   Acín was a committed anarchist, who was killed at the beginning of the Civil War when he gave himself up to an extreme right-wing group that had arrested his wife, who was shot alongside him.

19.   Buñuel had studied entomology at university.

20.   The group included Benavente, the Álvarez Quintero brothers (authors of *zarzuelas*) and Carlos Arniches (the author of *sainetes*).

21.   Hence the oxymoron of the film's title: a *morena clara* is a 'light-skinned dark' person.

22.   The film is based upon 'a comedy in three acts and an oral trial (*un juicio oral*)' by Antonio Quintero and Pascual Guillén.

23.   It was also in 1935 that Spain's first female director Rosario Pi, a Catalan, made her first film, *El gato montés* (The Mountain Cat).

24.   In the February 1936 election the Falange had failed to gain a single seat.

25.   Rey returned to Spain after the war to work for Suevia Films but, despite initial success, his films lacked the flair of his earlier works. In 1942 he even remade *La aldea maldita* as a quaint and bland rural melodrama. In 1949, when Argentina appeared at New York's Carnegie Hall, her concerts were picketed by Spanish exiles, who denounced her for collaboration with the fascists. She moved to Buenos Aires after the war and made several films there under the direction of Benito Perojo. Later she would return to Spain and make a few cameo appearances before starring again in José Luis Borau's *Tata Mía* (1986).

26.   It was this lack of studio facilities that forced Millán Astray and CIFESA to send film-makers to Lisbon, Rome and Berlin. Another such was Joaquín Reig, who went to Berlin with orders to produce a documentary entitled *España heroica* (Heroic Spain, 1937).

27.   This also allowed Buñuel to repay the daughters of Ramón Acin the money that their father had lent him (Buñuel, 1983, p.141).

CHAPTER THREE

Under Franco

Spanish cinema during the dictatorship

Cuts were called corrections by the censor. The Civil War was not a vile and bloody disaster but a holy, successful crusade. There were no other languages besides Castilian Spanish. There was no such thing as poverty, nor adultery, nor dissidence, nor differences of any kind. There was only Spain, favoured by God and Franco, watched over by the military and the Catholic Church. This, at least, was the cinematic version of life for Spaniards during the dictatorship. For close on forty years it was a regime that subordinated all media to its conservative and nationalist discourse. Through censorship and dubbing, the supervision of scripts and shoots, the rationing of permits and licences, and the imposition of prohibitive film classifications, Spanish cinema was press-ganged into the rewriting of history and the dissemination of fascist propaganda. Nevertheless, as the historian Paul Preston has stated: 'The hostilities of the Spanish Civil War ended formally on 1 April 1936 but the war went on, in the form of . . . a resistance movement until 1977' (1999, p.5). Accordingly, a cinema of opposition did emerge in the films of Juan Antonio Bardem and Luis García Berlanga, with reinforcement from the exiled Luis Buñuel. Like advancing snipers, their efforts paved the way for many and ensured that an otherwise stagnant period was vivified by their innovation and nerve.

During the Civil War the Republicans had held on to the film studios in their sections of Madrid and Barcelona and made propagandist newsreels for fund-and-army-raising screenings abroad, while the fascists took heart from the righteous, bombastic product of their German and Italian allies. Post-war the Spanish film industry, like all things, surrendered to the state, which determined to establish a loyal and useful national cinema by means of both protective and repressive measures. No leeway was granted: shooting scripts were submitted for approval to a jury made up of priests and bureacrats, while the finished films were recalled again and, if found to be in need of correction, either cut or confiscated.[1] On the other hand, those films that upheld fascist values were awarded the title 'of national interest' and their producers were rewarded with lucrative licences for the distribution of foreign films. Consequently, self-seeking or servile companies made *cine cruzada* – films that celebrated Spanish imperialism or retold legends of Nationalist heroism in the Civil War, of which the most notorious was *Raza*, based on a semi-autobiographical novel-cum-script by Franco.[2] There were even state-sanctioned sub-genres such as *cine de curas* (priest cinema) about heroic missionaries and their like, which made a change from the multitude of *españoladas*[3] and melodramatic morality tales featuring singing prodigies, the so-called *cine con niño* genre (cinema with child).

Chief amongst these opportunist production companies was Vicente Casanovas' CIFESA. Formed in Valencia in 1932 in order to distribute the films of Columbia Pictures in Spain, CIFESA had also achieved popular success with its own adaptations of light operettas. During the Civil War CIFESA specialised in the production of newsreel for the Nationalists and so was ideally placed to claim privileges from the victorious new regime.[4] What Franco wanted were films that celebrated the greatness of Spain. What he got were grandiloquent military epics such as Antonio Román's *Los últimos de Filipinas* (Last Stand in the Philippines, 1945), which opens with an overture accompanying a map of the Philippines, thereby locating us firmly in the genre of such golden-age adventure films as *Gunga Din* (1939) and *The Four Feathers* (1939). A firm voiceover informs us that 'a handful of men far from their fatherland maintain their flag aloft' and then lists the horrors that they face – 'isolation, heat, fatigue, struggle, solitude and homesickness.' This may be 1898 and the last stand for Spanish colonialists in the Philippines, but the film is only a metaphor for the condition of Spain in the Europe of the 1940s. Having gambled on the success of the Axis powers, Spain found itself rebuffed by the victorious Allies, who resented but tolerated the survival of a fascist dictatorship in western Europe. In commemorating the battalion that held out for almost a year after Spain had been forced to forfeit the Philippines in the Treaty of Paris, *Los últimos de Filipinas* sought to explain the post-World War Two isolation of Franco's regime as a comparable affront that would be similarly overcome. The soldiers (including a young Fernando Rey) suffer terrible physical degradations but also appear to approximate ecstasy as their moment of sacrifice draws near. Their quasi-erotic ritual of martyrdom in the cause of Spain is presented in scenes of Hawksian fraternity amongst the soldiers, who at one point stand gawping, more homesick than lovestruck, as a 'civilised' Philippine singer (i.e. she sings in perfect Castilian) reminds them all of home – a united Spain that is deliberately exaggerated in the surnames called out by the postmaster (Luis *Segovia*, Gregorio *Catalán*, Luis de *Levante*, etc.). But what's this? A seditious poster in the drawer of the Philippine barkeeper! Quick men, to the church! And off they march into the last refuge for Christian warriors such as they, where a low-angle camera keeps them permanently under the protection of the cross. Most men who die do so shouting '¡España!', except for the fever-ridden captain, whose last order is for the remaining thirty men to save ammunition and forgo his funeral salute. The Filipinos are cunning (and sweaty): 'They're alone,' sneers one, 'we could make them remember that women exist!' Thank goodness the Spaniards have the Catholic priest to protect them. In return, he gets to deliver the Christmas mass with the help of a choir of soldiers, whose carols are strangely echoed in those of their enemy. 'It's the work of Spain,' explains the priest, 'it's the labour of centuries. And even though we might one day have to leave, here will remain the faith and the language forever.'

Casanovas based CIFESA on Rome's Cinecittà studios, which had opened in 1937 to make propaganda for Mussolini, but it grew to resemble an old-time Hollywood studio with its own roster of directors (Rafael Gil, Juan de Orduña, José Luis Sáenz de Heredia) and bevy of starlets (Aurora Bautista, Amparo Rivelles).[5] Under the aegis of Admiral Carrero Blanco (Franco's hardline right-hand man, fellow film fan and strict Catholic) CIFESA served the regime faithfully and in 1941 made eleven films, thereby gaining the licences to distribute twenty-two. Sumptuous, fictionalised biographies of previous Spanish monarchs[6] such as *Locura de amor* (Madness of Love, 1948), *Agustina de Aragón* (1950) and *La Leona de Castilla* (The Lioness of Castile, 1951) were a speciality, but it wasn't only history that was rewritten; the present also took on a propagandist spin in the official NO-DO newsreels, which not only insisted on an adjusted version of events but also took up the space on the cinema programme that might otherwise have been used for short films and animation – a traditional training ground for future film-makers. Spanish cinema was being used to rewrite the past and dictate the present in order to posit Francoist Spain as the culmination of a struggle through the ages and a beacon of sinlessness in an otherwise pagan world. Newsreels of Franco and the deeds of his regime were a prelude to bellicose and bigoted epics. The line between spectacle and propaganda disappeared; but the hype was so overblown that it burst with *Alba de América* (Dawn of America, 1951).

CIFESA won the commission to make *Alba de América* in a dubious competition for the privilege of producing a biopic of Christopher Columbus. The honour came with a 10 million peseta budget, massive government support and the personal involvement of Carrero Blanco, who had led the competition jury and already ordered the building of a replica of Columbus' ship, the Santamaría. The screenplay, meanwhile, came from the Institute of Hispanic Culture and was intended as a corrective to Hollywood's overbearing *Christopher Columbus* (1948, directed by David McDonald). Directed by the favoured Juan de Orduña and starring a wooden Antonio Vilar as the

Messiah-like Columbus, *Alba de América* is a didactic pantomime. It begins at the point of mutiny and then unfolds as a flashback that recounts the crusade of Colombus until the moment when land is sighted and the Spanish empire begins in earnest. Characters tend to pose before they speak, then recite portentous prose with hands on waists. Columbus is 'as sure as there is a God' that the promised land awaits and, with the assistance of various monks, makes his case to the glamorous Queen Isabella (Amparo Rivelles), who is otherwise bothered by the 'hard war of Granada' in which the Arabs and Moors are being driven out of Spain. Thus another neat parallel presents itself with the Spanish Civil War, in which a union of the Church and the military drove out the infidels and set about reclaiming the glory that was Spain. Moreover, in this hagiography of Columbus, it is important to note that Carrero Blanco was himself an admiral, and that Columbus' mission is not to open up trade routes (something still unfeasible for Spain in post-war Europe) but to 'go and spread the word'. 'Thank you God for using us to do your will' says Colombus upon his arrival in the 'new world', where salvation, instead of slavery and syphyllis, is the fate of the indigenous people. The film ends with the baptism of a troupe of natives before the Spanish court, one of whom recites a Catholic prayer in perfect Castilian Spanish.

Alba de América was built to be a blockbuster: instead it symbolised the stagnancy of a national cinema that was so fixed on a romantic view of the past that it ignored the problems of the present. Italian propagandist features may have served Mussolini in the same way but, following the end of the Second World War, Italian cinema was revitalised by neo-realism, whereby the condition of ordinary people was represented in films shot in the streets with often non-professional casts. Spanish cinema, on the other hand, remained the tool of an extant fascist dictatorship and entered the 1950s – a decade of growth and reconstruction for all other European nations – with little to commend its rather threadbare and duplicitous view of Spain. So it was with tremendous nerve that José María García Escudero, the new minister for film, withheld the classification of 'national interest' from *Alba de América*, thereby ignoring Carrero Blanco's personal involvement in the feature, and awarded it instead to *Surcos* (Furrows, 1951), the first instance of Spanish-style neo-realism and a picture of society that was anything but propagandist. Directed by José Antonio Nieves Conde, whose fifth film this was after an apprenticeship to Rafael Gil, *Surcos* owes more to American realist films such as *The Grapes of Wrath* (1940) than it does to those of Italian neo-realism, which at that time had hardly been seen in Spain. *Surcos* tells of peasant emigration to the cities and includes scenes of prostitution and black market dealings that muddy the melodrama and moral. A family arrive in Madrid, enthused by the news from their eldest son who has just completed his military service there; but problems of homelessness, unemployment and delinquency build to an almost sacrilegious denouement – the disintegration of the family unit that was so central to the doctrine of Franco and the Catholic Church. *Surcos* ends with the family returning to its village, but dares to twist its moral with a final shot of the eldest daughter jumping from the train and another family arriving to take their place. Or it would have done: that scene was corrected (i.e. cut).

Progressive critics rallied to the film: the Catholic Church railed against it. Escudero was obliged to resign and a few weeks later the film's 'special interest' classification was reneged and returned to *Alba de América*. Nevertheless it was the first incidence that a more truthful reflection of contemporary society had reached the screen and more changes would come. It wasn't just this internal opposition to the dictatorial view, the regime itself was responding to economic and political pressure from outside by softening its fascism in order to attract foreign capital and investment. This makeover allowed for the establishment of an official film school, which opened in Madrid in 1947 with an intake of one hundred and nine students, including two who, ironically, would spearhead the cinema of opposition – Juan Antonio Bardem and Luis García Berlanga.

Bardem was born into a theatrical family in 1922. His mother was a comic player and his father a supporting actor in melodramas, his grandmother and two aunts were actresses.[7] At the age of six months they took him on tour in South America and, sometimes out of necessity, wrote him into the play. Eighteen months later the family returned to Madrid, where Bardem developed an interest in film-making that began with the Christmas present of a Pathé baby projector and cartoon reels of *Felix the Cat*. During the Civil War the family moved first to Barcelona, then San Sebastian, where Bardem was obliged to join the *Falange Juvenil* (Franco's 'Hitler Youth') at the same time as his own political ideas began forming in direct opposition. After the war he returned to Madrid, where he joined the illegal and clandestine Communist Party (PCE) and learnt about film-making from the illicit writings of the Russian theorists Kuleshov and Pudovkin. He studied agronomy and joined the film department of the Ministry of Agriculture in 1946, only to leave the following year for the new film school, the Instituto de Investigaciones y Experiencias Cinematográficas (IIEC). There he met Berlanga and the two were soon so conjoined that they both wrote for the university magazine *La hora* (The Hour) under the interchangeable signature of 'B'. In 1948 Bardem won a prize from CIFESA for the best student of the year, but he never graduated. University authorities claimed that he had used up his quota of film stock all too soon and excluded him on grounds of 'technical insuffiency' – a term that was probably invented in order to derail the career of a student whose political leanings were already apparent in Bardem's final project, an unfinished documentary on Madrid's Barajas airport. Yet he stayed close to

Berlanga and they continued writing scripts together in the hope of interesting the few independent film companies that had emerged after the dethronement of CIFESA following the commercial debacle of *Alba de América*.

Berlanga was born into a wealthy Valencian family in 1921. In order to divert attention from his father's republicanism, he had enrolled in Franco's elite Blue Division and fought on the Russian front in the Second World War. Next to Bardem, however, Berlanga seemed apolitical: his inspiration for film-making came not from theory and politics but from the Spanish literary traditions of the *zarzuela* (light operetta), the *esperpento* (an absurd and grotesque but colloquial theatrical genre) and the *sainete* – a farce that more affectionately caricatured common folk. Their first film together, *Esa pareja feliz* (That Happy Couple, 1951), was a gentle, buoyant comedy of contemporary life that concealed a diatribe against consumerism, thereby revealing both the common ground and divergent intent of the writers. It begins with a spoof of CIFESA and its pompous epics: an uproariously stilted conversation between noblemen and the suicide of their queen, who jumps from the ramparts and lands on Juan (Fernando Fernán Gómez), whose mission as production assistant is to catch her. The parody is an immediate affront to the so-called 'national interest' cinema in Spain, in place of which Bardem and Berlanga focus on Juan as a much more genuine example of Spanishness. In

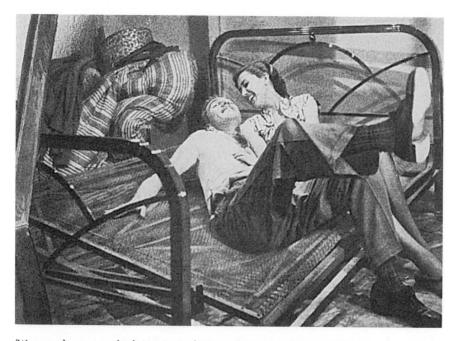

'We were happy, we had no money.' Fernando Fernán Gómez and Elvira Quintillá in *Esa pareja feliz* (Luis García Berlanga and Juan Antonio Bardem, 1951)

his memoirs, Fernán Gómez describes this opening as 'a declaration of principles' and explains that the purpose of *Esa pareja feliz* was 'to entertain the public by showing them a piece of reality.' He also recalls the comical consequence of the overwhelming mutual respect that existed between himself and his debutant directors. On the first day of filming he found clothes in his dressing-room that he took to be his costume. 'I looked in the mirror and I looked terrible,' he remembers, but he turned up on set anyway and asked his directors for their opinion, both of whom approved. It was only some years later they discovered the clothes had been left there for throwing out and that all three had been too respectful to voice their distress. 'I wasn't about to start work by complaining and make those young men doubt their own ideas,' writes Fernán Gómez (1998, pp.379–80).

In his dishevelled suit, Juan is a near-Kafkaesque everyman. Leaving the make-believe of the film set he walks home to the grim reality of a house full of screaming kids and peeling paintwork, where he lives with his wife Carmen (Elvira Quintillá) in one of the separately rented rooms. Bardem would have had them recovering from the death of a child, but was overruled by Berlanga, whose own bias towards humour had already filled the other rooms with the gallery of raucous caricatures that would become his trademark. A note tells Juan to look for Carmen in 'the Atlantic', a crammed cinema, where she sits amidst an audience that is enthralled by the escapism on offer in the latest Hollywood romance. But Juan spoils the film for her and those around them by explaining the techniques and tricks of the film. Thus, in its first few scenes, *Esa pareja feliz* sets up both the CIFESA and Hollywood forms of escapism and knocks them both down with realism. 'Damn, they've cut the kiss!' complains Carmen, thereby adding censorship to the conspiracy that promises the audience of workers a happy ending but keeps it forever out of reach. The only possible escape might be if they were to win the competition to spend one day like royalty that is announced in the intermission: 'All of Madrid just for you!'

Juan's pondering on the chasm that exists between reality and his wife's fantasies introduces a flashback to them setting up home three years ago, meeting the neighbours and making do, just like everyone else of their social class: 'We were happy, we had no money.' Then, when that memory turns sour over recollections of power cuts and a correspondence course in radio engineering that turned out to be a scam, back even further to when they'd met in the hall of distorting mirrors at Madrid's Casa de Campo funfair: 'It's a mirror? Just as well, I thought that's what we were like.'[8] But any regrets are banished on the day they win the competition and are chauffeured around Madrid in an orgy of orchestrated consumerism, collecting presents from competition sponsors, dining out and dancing until the day ends and the chauffeur dumps them back down to earth, so overloaded with packages that they cannot even kiss. Their resolution is to share out their gifts to sleeping tramps; Carmen even leaves her new Italian shoes behind and stands on stockinged tiptoe for their kiss. As a rejection of fascist and consumerist culture this bittersweet final scene caused friction between the directors and is undeniably forced: but it works. A Capraesque triumph of love over the class struggle provides a heartwarming fade-out that also celebrates the class consciousness and solidarity of the protagonists.

Esa pareja feliz was shot piecemeal by a hastily assembled production company called Altamira that utilised the students and staff of the film school, with Bardem directing the actors while Berlanga commanded the crew.[9] It has sprightly visual puns and well-juggled running gags, overlapping dialogue, personable leads and a number of political gibes that clearly went straight over the head of the censor, such as the panicking (politically perplexed) chauffeur – 'Right? Left? Right? Left? Where!?' – and the disarray of a light opera on a nautical theme, in which a singing, sinking admiral suggests a daring parody of Carrero Blanco. The episodic production schedule allowed the co-directors to adjust their script and style in order to reflect their affinity with the Italian neo-realist films that were beginning to reach Spanish screens, many of which would be screened in a special week-long season in Madrid's Italian Cultural Institute in November 1951.[10] An argument raged over whether neo-realism was a style or an ideology, but the films inspired Spanish film-makers to make films cheaply in the streets with recognisable characters, thereby promoting an alternative perspective on Francoist society to that which was sanctioned by the state. Neverthless, there were differences: Spanish neo-realism swapped indigenous black humour for Italian sentiment and was rather less enamoured of Hollywood. Also, Italian neo-realism depicted the poor, whereas the Spanish kind was made appropriate for all marginalised folk, whether economically, socially or politically.

Esa pareja feliz received the lowest classification from the censor, which meant that its chances of distribution were minimal. A private screening was organised to raise support for Bardem and Berlanga, but the film would not be released until 1953 on the back of their second collaboration. Of the few independent film companies that had sprung up to challenge CIFESA, UNINCI was the most politically motivated and therefore the keenest to recruit the makers of *Esa pareja feliz*. UNINCI had been formed in 1949 and included amongst its founders Francisco Canet Cubel and Ricardo Muñoz Suay, who were both, as was Bardem, members of the illegal Communist Party. Their aim was to make films that might counter the propaganda of CIFESA and they commissioned a script from Bardem and Berlanga, with the provisos that it should include five songs from Lolita Sevilla and, accordingly, have an Andalusian ambience. The result was *Bienvenido Mister Marshall* (Welcome, Mister Marsall, 1952), an ingenious farce that used a microcosmic village as the setting for a state of the nation address, in which mordant satire was made palatable by being flavoured like an Ealing comedy such as *Passport to Pimlico* (1948). UNINCI paid Bardem and Berlanga in shares and brought in Miguel Mihura, a comic playwright, to polish the script, but Bardem was forced to surrender his shares along with the chance to co-direct when he found himself close to indigence. The film was therefore helmed by Berlanga, who suffered various disagreements with his more experienced cast and crew, but who would be fêted by international critics and film-makers following its screening in Cannes in 1952, while Bardem barely managed to make the film festival on his third-class train ticket.

An introductory prologue uses freeze-frames and jump cuts to introduce a multitude of characters with comic potential in the long-dormant Castilian village of Villar del Río, all of whom are described in a wry voiceover from Fernando Rey, who whispers so as not to wake the council secretary and even apologises for pausing the film while one character is lifting a heavy can of film. Then even Rey is quietened by the mini-motorcade that brings a minor official with an urgent message for the deaf mayor Don Pablo (José Isbert). The Americans are coming, and every village in Castile is under orders to make a good impression on a nation that might deign to rebuild it with a handout from the Marshall Plan.[11] 'Tell them about the industry.' 'What industry?' asks Don Pablo. 'It doesn't matter, they only speak English. But don't forget they carry dollars!' Don Pablo calls an emergency meeting to plan how best to impress the Americans (where one of the best suggestions is a sack race!) before Manolo (Manolo Morán), who is trawling his singing starlet (Lolita Sevilla) around the bars of Spain, suggests they all dress up as Andalusians and do the village up as well, because that's the only Spain the Americans know. Thus the town is rebuilt like a film set, with whitewashed walls, geranium-filled window boxes and strolling guitarists, while the villagers study how to fight bulls and dance flamenco. The tone is affectionate, but there is no mistaking the satire that rails at what Spanishness had been reduced to, not only in the eyes of foreigners but in the *españolada* films as well (though, ironically, the setting of Guadaliz de la Sierra itself had to be redressed by Berlanga with a cardboard fountain for the purposes of the film).

Night falls and the villagers dream of what their new lives might bring, prompting parodies of various film genres. The mayor, for example, dreams himself into a western movie, with saloon brawl included, while Don Luis, the gentleman, starts an empire in the style of *Alba de América* but is eaten alive by natives.[12] Then the big day dawns, with the villagers done up like the cast of a very kitsch *Carmen*: and the Americans drive straight through without stopping. Now the villagers have to pay for the expense and try not to blame anyone, because, as Rey's returning voiceover attests: 'He who asked for a tractor yesterday is hard-pressed to give a bag of potatoes today.' As with *Esa pareja feliz*, the resolution of *Bienvenido Mister Marshall* is based on solidarity amongst the poor and marginalised in Spanish society. 'Sometimes things happen,' concludes Rey, 'but then the sun comes out again.' It's not much, but in the backwater country that was post-war Spain it was all that many Spaniards had. Spain never received a cent from the Marshall Plan, though Spaniards could derive some compensation from the fact that 'Mister Marshall' was duly insulted by the film, with Cannes jury member Edward G. Robinson protesting that it was anti-American, and the new American ambassador to Spain being severely disconcerted by being driven under a banner that said 'Bienvenido Mister Marshall' on his arrival in Madrid. The Spanish foreign minister, apparently, was hard-pressed to convince him that it was only publicity for a film.

Berlanga continued in the same vein for his following films, choreographing multi-player microcosms of mediocrity under Franco but, by dint of censorship, *Novio a la vista* (Boyfriend in Sight, 1953, co-written with Bardem), *Calabuch* (1956) and *Los jueves, milagro* (Every Thursday a Miracle, 1957) were weaker in their satire and a disillusioned Berlanga would not return to film-making until 1961. For Bardem, on the other hand, politics and film-making were an inseparable vocation that would lead him to a monumentous showdown with the state. Anyone with dissident political beliefs or an urge to be creative in the arts would have been frustrated during the dictatorship, to have both was surely unbearable. Bardem's frustration, being equal to his commitment, was partly surmounted by the second week of Italian neo-realist films in 1953 and the publication of nine issues between 1953 and 1956 of the magazine *Objetivo*, in which he expounded his views on film theory in terms that championed mostly unseen films from the Soviet Union and thereby communist ethics. Film-wise, his semi-autobiographical *Cómicos* (Comics, 1954) was a hard spin on *All About Eve* (1950, Joseph L. Mankiewicz) that explored the sacrifice and struggle of the theatre, a world to which his family and childhood belonged: 'It was nothing more than vomiting memories' (Cerón Gómez, 1998, p.101). *Felices pascuas* (Happy Christmas, 1954) meanwhile (for the films were made almost simultaneously) was a tender comic odyssey in which a family loses the national lottery but wins a lamb from the neighbourhood butcher. The idea is to fatten the lamb for Christmas, but 'Bolita' quickly becomes a pet. One day Bolita is stolen by Gypsies, causing the father (Bernard Lajarrige) to follow its descent through a police station, a convent and a military barracks until he finds it, seconds before the axe, in a slaughterhouse. Although it's a little muddled by shifts of tone and the religious context and symbolism, Bardem's theme once more illustrates the acquiring of social conscience and class consciousness. What Berlanga would have overlaid with irony and humour Bardem undercuts with realism and militancy. In his attempt to rescue the lamb from what are, respectively, the forces of law and order, the Catholic Church and the military, the father becomes proactive, even though, in the final scene of the family sitting around a table on Christmas Eve, lamb included, he also ends up hungry.

But never mind the consequences, activism was the thing – an activism that would culminate in the Salamanca Congress of 14–19 May 1955, when Bardem seized the opportunity of a conference organised by the film club of the University of Salamanca, Basilio Martín Patino and the editorial staff of *Objetivo* to launch a denunciation of the state's stranglehold on a national cinema that he described as 'politically, useless; socially, false; intellectually, base; aesthetically, void and industrially, stunted.' The problem with Spanish cinema, he claimed, was that it had no problems, it was 'a cinema of painted dolls' that had simply renounced its role as 'witness to our time' and was complacently, vacantly, toeing the party line. But his criticism was also constructive, and for this he attracted the support of a wide spectrum of people that included the ousted García Escudero, the Falangist director José Luis Sáenz de Heredia, the young Carlos Saura and, of course, Berlanga. Bardem's demands included the clarification of the code of censorship ('Destroy the labyrinth!'), the end of exclusivity for the NO-DO newsreel, protection for Spanish cinema against an influx of foreign films, the establishment of a national network of deregulated film clubs, vindication of the role of cinema in society and an appreciation of social realism in achieving this aim: 'Film is not a means,' he cried, 'but an end!' As examples of the type of cinema that was needed the Congress also hosted screenings of De Sica's *Bicycle Thieves* (1948), *Bienvenido Mister Marshall* and Bardem's latest, *Muerte de un ciclista* (Death of a Cyclist, 1955), straight from winning the International Critics' Prize in Cannes. This was the moment to which Bardem aspired, when politics and film-making fused. He stood up to the dictatorship in defence of Spanish cinema and offered this film as his manifesto.

The theme, as always, is conscience. A couple of bourgeois adulterers, hurrying back to the city, knock down a cyclist and leave him to die. Juan (Alberto Closas) was once a soldier in Franco's army and is now a well-placed academic (his brother-in-law is the dean), but the cold-bloodedness of his lover, María José (Lucía Bosé[13]) disturbs him enough to reject the supposedly superior morality of a society that condemns their adultery but, both literally and symbolically, condones, even sanctions, their murder of the working class. And this was no abstract metaphor: on viewing Bardem's script the state censor actually demanded retribution for their adultery before the end of the film and let the killing pass. In this Francoist *Bonfire of the Vanities* Juan is consumed by guilt and attempts to separate himself from the hypocrisy by which he maintains his social status, but in so doing he antagonises friends and family (i.e. those members of his class and generation who won the Civil War and profited accordingly) and is identified as a traitor to the Francoist

'He's still alive . . .' Lucía Bosé and Alberto Closas in *Muerte de un ciclista* (Juan Antonio Bardem, 1955)

regime. He tries, for example, to make amends to the dead man's family in their almost medieval slum; he also berates María José and those who find amusement in the tribulations of the poor.

In expressing the shifting sands of Juan's morality and conscience Bardem constructs *Muerte de un ciclista* upon a juxtaposition of ideologically charged film styles that maintains the vibrancy and spectacle of the political parable. For the scenes which take place in the Madrid slum, for instance, Bardem employs the neo-realist aesthetic, a distant observation of events and people that allows no privilege in the frame, while, for the society balls and dinner parties he utilises the dialectically opposite aesthetic of lush Hollywood melodrama, with its abundance of privileged close-ups.[14] The only link between these two worlds is a Wellesian depth of field that combines the two styles by keeping Juan in close-up, while the real world appears behind him in a focus that is just as sharp and therefore, equally consequential. In visual terms Juan is thereby identified as a prisoner of privilege and, at the same time, a protagonist in the grim reality of most Spaniards. In other words, in his juxtaposition of neo-realism with the *mise-en-scène* of melodrama, Bardem effects a grammar of film-making that maximises and antagonises the political implications of both. The sentimentality of Italian neo-realism often displaced the political discourse, while Hollywood melodramas presented any moral or social problem (e.g. divorce, illegitimacy) in such resolutely personal terms that any political dimension was jettisoned in favour of the star's histrionics. Bardem, on the other hand, recognises the political associations of both styles and creates an ideological discourse from a contrast of their aesthetics: the melodrama of the upper classes uses up all the sentimentality that might otherwise have weakened the political impact of the realism of the poor, and vice versa, the realism of the poor invalidates the sentimentality of the rich.

At times Bardem is overemphatic in his composition and montage, but his discourse clearly adheres to the Soviet style of film-making that was a large part of his political and cinematic education. For example, in one of the dinner parties that María José describes as 'a benefit for something, poor kids, stupid kids, some kind of kids', Bardem reveals Juan's paranoia as he tracks a whispered secret around the room by squeezing a stark, Soviet-style montage of battleship-(Potemkin)-sized proportions into a society drawing-room. Consequently, in this jarring sequence of rapidly edited, off-centre close-ups without dialogue, Bardem employs the film aesthetic associated with communism to deconstruct the tyranny of the bourgeoisie. Bardem even samples a noirish expressionist aesthetic when Juan, walking in the streets at night ('for something bad I did once'), has his conscience assailed by the sound of bicycle bells. Accordingly, *Muerte de un ciclista* could be considered a derivative hotchpotch were it not for the force of its rhetoric and the always relevant appropriation of the disparate aesthetics for their political meaning. Juan rejects the bourgeois lifestyle in order to live up to his newly awakened social conscience: he resigns from his post and makes plans to confess, but María José is too self-serving to comply. In an attempt to convince her of the immorality of their privileges, Juan takes her to where they killed the cyclist and recognises the place as a battlefield where he had recently fought, thereby connecting the death of the cyclist to the killing of thousands just like him in the Civil War. Terrified by his demands for penitence, María runs down Juan and races home to her husband, only to lose control when swerving to avoid another cyclist and career over the side of a bridge. The final shot is of her bloodied face in 'privileged' close-up as she hangs upside down from the wreckage of her car, while the cyclist stands on the bridge, equally in focus though distant, before cycling away for help. His compassionate action is Bardem's testament to the moral superiority of the working class, though this conclusion was accepted by the five-man board of censors, which only objected to a scene of students demonstrating against the nepotistic employment of Juan. The protest scene was largely cut, but at least in the few frames that remain there is evidence of a new voice and a new generation in Spain. 'This lack of selfishness, this solidarity,' remarks Juan in support of those who wish to oust him, 'they can shout ¡*Viva!* (Long live . . . !), ¡*Fuera!* (Out!) or ¡*Abajo!* (Down with . . . !): The important thing is to shout!'

In the Salamanca Congress, too, the important thing was to shout. But, with the exception of a new federation of film societies and a revised system of quotas for the distribution of Spanish and foreign films, Bardem's demands were ignored, but noted. Shortly thereafter, while filming *Calle mayor* (Main Street, 1956), he was arrested and held without being charged, though the vaguest of explanations suggested he and *Muerte de un ciclista* had incited a student demonstration in which a Falangist was injured. However, *Calle mayor* was a co-production with France and Bardem's arrest drew immediate protests from such as Jean Cocteau and Jean Paul Sartre. The publicity was a major embarrassment for the Spanish authorities, who had only recently won an international public relations campaign for Spain to be accepted as a member of the United Nations. Bardem was now a potent symbol of opposition to the regime and his unlawful jailing was liable to prompt the UN into taking a second, closer look. Bardem's lead actress, the American Betsy Blair, visited him in jail and refused to continue filming until he was released two weeks after his arrest.[15] United and retaliatory, their renewed collaboration on *Calle mayor* would result in one of the most brilliant and searing indictments of society in Spanish cinema.

At the behest of the censor, who had already cut twenty scenes from the original script, *Calle mayor* begins with a declaration of universality: this is most definitely not Spain (it says here) but 'any city, in any province, in any country.' Protesting too much, however, only serves to focus our attention on the Spanishness of the titular main street in which a single, monotonous church bell is enough to identify the Spanishness of the setting and therefore the specificity of its theme.[16] Inspired by the play *La señorita de Trevélez* (The Young Lady from Trevélez) by Carlos Arniches,[17] *Calle mayor* recounts a few weeks in the life of Isabel (Betsy Blair), a convent-educated, small-town spinster who becomes the butt of a cruel practical joke when she falls for Juan (José Suárez), who is then goaded by friends into courting her so they may enjoy the punchline of him dumping her at the annual dance. Similarly, Bardem wrongfoots his audience by beginning his film with a promise of a black-humoured *sainete*, when a crane shot introduces a practical joke in which undertakers deliver a coffin to a man who is still alive; but this nifty seduction quickly turns sour as Bardem embroils us in the antics of the joke's perpetrators as they set their sights on Isabel. Consequently, it is the inner struggle of Juan, initially virile and handsome but increasingly sickly and weak, that gives Bardem his patient for a social X-ray of a very infirm society.[18]

In a delicate and affecting focus on Isabel and her traitorous beau, *Calle mayor* avoids the rhetoric of *Muerte de un ciclista*, and even expresses pity for the perpetrators of her humiliation. Juan's friends are not evil, just bored: 'no worries, no ambition' remarks Federico, a visiting writer and the film's voice of conscience.[19] 'Like children playing with ants' they torture innocents such as Isabel, because of ennui brought on by too much privilege, but in their lack of empathy and compassion there lies the most understated critique of the ruthlessness of the Francoist regime. For all the tumult that accompanied its making, *Calle mayor* is a sincere and intimate film, firmly focused on the heartbreaking performance of Blair. Her stifled intelligence becomes a tangible force for change when awakened by the attentions of Juan. As the ruse spirals out of control Juan finds himself accompanying her to a building site where she plots out their future home: 'The children here . . . and the bedroom here. How many beds? Always two, like in the cinema? I heard it was because of the censor. But I want one just for us!' Blair is such an intelligent and self-effacing actress that Isabel becomes a credible and not altogether likeable character, thereby transcending any accusations of pamphleteering that Bardem and his film might otherwise have suffered. She whitters on incessantly about how miserable life was before Juan, spiking her monologues with sarcastic imitations of the idly sadistic townspeople, while displaying a self-awareness that is honest to the point of masochism: 'Do you know what I do? I dream.' But then her flowering is a magnificent thing: that first time in church as she struggles to suppress a smile that comes from knowing Juan is waiting for her at the back, the way she skates girlishly across the polished dance floor believing it will be the setting for her betrothal and, most remarkably, the erotic abandon with which she repeats Juan's name over and over, trying out different intonations that might be suitable for a myriad of potential situations together, some of them clearly sexual.

Bardem adheres to a neo-realist aesthetic but does not overload the film with rhetoric. Isabel is indeed a tragedy of wasted life under Franco, but Suárez's more muted Juan is an equal victim of the sacred status attained by machismo in a patriarchal state. Once goaded into the role of seducer on account of his handsomeness and faint heart, he has little option but to allow Isabel to suffer for his own cowardice. 'I love her,' he concedes, 'like a dog or an ill person.' He considers suicide (till Federico reminds him he's a coward) then runs away from this viciously twisted *sainete* and *Calle mayor* ends abruptly with a shot of Isabel trapped behind a rain-spattered window. She is certainly a victim of social prejudice as well as the dastardly prank, but no succour is offered in this brutal final framing of her helplessness; for Bardem derides inactivity as the true crime and Isabel is therefore her own gaoler. Like the students in *Muerte de un ciclista*, the important thing is to shout, but Isabel does not utilise her own intelligence, nor even believe in the brief realisation of her potential: she simply waits for a man to rescue her and gives up on life when one doesn't. A conscience is useless without proactivity and Isabel, for all her victimhood, does nothing to protest her true worth.

Calle mayor was a French entrant in the Venice Film Festival, where it won the international critics' prize, and achieved considerable success in New

York, where critics compared it favourably to *Washington Square* by Henry James. In Spain it played for a month in Madrid's prestigious Gran Vía cinema after a premiere that was interrupted several times by ovations for the director and his cast. Bardem rejoined UNINCI and set about more ambitious projects that expounded upon the principles of communism, but both *La venganza* (The Vengeance, 1957) and *Sonatas* (1959) toppled over into dogma. His extremism alienated audiences, critics, producers, new-bloods such as Carlos Saura and even old friends including Berlanga;[20] but it did attract Luis Buñuel, who wrote: 'My friend Julio Alejandro helped me write [*Viridiana*], but pointed out that we'd have to make the movie in Spain. I accepted on the condition that we work with Bardem Productions, since they had a reputation for opposition to Franco' (1983, p.234).

Buñuel was born in Calanda, Teruel in 1900 and, following a strict Jesuit education, had gone to university in Madrid, where he befriended Salvador Dalí and Federico García Lorca. Enthused by film, he moved to Paris in 1925 and worked as production assistant for Jean Epstein before embroiling Dalí in a plan to make a feature that would warrant their entry into the Surrealist group of André Bretón. *Un chien andalou* (An Andalusian Dog, 1925) remains a touchstone of surrealist art; its flagrantly irrational images are blasphemous, putrid, disturbing and possessed of a mad beauty, often all at the same time. *L'Âge d'or* (The Golden Age, 1931) was their follow-up, a sadistic, anti-clerical travesty whose nightmarish imagery was grounded in Rabelaisian wit. Returning to Spain, Buñuel inserted the surrealist ethos into *Tierra sin pan* (Land Without Bread, 1932), a consequently contradictory documentary on a desperately impoverished area of Spain, which was prohibited by the coalition conservative government. Following brief employment in the production company Filmófono, Buñuel fled to Paris at the beginning of the Civil War and in 1938 reached the United States, where he supervised Republican propaganda films and edited documentaries for New York's Museum of Modern Art. Unable to return to Spain at the end of the Civil War, he worked briefly for Warner Brothers, dubbing films into Spanish, and in 1946 moved to Mexico City, where he remained in exile until Bardem and UNINCI invited him back. In the meantime Buñuel had become a prolific and internationally renowned film-maker. His work was hardly seen in Spain, except in semi-private screenings, but in films such as *Los olvidados* (The Forgotten Ones, 1950), about the slum kids of Mexico City, he was known to have explored a way out of the dead-end streets of neo-realism by employing hallucinatory images and nightmares to illustrate the subconscious of his protagonists. Even by rumour and reputation he was a film-maker to follow. The very fact that he was a Spanish film-maker working beyond the reach of the dictatorship made his life a legend. In exile, he was a down-to-earth Dalai Lama for the film-makers left behind. And so, at a time of discreet hope for the Spanish film

Fernando Rey and Silvia Pinal in *Viridiana* (Luis Buñuel, 1961)

industry, Buñuel, the greatest Spanish film-maker of all time (and ever the forceful conundrum) returned to make the second of only three films he ever made in Spain.

Viridiana (1961) was financed by the Mexican Gustavo Alatriste (and starred his wife, Silvia Pinal) but was supervised by UNINCI and Films 59.[21] In recounting the tribulations of a naïve ex-novice nun *Viridiana* plays like a Mexican melodrama in the style of classic French cinema, but in its churning insides lurks the virulence of the vanguard and the subversion of the Surrealists.[22] Viridiana (Pinal) is released from holy vows to serve her gentleman uncle, Don Jaime (Fernando Rey), who promptly drugs her, dresses her in his dead wife's bridal gown and attempts to rape her, before the magnitude of his perversion (incest, necrophilia, sacrilege, etc.) sends him scurrying away to seek exorcism by suicide, which, ironically, in terms of Catholic doctrine becomes his greatest sin. As heiress to her uncle's wealth Viridiana proposes to practise Christian charity in the real world and fills his mansion with beggars, but finds herself prey to the advances of his lecherous nephew (Francisco Rabal) and the grubby instincts of her Goyaesque charges.[23] Spiritualism turns to carnality, reason surrenders to instinct and order descends into chaos, until, in its accumulation of detail and denouement, religiosity is at the mercy of Buñuel's atheistic zeal. Gleefully parodic, the film explores the fetishisation of sacred acts and artefacts until they become the very essence of sin: the bridal robing of a drugged Viridiana and, later, a leprous male pauper, a dagger in the form of a crucifix and, most notoriously, a mock-up of Leonardo da Vinci's *The Last Supper* with degenerate, lousy beggars for disciples around a blind and lecherous Christ. The scene was largely improvised (and required four hurriedly disguised extras to make up the required number of beggars) but, in its twisted hierarchy and display of moral and physical corruption and decay, Buñuel effects a microcosmic snapshot of Spanish society with all the delight of the slattern who lifts up her skirt to take a photograph of the *tableau vivant* 'with a camera my daddy gave me.' Unlike Viridiana, Buñuel clearly does not subscribe to a romantic notion of the nobility of the poor. Good deeds are irrelevant, mankind is basically rotten and Viridiana, for all her spirituality and purity, is an idiot. Until, that is, her final transformation into a flesh-and-blood woman. And it is here that the board of censors played its most celebrated hand, for the script, which had ended with Viridiana knocking at her cousin's bedroom door and entering, was 'corrected' to conclude with her joining him and her maid (his lover) in a card game, thereby implicating all three in a *ménage à trois* that Buñuel was quite envious of not having invented for himself.

In 1960 an official committee had been established to select Spanish films for foreign festivals.[24] The inclusion of film professionals as well meant that Bardem as a member could browbeat the usual bureaucrats and clerics, with the result that *Viridiana* reached Cannes and won the Golden Palm.[25] Despite being entered as a UNINCI production, the head of the cinema institute in Madrid, José Muñoz Fontán, took it upon himself to claim the prize for Spain. The morning after he did so, however, a raving review appeared in the Vatican newspaper *L'Osservatore Romano* accusing the film of being 'blasphemous, anti-religious, scornful of the poor, morbid, brutal, poisonous and the product of a delirious mind.' Muñoz Fontán was immediately sacked and all copies of *Viridiana* in Spain were confiscated and destroyed.[26] UNINCI was outlawed and Buñuel was ushered back into exile (and prohibited from ever entering Italy) while the original filming permit was retroactively rescinded from its application date. *Viridiana* officially ceased to exist until after the death of Franco, when it received its belated premiere on 9 April 1977, the Saturday of Holy Week and the day that the Spanish Communist Party was legalised.

The results of this official reaction were severe but necessarily brief. In the early 1960s Spain was suffering the consequences of isolation, industry was antiquated and an inability to produce its own plant and machinery gave Spain no hope of catching up. A massive import bill, spiralling inflation and a worsening trade gap pulled Spain into debt that would have caused its collapse had not the United States persuaded the International Monetary Fund to extend existing loans in return for changes in Spain's economic policy. A new age of openness (*aperturismo*) dawned that was designed, largely by technocrats, to ensure Spain's partial integration into the world economy. Foreign investment poured in along with tourists, passing Spaniards who were at last allowed out to look for work abroad. In 1962 Spain joined the Common Market and made plans for the nurturing of sportsmen and film-makers who might carry the flag, win prizes and bring home honour from abroad. The liberalising Minister of Information Manuel Fraga Iribarne reinstated García Escudero to his previous position as Minister of Film, from where he revised the censorship code in accordance with the demands of Bardem and established special art-house cinemas to screen foreign features and those Spanish films in the new 'special interest' category – a classification bestowed upon films that dared to express alternative perspectives on Francoist society, most of which came from the graduates of the relaunched Official Film School in Madrid.[27] Independent producers such as ex-footballer Elías Querejeta became a focus for the spirit of invention and dissent that characterised the so-called New Spanish Cinema and, in the next five years, almost fifty new directors made their first films while Carlos Saura became an internationally acclaimed film-maker on the basis of his personal and prolific cinema of opposition.

Invigorated but dubious of this new spirit of tolerance, a pent-up Berlanga returned to test the water with *Plácido* (1961), a raucous, frenzied comedy that skids perilously close to chaos.[28] The plot of *Plácido* is more of a breathless running gag that sees Plácido (Casto Sendra) tearing around the streets of Madrid on Christmas Eve in his three-wheeler van with a massive star on top (he should be in a festive parade) in a desperate attempt to pay off the first instalment on his transport; but this is merely the thread that allows Berlanga to interweave grotesque vignettes of the class divide. The pungent script was the fruit of his collaboration with the scriptwriter Rafael Azcona, who had already earned a reputation as a satirist in both his work for the magazine *La codorniz* (The Quail) and two mordant scripts for the Italian director Marco Ferreri: *El pisito* (The Little Flat, 1958), about a young man who marries an eighty-year-old spinster so that he can inherit her flat, and *El cochecito* (The Little Car, 1960), which took the Critics' Award in Venice and the prize for Best Film in London. These films' satire was indeed so caustic that Ferreri's residency visa was rescinded, but Azcona found an even greater sparring partner in Berlanga. *Plácido* races from Pythonesque credits to its frenetic first scene in a public toilet, whereupon Plácido is waylaid by a photographer (José Luis López Vázquez) who is frantically orchestrating a public relations campaign in which rich families invite paupers to their tables for Christmas dinner.[29] In the midst of bedlam involving starlets, rogues, bureaucrats and beggars, the film strikes at the social hypocrisy and tyrannical mediocrity of the middle class. Worried sponsors are shown competing for the cleanest beggar, one vagrant has to suffer his host's dog, which sits at the table in a baby's high chair, while another suffers a heart attack and is married despite his protestations by hosts who won't abide him dying in sin. The humour turns black as night, despite bitterly jaunty music, till Plácido has to transport the unhappily married corpse through the town and get back to his hovel in time for his own poor man's supper, whereupon a final Christmas carol provides the ironic anthem for his stupidly steadfast belief in goodwill and Christian charity.[30]

If the censor grinned and bore *Plácido* it was probably because at the speed the film was going there was barely time to jot down an iniquity before the next ten came along. Berlanga's *El verdugo* (The Executioner, 1963) was very different. Based on a true story of a state executioner who needed to be tranquilised before he could perform his lethal act, this Spanish–Italian co-production is an elegant, formal tale that lays bare the social basis of Francoism by exploring the psychological dilemma of its protagonist as an example of sociological malaise. José Luis (Nino Manfredi) is an undertaker with dreams of training as a mechanic in Germany. He meets the shambling executioner Amadeo (José Isbert) and is pressured into apprenticeship when he gets his daughter (Emma Penella) pregnant and they all three move into a new flat that comes with the job. Terrified of ever having to carry out a garrotting, José Luis nonetheless conspires to live well by assuaging his conscience with Amadeo's assurances that most criminals either die first or are pardoned. He even takes to interceding in petty arguments between passers-by in case one of those involved resorts to murder. And all goes well, until he is ordered to report to Majorca, where a condemned man awaits him. His wife takes the trip for the honeymoon they never had, but even she is shocked by the outside world's invasion of an island that is waking up to tourism and full of carefree foreigners. Luckily the condemned man falls ill and the holiday is prolonged: unfortunately he gets better and can be killed. A distraught José Luis is plied with champagne and manhandled to his duty in a magnificently choreographed, high-angle, single take that makes for an increasingly stark and abstract composition out of one corner of the jailyard as it slowly empties of those attending this act of justice of the state. 'Never again!' cries José Luis, when he is reunited with his family on the departing ferry. 'Bah, I said the same thing my first time,' replies Amadeo.

Just two weeks after the execution of two anarchists in Spain *El verdugo* was shown in the Venice film festival, from where the Spanish ambassador to Italy, Alfredo Sánchez Bella, wrote an urgent letter to Franco denouncing the film as 'one of the greatest libels ever made against Spain, an incredible political pamphlet, not only against the regime but against all society too.' In truth, Sánchez Bella was most astute: this portrait of an executioner in need of a successor was easily interpreted as a parody of an ageing Franco, while deliberations on the death penalty transcend the political context of the film's making to attain a universal resonance. Inhumanity is not the reserve of a fascist dictatorship, and neither is careerism or self-interest the localised crime it might seem. In 1963 the Francoist regime was barely halfway through its tenure of tyranny, but foreign powers were only too willing to turn a blind eye to Spain's pitiful human rights record in return for its sunshine and investment opportunities.

Openness was an experiment for the regime, which soon discovered that the flood of foreign funds and tourists were unconcerned about the personal freedom of Spaniards. Thus in 1967, following an escalation in the activities of the Basque separatist group ETA, disruptive action from clandestine workers' unions and protests from the businessmen of Catalonia, the reins of the dictatorship were tightened by Admiral Carrero Blanco, newly appointed to the vice-presidency, who took up the slack from Franco's ailing grip and twisted them into a noose around any possible dissenter. García Escudero was kicked out once more for allowing the Barcelona School of film-makers to hold a similar conference to that of Salamanca, and in his place came Alfredo Sánchez Bella, the returning Spanish ambassador to Italy, who promptly banned all films by Fellini. The Spanish film industry collapsed into a state of fear and disarray that was only briefly enlivened by Buñuel, who carried out another hit-and-run with *Tristana* (1970). This tale of another young maid (Catherine Deneuve) and her lecherous uncle (Fernando Rey) was filmed under cover of being a formal adaptation of the novel by Benito Pérez Galdós; but beneath its dull veneer of respectability there lay virulent anti-clericalism and a treatise on the stagnancy of Spanish society that was too much to bear. Unable to say exactly why the film was so contentious the censor banned it for a reference made to duelling.

The changing fortunes of the dicatorship had all been felt on film. In its beginning, for example, Carrero Blanco had supported the notion of utilising the cinema to dramatise and inculcate patriotic sentiments and had once personally overseen *Alba de América*, a bombastic epic that might have served as a model for those who wished to reclaim the Spanish empire. Then, during the brief period when the youthful protests of Bardem and Berlanga were heard, he had been the target of parody in *Esa pareja feliz*. But, in addition to his personal friendship with Franco, Carrero Blanco enjoyed prestige within the regime, was supported by conservatives, technocrats and the military, and through four decades had personally interceded on matters of censorship and the administration of the film industry as part of his duty to the regime. He entered the 1970s as the obvious successor to a moribund Franco; but on 20 December 1973 this despot-in-waiting was blown sky-high by ETA. The force of the explosion was such that his car flew over the roof of the church he had just been attending. Those investigating the crater concluded that a gas main had ruptured and it was only some time later that the wreckage was noticed and Spaniards discovered that the dictatorship had been left without an heir. Peter Besas reports that only a few days prior to his death Carrero Blanco had gone to the cinema to see Fred Zinnemann's *The Day of the Jackal* (1973), about an assassination attempt on General De Gaulle (1985, p.xvi). His verdict? 'That sort of thing only happens in the movies.'

Notes

1. Censorship and dubbing (including the imposition of rewritten dialogue) took care of any alternative or dissident elements in films from abroad: De Sica's *Bicycle Thieves*, for example, had its title changed to the singular in Spanish (thereby annulling the film's universality) and suffered a spoken epilogue that assured the audience of a happy future for the protagonists. Only very occasionally might something risqué slip through: *Gilda*, for instance, in which not only was the homosexual subtext too subtle for the censor to notice but Rita Hayworth's famously erotic striptease (in which she removes nothing more than her elbow-length gloves) was too abstruse for scissors to sensibly intercede, though it did have priests picketing cinemas and threatening excommunication for those who dared enter. I am indebted to Alfredo Santamaría for his personal recollection of braving the picketing priests.
2. *Raza* (Race, 1941) was directed by José Luis Sáenz de Heredía (first cousin of previous dictator Primo de Rivera) and featured Alfredo Mayo as José Churruca, a thinly disguised version of Franco.
3. There was also the sub-genre of *andaluzadas* for films that exploited the Francoist version of flamenco.
4. Because of this, CIFESA was blacklisted by Columbia and other American companies.
5. The influence of the prototypical Italian epics even extended to the importation of directors such as Augusto Genina, who directed *Sin novedad en el alcázar* (All Quiet at the Fortress, 1940).
6. Paul Preston notes that 'Franco had delusions of being a royal personage, his pride demanding that he could be succeeded only by someone of royal blood' (1999, p.70).
7. The Bardem dynasty continues. Pilar Bardem (*Nadie hablará de nosotras cuando hayamos muerto* (Nobody Will Talk About Us When We're Dead)) is Juan Antonio's sister, which makes Javier Bardem (*Jamón, jamón* and *Carne trémula* (Live Flesh)), his nephew.
8. The use of distorting mirrors relates to the work of Valle-Inclán, the creator of the *esperpento*.
9. A first attempt at making a film called *La huida* was abandoned due to their inexperience.
10. Román Gubern has described this season of Italian neo-realist films as 'a mythic reference point' for Spanish cinema (1997, p.280); while Marsha Kinder dates the movement known as New Spanish Cinema from its occurrence (1993, p.3).

11. The Marshall Plan was a programme of American economic aid for the reconstruction of post-Second World War Europe (1948–52). Spain received nothing, but in an effort to curry favour with the lesser evil of the western powers during their cold war against the Soviet Union, Franco did suffer American military bases in often dangerous proximity to Spanish cities in exchange for American economic support.

12. Due to budget limitations Berlanga had to cut a dream sequence belonging to the spinster schoolteacher (Elvira Quintillá) in which she was ravaged by a football team. It would probably have been cut anyway.

13. Lucía Bosé had played an adulterer in Antonioni's *Chronicle of a Love* (1950), which has a similar plot to *Muerte de un ciclista*. She is the mother of Miguel Bosé, star of Almodóvar's *Tacones lejanos* (High Heels, 1991).

14. Marsha Kinder has written an insightful and compelling essay on the subversive reinscription of melodrama in *Muerte de un ciclista* (1993, pp.54–86).

15. Bardem met Blair in Cannes in 1955, but he had admired her work since seeing her in George Cukor's *A Double Life* (1948). Blair had been nominated for an Oscar for best supporting actress for *Marty* (1955).

16. Bardem filmed in Cuenca and Logroño under strict instructions to avoid filming giveaway landmarks.

17. This play had been filmed previously by Edgar Neville. *Calle mayor* also owes some debt to Federico García Lorca's *Doña Rosita la soltera* (Doña Rosita the Spinster).

18. Curiously, almost all of Bardem's protagonists are, like him, called Juan.

19. Federico (the voice of conscience) is played by the French actor Yves Massard and therefore, ironically perhaps, dubbed (by Fernando Rey).

20. UNINCI, under Bardem, rejected two of Berlanga's projects and picked up but squandered the opportunity to produce Saura's first film, *Los golfos*. In later years Bardem would make documentaries that he financed by stints as a director-for-hire on cheap genre films and opportunist star vehicles for an ageing Sara Montiel (*Varietés*, 1971) and the newly adult, newly sexy singing star Marisol (*La corrupción de Chris Miller*, 1972; *El poder del deseo* (The Power of Desire, 1975)). Despite his consecration in post-Franco Spain Bardem would only work intermittently in television, directing somewhat stilted biopics of Lorca (*Muerte de un poeta* (Death of a Poet, 1987)) and Picasso (*El joven Picasso* (Young Picasso, 1991)).

21. The invitation to make a film in Spain came from Ricardo Muñoz Suay while in Mexico making Bardem's *Sonatas*, but was only ratified after Buñuel met Carlos Saura at the Cannes Film Festival.

22. The story was based upon a play called *El pozo* (The Well) by Julio Alejandro, though Buñuel was also heavily inspired by a portrait of Santa Viridiana in the Museum of Mexico City that shows her with cross, crown of thorns and nails (Pérez Turrent and de la Colina, 1993, p.117).

23. The actors playing these beggars were dressed in clothes that had been acquired in exchange for food from Gypsies who lived under a bridge in Madrid, but the cast also contained real-life beggars including the deranged leper, who once caused a power cut by urinating on a fuse box and played the final scene of the beggars' attempted rape of Viridiana with his trousers full of faeces (Pérez Turrent and de la Colina, 1993, p.120).

24. Carlos Saura's neo-realist *Los golfos* (1959) had been the first choice of the jury the previous year.

25. *Viridiana* was screened on the last day of the festival, prompting the jury to reconvene and reconsider their vote so that *Viridiana* shared the Golden Palm with Henri Colpi's *Une aussi longue absence.*
26. Fortuitously, a copy of *Viridiana* was smuggled out of Spain to Paris.
27. Previously the IIEC, it became the EOC in 1962.
28. The title is highly ironic as *Plácido* means peaceful in Spanish.
29. The title of the campaign: 'Seat a poor person at your table' was the original working title of the film.
30. Ironically, this ending no longer works. The 'poor man's supper' is bream, then the cheapest of fish, now a luxury affordable to the few.

CHAPTER FOUR

Another reality

Carlos Saura

Film-making for me has never been a tragedy. On the contrary, it's always been a great pleasure, enormous fun, a wonderful game. You're doing what you love, making what you've written, putting into practice a series of ideas that are sometimes absurd, sometimes not. This creation of another reality is what fascinates me and I've been working on it for a very long time, whenever I can.[1]

Longevity and fulfilment grants the last laugh to Carlos Saura, who appears to have thrived on the struggle, both political and creative, to realise a better world on film. His early films placed him at the forefront of the cultural resistance to the dictatorship: they were complex, allegorical and subversive, revealing closed worlds and microcosms that provided a much-needed critical perspective on the Francoist regime. His personal creativity was celebrated as a response to autocracy. Yet, far more than pamphleteering, these films investigated the role of the imagination in politics (and vice versa) and revealed a skill with metaphor that was allied to a keen sense of theatricality and ritual. Following the dictatorship Saura's compulsive reworking of these themes alienated many who accused him of stagnancy, but he continued to mark the early years of the democracy with works of wilful idiosyncrasy, subtlety and experimentation. From them would emerge a new way of utilising dance on film and, incidentally, his greatest international success.

Saura was born in Huesca in the province of Aragon in 1932, but grew up in Madrid during the Civil War amidst the cultural detritus and poverty that formed the punishment handed out to the vanquished Republican zone. As he recalls, family life was complicated by its own internal tensions:

My parents were Republicans but my mother was Catholic. She didn't go to mass but, like so many Republicans, she was devout in her own way. Everyone thinks they were all atheists and communists but it wasn't so. In Spain it's not hard to find these extremes. And my father was liberal with an open mind and Republican in the sense that he worked as secretary for the Ministry of Finance and had always lived in the Republican zone.

There were times when Saura's parents sent him to live with his maternal grandmother in her right wing, profoundly Catholic household, but he returned to attend a Marist school, when not skipping classes to see three or more films a day (sometimes the same film over and over again) until his father found out and forbade him. Nevertheless, he learnt to read from an uncle priest that his parents sheltered in their flat and, alongside his brother Antonio's passion for painting, he developed an interest in photography: 'When I was seven I already knew I loved making pictures.'

In time Antonio would become a leading exponent of modern art in Spain,[2] but engineering seemed the probable career path for Carlos, until its study depressed him too much to continue:

Fourteen or sixteen hours studying mathematics! That was a mental wasteland. It was dreadful. I realised that my brother, who was a painter, evolved intellectually and I became more of an imbecile every day. So I decided to abandon it and dedicate myself to photography. That's how I found out who I was.

He published pictorials on music festivals and other travelogues in Spain, pursuing the same social realism in his photographs as he had witnessed in Rossellini's *Rome, Open City* (1945). Indeed, it was a season of Italian neo-realist films in Madrid's Italian Institute in 1951 that inspired many Spanish film-makers, with its revelation of a new type of documentary-style cinema that could be made in the streets with ordinary people; especially Saura, whose wish to make a documentary spurred his successful application to Madrid's Official Film School.

The early 1950s were a galvanising time for those Spanish film-makers who were opposed to the regime. A move towards social realism was led by Juan Antonio Bardem and Luis García Berlanga's *Esa pareja feliz* (That Happy Couple, 1951), Nieves Conde's *Surcos* (Furrows, 1951) and Berlanga's *Bienvenido Mister Marshall* (Welcome, Mister Marshall, 1952). New magazines such as *Objetivo* advanced the theory of the form in terms of veiled communist ethics, while the infamous Salamanca Congress (14–19 May 1955) provided a forum for these film-makers to publicly denounce Francoist cinema and turn the revitalisation of the industry into a political and social imperative. In this they were encouraged by the establishment of Spanish television in 1956 and the appointment of liberal film-fan José María García Escudero to the position of ministerial responsibility for film. Escudero revised the system of government subventions, which had previously only rewarded film-makers who complied with the dictum of 'national interest', and made funding available for those who might attempt films of 'special interest', thereby opening the way for alternative points of view. Consequently the film school became a focus for would-be *auteurs* who were ill-served by existing resources; films were talked about but hardly ever seen. Saura collaborated on short documentary features and graduated in 1957 with *La tarde del domingo* (Sunday Evening), a sentimental, neo-realist short that was the first student film in 35 mm. Seeking realism, he filmed with a handheld camera and, in the scene that takes place during a public dance, simply pushed his actors into the crowd and began filming. 'I started making documentaries,' he recalls, 'and soon I felt documentaries were limited and I wanted to tell stories so I started making fictional films. It's all been quite smooth.' As the only student to graduate that year Saura was quickly recalled for teaching duties and would spend the next six years training students including Víctor Erice, Mario Camus and Pilar Miró. But he also made films: *Cuenca* (1958), a documentary on the medieval city that expressed an uneasy contrast between tradition and social progress, and the full-length feature *Los golfos* (The Louts, 1959).

Los golfos is a film about the marginalisation, self-determination and frustration of Juan (Oscar Cruz), who works in a market in Madrid's working-class district of Legazpi and dreams of making it as a bullfighter. As he is unable to raise the money necessary to secure a trial in the bullring his friends provide him with their gains from petty theft. Made without means, *Los golfos* emulates the neo-realist style of film-making out of necessity, but avoids the manipulative search for poignancy that characterises many of the Italian films. Instead Saura builds his narrative upon a series of disjointed, open-ended scenes that, coincidentally, render the film closer in spirit to the ideology of the French New Wave. His actors were mostly non-professional and included two leads who could not read and had to be told their lines. Consequently Saura allowed his scenes to develop around the improvisation of his cast, most explicitly in the final bullfight, where Cruz refused to comply with the scripted defeat of his character. Seizing the opportunity for realism, Saura struck a deal with the actor by agreeing to end *Los golfos* on whatever was the outcome of the *corrida*. In the event the actor's performance was a disaster and Saura got the pessimistic ending he had wanted, now ratified by actual events.

Nevertheless, in the first of many altercations, the censor objected to the film's moral ambiguity and nihilism: Saura surrendered ten minutes of the final film and the line, 'It's hard to become someone here', that was spoken in a scene of the friends looking at Madrid from its outskirts, thereby contextualising their delinquency as a response to the indifference of the state. In addition, the film was classified of negligible interest and its distribution was held up for three years. However, it did reach the Cannes Film Festival,[3] where its social realism was celebrated for upholding the legacy of Luis Buñuel's film about slum-kids in Mexico City, *Los olvidados* (The Forgotten Ones, 1950), despite the fact that Saura had never seen it. In fact *Los golfos* is best considered as part of a Spanish literary tradition of low-life realism established by Pío Baroja in *La busca* and Benito Pérez Galdós in novels such as *Misericordia*; but, at that moment, the Cannes success established an international reputation for Saura that would prove essential to maintaining his creative freedom within Spain. In addition, Saura's main reward at Cannes was a hug from fellow Aragonese Luis Buñuel and the beginning of a friendship that saw Saura pave the way for Buñuel's shortlived return to Spain from exile; though, unfortunately, the ensuing *Viridiana* affair (see Chapter 3) would effectively curtail film-making in Spain for the following three years.

Saura's next script was to have been a rural reinterpretation of the themes of *Los golfos* but this was censored beyond all hope of its filming.[4] He stuck with teaching until his film course was assimilated into a recognised university degree and he lost his job to those with more academic qualifications. A blessing in disguise, Saura returned to film-making with *Llanto por un bandido* (Lament for a Bandit, 1964), a mix of epic, period film and intimate drama that in scale and form, if not in its theme of the subjective branding of marginalised characters as criminals, was the complete opposite of *Los golfos*. The film starred Francisco Rabal and was set just after the Napoleonic wars of the early nineteenth century, but was a particularly frustrating experience for Saura, who gamely attempted an epic with only five metres of camera track.[5] Individual scenes are striking, such as a duel with cudgels that recreates the 'black painting' *Duelo a garrotazos* (Duel with Clubs) by Goya, but the film was butchered by Italian editors, who wanted an action adventure, and the Spanish censor, who excised an opening scene in which Luis Buñuel and fellow anarchists played executioners who garrotte seven bandits.[6] Resolving to take more control of the film-making process, Saura sought the assistance of the independent producer Elías Querejeta, who would become a key player in Spanish cinema by fostering the careers of many. Their collaboration would generate a thirteen-film attack on Francoism and its legacy that began in 1965 with *La caza* (The Hunt).

La caza opens on a close-up of ferrets in a cage. Trapped together and potentially vicious, they provide the first clue to a metaphorical reading of the film by symbolising the true nature of the protagonists – ex-combatants in Franco's army on a rabbit hunt in a valley that was once their battlefield. 'Lots of people died here,' says Paco (Alfredo Mayo), 'it's a good place to kill.' But Paco is one of the victors: he'd driven a lorry before the war and has since done well in business.[7] On the other hand José (Ismael Merlo) has fallen on hard times and hopes to use the hunt as a means to ask Paco for money. Luis

Emilio Gutiérrez Caba, Alfredo Mayo and José María Prada in *La caza* (Carlos Saura, 1965)

(José María Prada) is a mean-spirited, disillusioned drunk who works for José, and Enrique (Emilio Gutiérrez Caba) is Paco's young brother-in-law, a member of the new generation and clearly identified as Saura's witness to the unfolding drama by his wielding of a camera. Over the course of a sweltering day the three ex-soldiers will quarrel, beg and taunt each other, while Enrique's constant questioning identifies a chain of favours and dependencies that twists Darwinian concepts of survival into a critical treatise on the unnatural consequences of the Spanish Civil War.

In his innovative use of high-contrast film stock, Saura evokes the bleaching heat that keeps an overpowering sense of menace and tension simmering until the violent impulses of each man are ultimately directed against each other.[8] Although they appear to accept their revised social hierarchy their dreams and voiceovers compete against each other between scenes of them preparing their rifles as if for war. 'What war?' asks Enrique, but it's a question that goes unanswered, for the censor clearly twigged Saura's critique of Spanish society and countered his audacity by cutting all mention of the Civil War. Yet, rather than weaken the analogy, such censure only served to strengthen Saura's argument by its illustration of the problems of representation and social realism, for, as Marvin D'Lugo has stated, the debate that Saura intended was intensified by making 'social reality self-consciously a problem of representation for the characters in the film' (1991, p.56). That is to say, Saura's obedient censoring of specific social, political and historical references left his characters in a vacuum that, with powerful irony, was wholly representative of Saura's view of contemporary Spain as a place of fear, denial and falsehood. The final blurred freeze-frame of Enrique fleeing towards the camera recalls both Robert Capa's photograph of a Republican soldier at the point of death and the celebrated final shot of Truffaut's *The Four Hundred Blows* (1959). Thus *La caza* marks a transition in Spanish cinema, with both past and future caught on film in the young man's anguished attempt to escape the frame.

La caza would be held up by the censor, but in 1966 it won the Golden Bear in the Berlin Film Festival, where it was championed by jury member Pier Paulo Pasolini. Thus Saura and Querejeta added more international film-makers and critics to their supporters from Cannes (including Sam Peckinpah, who cited *La caza* as a major influence on *The Wild Bunch*[9] (1969)) and thereby achieved an international status that translated into a singularly privileged relationship with the state in Spain. In part this was maintained by Querejeta's ruse of using double scripts: one went to the censor to froth over while the other was filmed as written. The censor inevitably returned the first script in butchered form, but this was already irrelevant to the actual film being made. When the finished film was presented to the censor it would be too late for a reprimand as it was clear that Querejeta would gladly use his contacts to stir up an international outcry if anything was cut. Fearful of the scandal, the Spanish censor would have to put up with the creative tandem of Querejeta–Saura for the next decade. 'Truthfully, the battles have been fought by my producers more than me,' reflects Saura, 'but there have been times of great difficulty and disappointment and there have been films that I never got to make.' Nevertheless a faithful and committed crew united around this union of producer and director: Luis Cuadrado as director of cinematography, Teo Escamilla on camera, Primitivo Álvaro as head of production and Pablo del Amo as editor. 'A director is like a vampire,' says Saura, 'your collaborators must be the best possible. The better they are the more they give me.' The team would be completed on *Peppermint Frappé* (1967) with screenwriter Rafael Azcona, and Saura's personal and professional union with the actress Geraldine Chaplin.[10]

They never married, but Chaplin's deceptive fragility, introspection and foreignness were a deliberately incongruous presence in Saura's next ten films. Her collaboration tempered and humanised that of Querejeta, who seemed to be pushing Saura into a creative cul-de-sac of dissident film-making. With Chaplin as his collaborator and muse Saura abandoned the realism and rural setting of his first three features and relocated his intimate dramas in an increasingly circumscribed universe, thereby nurturing a theatricality that was based upon the basic, psychological metaphor of many of Saura's films: an isolated country house close to Madrid, with dark passages and many rooms, whose decoration has been aptly described by Marsha Kinder as 'the carefully controlled fetishization of objects in the dual context of traditional orthodox Catholicism and postmodern consumer Capitalism' (1993, p.165). In such an ideologically charged setting Saura's characters slipped in and out of mirrors, make-up and role-plays, exchanging psyches and intermingling hallucinations, dreams and memories. In time Saura would move closer in to Madrid, the geographical, political and metaphorical heart of Spain: a suburban townhouse in *Cría cuervos* (Raise Ravens, 1975), a grand apartment in *Dulces horas* (Tender Hours, 1981), a dance studio in *Carmen* (1983) and a modern flat in *Taxi* (1996); yet this basic metaphor would remain the key to an understanding of his cinema: 'I've always loved the theatre,' says Saura, 'but only inside a film.'

A primary cause of this theatricality was Saura's way of cutting abruptly between scenes. His narratives resembled disjointed acts in a play, as if in the context of such theatrics resided some undeniable sense of realism, that what cannot be ignored is the consciously representative nature of the film itself. Indeed it is precisely this foregrounding of artifice that reveals Saura's warning against taking the cultural propaganda of Francoism at face value. In *Peppermint Frappé* (1967), for example, Julián (José Luis López Vázquez) is a doctor in Cuenca, whose eroticised memory of an anonymous young woman (Geraldine Chaplin) at a religious festival provokes an obsession with Elena (Chaplin again), the foreign fiancée of his childhood friend Pablo (Alfredo Mayo).[11] Bubbly blonde Elena was clearly modelled on the myth of the female tourists – generically termed *suecas* (Swedes) – who were beginning to flock to Spanish beaches, bringing with them a desirable but disruptive liberalism that contrasted dramatically with the circumscribed role of women in Spain. Julián, for instance, clearly suffers from a frustrating inability to function around this independent woman. When Elena dances to raucous pop music his response is to pick up his camera, thereby retreating to a safe, objective distance that simultaneously allows him to indulge in an act of voyeurism. His response to her independence is to transform his meek, adoring nurse Ana (also played by Chaplin) into her double and then murder Pablo and Elena. Just like the men in *La caza*, therefore, Julián responds to representations of femininity with violence, for, apart from the murder, he also symbolically rapes her drugged near-corpse by ripping off her false eyelashes and smearing her lipstick.[12] His final orgasmic union with the transformed Ana, who now appears dressed as the young woman from his memory, is conveyed in a Hitchcockian vortex of vertiginous camerawork that befuddles Francoist doctrine in its twisted reinstatement of gender roles, patriarchy, machismo and religiosity. That is to say, a devoutly Catholic, middle-class professional such as Julián is revealed as a murderous pervert precisely because he embodies many of the precepts of the state. His ritualised murder of Pablo and Elena may therefore be seen as a sacrifice in accordance with the propaganda and doctrine of the state that has formed him. Of course the audience would only reach this conclusion by deconstructing the narrative in order to diagnose the psychological delusion of the character and the correlative artificiality of the social context which he inhabits. But this was precisely Saura's intent, for as Marvin D'Lugo has perceived, his films reveal an 'implicit desire to demystify aspects of the cultural mythology of Francoism' (1991, p.29). In other words Saura wanted his audience to recognise its own reality as a lie.

Francoist Spain had presented itself as the last stronghold of faultless, mighty Catholicism in an otherwise pagan world. Saura's response was to explore this self-righteous concept in films that stressed the injustice of a female's fate as a criticism of its supposedly state-sanctioned lawfulness. In *Stress es tres, tres* (1968), the infidelity of a wife (Chaplin) and the murder of her lover are revealed to be the masochistic fantasy of her husband. Thus not only is her ostensibly transgressive behaviour revealed to be the product of a deranged male subjectivity, but the originator of the moralistic discourse is identified as the perpetrator of an indoctrination which demands that the female be punished for what is, in effect, his own transgressive fantasy. Saura's aim was to reveal the enemy as a holy alliance between the deep-rooted sexism of an elitist society and the dictatorship. Consequently his films repeatedly challenged the privileged perspective of the male and the concomitant objectification of the female by encouraging his audience to perceive the false axiom of male superiority and the moral corruption of its originators. By these means his audience were inspired to form their own critical perspective on the state as they viewed the distorted images of a dictatorship that had not only constructed their own way of seeing, but had made them accomplices to their own victimisation.

During the worldwide cultural and philosophical upheavals of the late 1960s Saura's films found an increasingly appreciative audience abroad. Following *Los golfos* and *La caza*, Saura was invited back to Cannes in May 1968 with *Peppermint Frappé*, but the screening took place in the middle of a month of rioting in Paris. Jean-Luc Godard, François Truffaut and others had already seized the festival hall in the name of the Parisian Committee of Occupations and four members of the jury had resigned in support, but others tried to keep the festival going with an evening showing of *Peppermint Frappé*. Saura tried to withdraw his film but was ignored, until the lights went down and he, Chaplin and the other film-makers held on to the curtains to stop them opening. The curtain went up anyway, with Saura and Chaplin hanging on. When they fell all hell broke loose, with *Peppermint Frappé* projected on top of the ensuing fistfight. The outcome of all this was the Marxist reorientation of many French film-makers and a black eye for Geraldine Chaplin. Meanwhile simultaneous student demonstrations in Spain had prompted a clampdown on cultural and personal liberties. However, rather than work freely in exile like Buñuel, Dalí and Picasso, Saura returned to the period of increasing tyranny that marked the last years of the dictatorship.

The metaphorical constructs of Saura's films were a practical response to censorship, but it also meant that his and Azcona's writing veered towards a schematic deployment of characters. *La madriguera* (The Warren, 1969) betrays this subterfuge in its limited focus on a bored, middle-class couple in a modern, bunkerlike chalet on the outskirts of Madrid. Stirred from ennui by the arrival of the furniture that constitutes her inheritance, Teresa (Chaplin, who collaborated on the script) takes to role-playing scenes from her childhood and gradually submerges into fantasies of suicide and murder. Here was the release of the imagination that had been celebrated in the movements of 1968, but turned on its head in the context of Francoist Spain so that Teresa's fantasy of a glorious past is signalled as a derangement that once more leads to violence. Her fetishistic use of mirrors relates to the Francoist propaganda that revised Spanish history and proclaimed this false image in films in order to present the dictatorship as the culmination of a holy crusade. Saura's message to his audience was that the past was false but that the madness of the present was real.

Deciphering the analogies of Saura's films was often easier when his themes and images could be contextualised within traditions of art and literature.[13] In his next film, for example, the audience would have known from the identically titled painting by Hieronymous Bosch, which hangs in Madrid's Prado Museum, how Saura intended for the family of *El jardín de las delicias* (The Garden of Delights, 1970) to be recognised as the inhabitants and progenitors of a world in moral apocalypse. An ageing, amnesiac, wheelchair-bound patriarch (José Luis López Vázquez) becomes a spectator to representations of scenes from his life that are performed by family members hoping to jog his memory for such financial secrets as the combination to his safe. It didn't take much to see the senile and infirm patriarch as a satire on the condition of Franco. The family, meanwhile, repesented the Spanish people, whose attempts to recreate scenes from their past are hopelessly staged and artificial because their patriarch has denied them any notion of themselves beyond his autocracy. The film ends with the family reduced to wandering aimlessly in wheelchairs around their patriarch, submitting once more to the only role model available. Unsurprisingly, distribution of *El jardín de las delicias* was withheld for seven months, thereby denying Saura the opportunity to screen it in foreign festivals.

Rather than bow to censure, however, Saura's response would be the rather more explicit critique of *Ana y los lobos* (Ana and the Wolves, 1972). Here the beleaguered female is an English au pair (Chaplin), whose resistance to the sexual, religious and authoritarian demands of three brothers (who function metaphorically as symbols of family, Church and military: the 'holy trinity' of the dictatorship) is deemed by their mother to constitute unlawful behaviour for which she is punished by being raped, scalped and executed. The film's minimalist, linear narrative certainly made the parable as explicit as possible: the matriarch was Spain, the three brothers represented Francoist doctrine and their children were the new generation of Spaniards under the supposedly pernicious influence of the foreigner – Ana, who was the quintessential victim of Francoism, martyred in a final shot that left no doubt as to the accusatory nature of the film. The censor, as expected, was staggered by the film's blatancy, but decided to grant it a release anyway, betting, correctly as it turned out, that its fleeting passage through a limited distribution would avoid a scandal rather more effectively than its prohibition.

Just warming up, Saura's next offering was *La prima Angélica* (Cousin Angelica, 1973), in which Luis, an emotionally stunted male (José Luis López Vázquez), relives scenes from his childhood and religious education during the Civil War, physically shifting back and forth between the past and the present in search of an explanation for the infantile psyche that resulted. López Vázquez played Luis as both man and boy and created an affecting portrait of a half-formed being who, with his sad-dog face and nervous shuffle, personified those members of a generation that had been suffocated by decades of obeisance to Francoist doctrine. Rather than continue his attack on the prosperous victors of the Civil War Saura made *La prima Angélica* a treatise on contemporary Spain from the perspective of the losing side. Perhaps most outrageously, the film ridicules Luis' falangist uncle Anselmo, who breaks his arm and has it set in plaster in a fascist salute. Clearly perceived as an affront to the moribund dictatorship, *La prima Angélica* was excoriated by the censor and the right-wing press. Cinemas suffered bomb warnings and attacks when they attempted to screen the film (as the second feature on a double bill with *Jesus Christ Superstar*!). It wasn't just the specific taunts that caused outrage; Saura's psychotherapeutic odyssey courted blasphemy by presenting the family unit as a medium of repression, servility and corruption. 'It's a Spanish problem,' explains Saura,

> I see the Spanish family as destructive; the kids are controlled and suppressed. It's part of the social and family culture. It's the mother, it's the father, it's the children: it starts off as a family and becomes a tribe, then a mafia. You start owing favours and when the family unit isn't so tight-knit it's prey to corruption.

The scandal ensured that *La prima Angélica* was celebrated in Cannes that year, but it also signalled a hiatus in the working relationship between Saura and Azcona: 'Suddenly I began to reject all his mysogyny,' explained Saura, 'because I'm the complete opposite' (Boyero, 1988, p.99). Perhaps as a corrective Saura's next film, *Cría cuervos* (Raise Ravens, 1975), avoided the tradition of female suffering on behalf of all marginalised people in Spain, and focused instead on the particular trauma of women. The film explores the real and fantastic worlds of little Ana (Ana Torrent) growing up in a house marked by death. Haunted, literally, by memories of her mother's wasting illness, and introverted by the death of her father, whom she believes she murdered, Ana struggles to make some sense of events and thereby define her own role in the transitional present. In this Ana is both aided and confounded by the tentative presence of Geraldine Chaplin as both her mother and her adult self, who recalls the events of the film from the other-worldly perspective of 1995. Consequently there is a cyclical aspect to the film that withholds hope about the post-dictatorship future even as it assumes the death of Franco, the patriarch of Spain. However, rather than reflect the tentative optimism that characterised the time of its making, *Cría cuervos* is mostly a hushed, still and sombre film, emanating a sense of exhaustion and melancholy that may have been partly inspired by the recent blindness of Luis Cuadrado, Saura's previous cinematographer, to whom the film is dedicated. Indeed the film's intense focus on the subjectivity of Ana (and so the eyes of Ana Torrent, which would become wholly emblematic in Spanish cinema[14]) is a poignant testament to the alternative perspective on society and the state that Cuadrado and Saura had presented.[15]

Cría cuervos marked the political transition in Spain and was duly celebrated with the Special Jury Prize at the Cannes Film Festival of 1976, but it also marked an impasse in the work of its director. The death of Franco had a bewildering effect on the Spanish people, who, like Ana at the end of *Cría cuervos*, would step into the blinding light of a different Spain. The end of the dictatorship and Spain's rapid acceleration towards capitalism and liberalism left numerous artists, film-makers and playwrights floundering in its wake. Many who had built their careers on the creative struggle against the totalitarian state were suddenly made redundant. Saura discovered that critics and public alike had ghettoised him as a director of anti-Franco parables that were now considered fossils from an extinct regime. In response, he has reflected:

In my films, like those of others, there was politics because we believed that we had to change things. Everything that happened to us, everything that worried us was connected to politics. So it's normal that it gave meaning to our lives, to mine. It was there in my stories. However, if you ask me, I'd have to say that I never wanted to make political films.

(Alameda, 1997, p.11)

Nevertheless, looking back from the perspective of 1999, Saura had to admit that:

Following the death of Franco I lost all interest in politics, because what there was before was so brutal, so potent, and what we had to destroy was so powerful, that what came after was nothing but little quarrels amongst uninteresting political groups.

The mark of Saura's disorientation was *Elisa, vida mía* (Elisa, My Life, 1976), an intimate, complex film, more Bergman than Buñuel, that removed itself from contemporary politics and hid out in a house in the country. There Saura observed the crumbling identities of a dying Luis (Fernando Rey) and his beloved daughter, Elisa (Chaplin), who clings to the flotsam of Spanish literary traditions in an attempt to define herself in a world beyond patriarchy. Luis has written a first-person account of his daughter's life that Elisa will appropriate for her own past and then continue writing in an act of self-determination that reveals her as the maker of her own future. This obscure, elliptical film traces the changing perspective of Elisa as she adapts to a world without authority, and it contextualises her evolution within a series of allusions to poetry, literature, opera, music and film. Most notably, Elisa takes over her father's duties in staging a version of Calderón de la Barca's morality play *El gran teatro del mundo* (The Great Theatre of the World) in the local school, whereby Saura makes the play's concept of human self-determination relevant to post-Franco Spain by revelling in both the amateurism (i.e. the realism) of the schoolchildren and their potential for autonomy.[16] Nevertheless the chaos from which Elisa's new self must emerge is compounded by the film's lack of any emotional or visual anchor: there is no child's gaze here with which to maintain a critical perspective, though Ana Torrent does appear as the young Elisa, with Chaplin as her mother and therefore Luis' wife, thereby accentuating the Electra complex that simmers between Luis and Elisa and the intertextuality with Saura's own *Cría cuervos*. Moreover this intertextuality originates more directly with Víctor Erice's *El espíritu de la colmena* (The Spirit of the Beehive, 1973), for the central premise of Saura's film was once the prologue to that of Erice, who discarded the notion at script stage against the wishes of his producer, Querejeta, who duly safeguarded the idea for a future project.

Saura's own father was ill at the time of the film's making and this passing of a generation placed a keen edge on his study of transition. Saura has referred to *Elisa, vida mía* as his first liberating film, but its success abroad, especially in France, was in contrast to its reception in Spain, where the critical reaction was typified by that of Fernando Trueba, one of the new generation of film-makers, who wrote that the film was 'sluggish and uncertain . . . a lamentable slump in the work of its author.'[17] *Elisa, vida mía* is certainly too personal to be wholly penetrable, but it did signal a conscious attempt at artistic reorientation by Saura, one that would see him turn gradually inwards, towards more intimate works which would oblige him to revise and even parody his own work in an attempt to liberate himself from the conventions of his own film-making.

Two years later *Los ojos vendados* (Blindfolded Eyes, 1978) seemed like an unnecessary postscript to his films of the dictatorship in its reaction against the last-gasp right-wing extremism of the time. It was the tale of a survivor of torture whose testimony is revised as a theatrical monologue. A game of mirrors and doubles culminates in the transfer of personality from the victim to the actress and the consequent execution of the latter. It reflected a recent spate of violent acts in Spain that included the beating given to Saura's own sixteen-year-old son by right-wing thugs, but it failed to find an audience in a country that was otherwise focused on liberalism and loathe to consider the darker side of accelerated change. Sidelined as a film-maker by the demand for soft porn and comedies that characterised the liberalism and relief of the immediate post-Franco era, Saura was unimpressed by a generation's misuse of liberty and democracy that would have grave consequences for their children in the 1990s: 'Spanish youth is disoriented by its freedom. They don't have the ties they used to. However their parents used to educate them, it might even have been wrong, but at least it was some kind of orientation.'

But the end of the dictatorship had also disoriented Saura. His privileged status was washed away by the influx of foreign films and a new generation of film-makers such as Pedro Almodóvar and Fernando Trueba, whose films revelled in the present with barely a glance back at fascism. Nearing fifty, Saura sought to revise his own outdated concepts of Spanish society in films which drew on his own art and experience in an attempt to find an overview that would reflect on the position in which he found himself. *Mama cumple cien años* (Mama Turns a Hundred, 1979) was a sequel of sorts to *Ana y los lobos*, in which the resurrected Ana returns to the country house where she was killed to find that the three murdering brothers had become parodies of their former selves: José (the military fetishist) has died, of course; Juan (the pervert and family man) has run off with the cook; and Fernando, the mystic, has taken to gliding as a substitute for levitation. Here was a new way of looking at the past, one that was no longer fearful: the film drew a line under the past that was strangely ratified by Saura's splitting from Chaplin.

Saura continued to revise his past accomplishments, like an artist who paints over his own canvases, by reviving the social realism, improvisation and amateur casting of *Los golfos* in *Deprisa, deprisa* (Fast, Fast, 1980), and reworking *La prima Angélica* as a rather stagnant self-parody in *Dulces horas* (Tender Hours, 1981). The first won the Golden Bear in Berlin in 1981 on the same day that Lieutenant-Colonel Tejero staged his attempted coup in Madrid's Congress of Deputies so that cynical cries of 'Thank Tejero!' accompanied Saura's acceptance speech. Meanwhile Spain's right-wing *ABC* newspaper criticised the film's social realism and accused Saura of paying his cast in hard drugs.[18] In contrast, the self-deprecating *Dulces horas* saw Saura spoof the introspection of his more theatrical films in a slight and stilted tale of Juan (Iñaki Aierra), who writes, directs and acts in an autobiographical play that allows him to wallow in a reconstruction of his childhood. His mother had committed suicide, but Juan's relationship with the actress (Assumpta Serna) who plays her reveals that his delusion of guilt is fruit of an Oedipal conflict that is celebrated rather than resolved in the final scene of the actress bathing him.

Saura received the most virulent critical attacks of his career for *Dulces horas*, yet the experience only seemed to redirect his anarchism towards a wilful subversion of expectations in the major international co-productions of *Antonieta* (1982) and *El dorado* (1988), as well as in more intimate dramas such as the May–December romance of *Los zancos* (The Stilts, 1984) and *La noche oscura* (The Dark Night of the Soul, 1989). The latter especially was reviled for its grim deliberation on the creative process of the Spanish mystic Saint John of the Cross (Juan Diego) and its staunchly anti-clerical vision of his historical rebellion against Carmelite doctrine. With *El dorado*, meanwhile, Saura confounded Spanish critics even more, along with politicians and the organisers of the quincentennial celebrations of Columbus by taking the biggest budget ever raised for a Spanish feature and using it to transform the legend of conquistador Lope de Aguirre and his incursion in South America into an allegory of imperialist corruption and the consequences of pitting Spaniard against Spaniard. 'I still have the tendencies of an anarchist,' admits Saura,

> but now the anarchy has to be kept inside. If you belong to an anarchist party you stop being an anarchist. Besides, absolute anarchy can never be carried out. Better said, it's a personal posture, something very particular that's sometimes in your work and sometimes not.

In response Spanish critics attacked him for whinging when Spain was supposedly a democratic country and a fledgling consumerist utopia. 'I've a bad relationship with most of the critics,' admits Saura:

They look on me as an enemy instead of a friend. But after thirty-odd films, I know that what's important is to follow your own path even when they tell you that you're going the wrong way. It's only if you're true to yourself, true to your own mistakes even, that you can make something personal.

(Alameda, 1997, p.11)

Foreign critics were rather more perceptive, with John Hopewell noting 'Saura's intriguing emotional changes from the late 70s, when he begins to respond far more to the southern Spanish side of his family' (1986, p.148). This change in sensibility involved a move away from claustrophobic films about the Castilian middle classes and inspired an enthusiasm for light, colour and movement that flourished in a series of films about the Andalusian culture of flamenco that were no less critical of contemporary Spanish society but far subtler in their anarchism. In part this enthusiasm stemmed from the autonomy afforded Saura by shooting on a soundstage. 'There are so many advantages to working in the studio,' he avers,

I'm interested in artifice, in taking the film beyond an easy realism. What I like is when the artifice allows you to believe the story that's inside all the artifice. It's a miracle that all these artificial elements can create something so real. That's why musicals have this great advantage. They allow for a much greater experimentation than normal films: the relationship of the camera to the music is so full of possibilities.

In post-dictatorship Spain the dancer and choreographer Antonio Gades had recuperated Lorca's play *Bodas de sangre* (Blood Wedding, 1933) with a flamenco dance version that replaced the text with movement, rhythm and gesture. This dance version accentuated the realism of the play by jettisoning Lorca's supernatural elements and foregrounding the social injustices that provoke the tragedy of the mismatched lovers, thereby adding political resonance to the characters' plight, trapped as they are by their society. Saura was unwilling to attend a rehearsal of the ballet, but had succumbed to the fervour of producer Emiliano Piedra. As Saura recalls: 'I'd never have dared to make a musical if it hadn't been for Emiliano telling me, "Hey, look, see if you want to do this," and then I was fascinated.' Saura's delight ratified his appreciation of flamenco as a medium for the expression of the dis-enfranchised and sharpened his contempt for its bastardised 'pop' form as a symbol of the corruption of Spanish ideals in the 1980s.[19] His collabora-tion with Gades and, later, cinematographer Vittorio Storaro, would see his enthusiasm for flamenco evolve into a unique critical perspective on con-temporary Spain.

Saura's *Bodas de sangre* (Blood Wedding, 1981) opens on a still of Gades' dance troupe in full costume and make-up, with the lead characters clearly identifiable in the social hierarchy that is required of a posed wedding photograph. The camera obliges the characters to hold these positions, though it also obliges the performers themselves to confirm their roles in both the semi-documentary film and in the closed community of the dance company. Similarly, the everyday costuming suggests a realism that Saura will underscore by structuring his film around an awareness that the world constituted in performance is not separate from the world outside, for the ballet itself is only reached after backstage scenes that establish the systematic sequence of events that is demanded by the performance: the arrival, the warm-up, the costuming and the rehearsal. Although many critics regard these scenes as a mildly interesting prelude to the ballet, Saura's structuring of *Bodas de sangre* emphasises the lifelong dedication of the dancers that is essential to the performance itself. Consequently Saura transforms the single indoor space of the dance studio into a microcosm of Spanish society. The dance troupe becomes an example of a social order that is expressed in the importance that Saura places on the lives and experiences of the dancers, in particular that of Gades, a committed communist, whose dance interpretation of the character of Leonardo, the instinctual and fateful outsider, is vital to the political undercurrent of the film.

As regards the ballet, Saura's experimentation and innovation transforms the performing space of the dance studio into something fluid and dynamic, for the camera's movement places the spectator aesthetically in constant motion in accordance with the rhythm of the music and the dance. 'You have to eliminate all superfluity,' says Saura, 'I film dance in minimalist terms and I think the music is the key. If we start from the music you can sing, dance or simply perform. But the most brilliant discovery is the music.' With *Bodas de sangre* Saura created a multi-layered illustration of the links between different systems (i.e. film, dance and theatre) and revitalised his own status in national and international markets. Moreover it established the importance of flamenco in his work as a medium for expressing his fears that, after just a few years of democracy, the Spanish people were once again in danger of losing their direction and identity.

Returning to flamenco and his collaboration with Gades, Saura came to film *Carmen* (1983) after rejecting an offer to make a gala version of the opera that subsequently fell to Francesco Rosi.[20] Similarly, he rejected Ángela Molina for the role of the mythic Gypsy and pursued his own concept for a revisionist version of the tale by casting an unknown.[21] Laura del Sol, with her black hair, almond-shaped eyes and full lips, suggested a Gypsy heritage that supported Saura's revindicatory use of genuine flamenco, while the independence and freshness of her Carmen embodied Saura's own reading of the myth as an exploration of gender politics in contemporary Spain. *Carmen* recounts the story of Antonio (Antonio Gades), who is searching for the music, dance styles, props and cast that will incarnate his dream of recapturing the essential Spanishness of the myth. As the film begins he is auditioning prospective leads, none of whom will meet with his approval. He stands facing a huge mirror at the front of the dancers and performs his concept of Carmen for them to copy; but, in performing the role for the female applicants, Antonio's ideal woman is shown to be a chauvinist concept that is the legacy of Francoist doctrine and its censure of the self-determining female. Saura contends that Antonio's deluded belief in the empiricism of the myth is an ultimately masochist self-deception, for his subsequent attempts to fashion a Carmen from the raw material of an authentic female will be thwarted by her independence. At the same time Antonio's endeavour runs parallel with his attempts to reinterpret Bizet's opera through the medium of flamenco, thereby suggesting that his attempt to make flamenco fit the text is analogous to the attempts of males in post-Franco Spain to make modern women conform to their previously circumscribed roles. His increasing desperation will see him struggle to reimpose the cliché on an elusive female and eventually resort to her murder.

In clarifying this analogy Saura develops a structural metaphor that reveals how Antonio's attempts at validating the myth, both in performance and in his relationship with his chosen dancer, only serve to create a fragmented narrative, in which the inability of an audience to distinguish between reality and fantasy mirrors Antonio's inability to function between the myth and the woman. Moreover, in targeting Antonio as an unwitting advocate of Francoism, Saura isolates him in his fantasy by insisting upon an alternative reality that is created by the fusion of a feminist sensibility, genuine flamenco and the affined perspective of his subjective camera. For example, Carmen and Antonio have sex, but Antonio's fantasy of taming the myth is a delusion that Carmen punctures by upping and leaving in the middle of the night. Aware of his objectification by this female and faced with subordination and emasculation, Antonio returns to the controllable world of his dance studio and resorts to subjugating the female by conjuring up and redressing his fantasy of Carmen with the archetypical props: 'And now with the fan, the comb, the flower, the veil. The cliché! What the hell?' Carmen is thus fetishised by Antonio: the image that she presents relates only to male narcissism and fear. 'You have to be more feminine' he shouts at her, but he clearly means 'more submissive.' Ironically, therefore, Del Sol's Carmen best incarnates the original myth because she refuses to submit to a male's demands that she conform to the adulterated myth of the Spanish female.

Saura contends that it is this Carmen's affinity with flamenco which evinces her authenticity, and this suggests that her dancing should be recognised as the politicised expression of female identity. Indeed, despite the frequent victimisation of the female in Saura's earlier works, there is much evidence in his later films that women were fighting back – literally so in ¡Dispara! (Outrage), in which a rape victim takes revenge on her attackers (before being martyred to the sensationalist press), and here, where Carmen's rebellion is allied to the vindication of flamenco. Her independence challenges and exposes Antonio's own crumbling ideology in accordance with the changes in contemporary Spain: 'Spain has changed so much in terms of freedom,' says Saura, a four times married father of seven,

and what's changed most is the role of the women in contemporary society. The female has stopped being just a mother and become a person who works, who seeks her independence, and I think that's great. But it means that all the old family values have changed too.

Consequently it is in the context of such social change that Carmen's protest – 'I want to be free and do as I feel!' – must be seen, for the myth of Carmen is open to many interpretations, but the independent woman, by her very nature, defies the imposition of them all. At the end Carmen storms offstage during the macho charade of Antonio's dance–duel with the bullfighter because the choice of partner is not theirs to make, it's hers. It's almost as if she were storming off the film set too. Indeed it would have been a total vindication of her rights if Saura had shown her stepping over cables, barging past cameramen and spotlights, ignoring his own calls to return, and leaving the artifice of the film set for good. But not even Saura dares save the life of this woman, so trapped is she in the tragic, fateful and fitting end of a typical protagonist of flamenco deep song. Antonio grabs her, pushes her out of sight and stabs her three times in her abdomen with a sexual rage that is alarming. She slumps to the floor and her bright red flamenco skirt suggests a terrible, incriminating flow of blood. Once again she is a martyr to male oppression, while her analogous relationship with flamenco represents its defamation by external forces such as Bizet, with his post-Napoleonic romantic fervour, and the similarly jingoistic appropriation of flamenco by the Francoist regime.

Franco? By the mid-1980s he was already a fading memory as Spaniards celebrated consumerism as an escape from backwardness and insularity. Flamenco was commonly decried as hackneyed folksong that let slip a whiff of primitivism; yet, as Carlos Saura suggested in El amor brujo (Love, the Magician, aka A Love Bewitched, 1986), this bastardised form of flamenco was merely the legacy of its transformation into a signifier of Francoist doctrine. Genuine flamenco has an anarchic, nihilistic sub-text that speaks of marginalisation and anguish: it was poles apart from the commercial, often ideologically opposite form of flamenco that had been popularised by the *españolada* musicals of the Franco era and the tourist board of the democracy. Thus, in *El amor brujo*, Saura underlines the incongruity of traditional flamenco in contemporary Spain, thereby signalling the estrangement of contemporary Spaniards from their cultural heritage and the effect of this alienation on individual and national identity. In terms of structure the linear narrative of *El amor brujo* certainly appears very different from Saura's dextrous and meaningful manipulation of space and time in films like *Cría cuervos*, *Elisa, vida mía* and *Carmen*. Saura had developed a motif of mirrors that forced an audience to recognise itself in these complex and profound dramas, but the superficiality of *El amor brujo* suggested that he was reflecting the lack of imagination of his contemporary Spanish audience, who, says Saura, 'don't know how to use their freedom' and were increasingly unwilling to engage in a process of national and self-analysis.

As if trapping his audience in a world of their own prejudicial notions of Spanishness, Saura begins *El amor brujo* with a shot of the door to his soundstage trundling downwards like a medieval portcullis and a slow pan of the camera on to the massive, illuminated Ciclorama that gives way to a recreation of a Gypsy encampment. This opening shot forces the audience to move from a subjective recognition of the world beyond the studio walls as their reality to an objective appreciation of the artifice that has been created within. Yet the camera does not stop there; it continues moving until its frame is within the limits of the encampment and the primacy of the setting is established. Consequently the camera is not signified as a means to artifice but as a portal to another reality, one that Saura will explore with an astute sense of irony. In accordance with the original tale of star-crossed lovers by composer Manuel de Falla, Saura presents his Gypsy community as the last territory of magic and myth, yet he also signals that the magic is merely cinematic, while the mythology is that which was established by the folklorist musicals of Francoist cinema. Indeed, this encampment is not all that different from the one in Saura's *Taxi* (1996) that is torched by fascist thugs, who then celebrate their self-righteousness (while Saura underlines their ignorance) by dancing to traditional (i.e. Gypsy) flamenco.

Saura starts the credits to *El amor brujo* by freezing the image of the child Carmelo as he watches the sudden betrothal of his sweetheart Candela to an indifferent José. He then effects a very slow dissolve from the child's face to that of Antonio Gades as the adult Carmelo, because, in effect, this dissolve is also a political transition: the child of Francoist Spain becomes the adult of the democratic 1980s. In addition, Saura's innovation of the character of Lucía (Laura Del Sol) introduces an independent, passionate female to the drama of *El amor brujo*, one who is continually presented in relation to traditional flamenco song and dance. The adult Carmelo is ultimately united with Candela (Cristina Hoyos) by sacrificing Lucía to the vengeful ghost of

José, but this dubious happy ending barely excuses the sacrifice that reorients the original work by positing Lucía as victim. Consequently her fate is allied to that of Saura's Carmen in the sense that both females are identified in relation to genuine flamenco and both are sacrificed to the enduring legacy of the Francoist regime and the indifference of contemporary Spain.

El amor brujo revitalised the wrath of Spanish critics, who either failed or refused to engage themselves with Saura's deconstructionist critique. Thereafter, apart from a brief reconciliation with the critics, the public and Rafael Azona in 1990 with *¡Ay, Carmela!* (a warm and spirited adaption of an ultimately tragic play about travelling players during the Civil War), Saura's films would most often be relegated to Spanish art-house cinemas, while he pursued a studio-bound experimentation with the relationship of music to the rhythm of editing and the movement of cast and camera – an endeavour that suggested he was boxing himself into the studio in order to provoke a reaction of creativity akin to that which he developed under the dictatorship. *Sevillanas* (1992) was a showcase for various interpretations of the eponymous dance in which Saura's blunt sequencing of performances avoided the constraints and distractions of a plot and focused instead on the performers. Its portrait of contemporary Spain incorporated regional differences, traditions and innovations in an act of social synthesis, whereby a diverse sense of Spanishness was anchored to the common root of the *sevillana* – a type of folk song that Saura had previously reinstated 'as a symbol of resistance and a reaffirmation of solidarity and integrity' in *¡Ay, Carmela!* (Jordan and Morgan-Tamosunas, 1998, p.29). The organisers of Seville's Expo' 92, where the film was intended to run for six months in the Spanish pavilion, initially rejected *Sevillanas* for being 'too traditional, too stereotypical' (Sharrock, 1992, p.26). Nevertheless the popular and critical approval awarded to Saura's *Flamenco* (1995) was even more testament to the rapidly changing face of contemporary Spain, for the success of this feature was an indication that genuine flamenco culture was finally able to reclaim its heritage from a history of such ignorance and oppression. In so doing *Flamenco* celebrated a new pluralist identity for modern Spain.

Flamenco, like *Sevillanas*, is an abruptly sequential series of performances with neither narrative nor commentary to distract. It opens on massive angled mirrors, monolithic shards that cut into the viewers' perception of depth and shatter the railway station setting of La Plaza de las Armas in Seville into mismatched images. This authoritative beginning suggests that we are to bear witness to various perceptions of flamenco: each song, each style, rhythm and dance, each colour, camera movement, frame or edit will reflect the same ideological framework that underpins the culture of flamenco, but in different ways. María Pagés, for example, performs against a backdrop that is redolent of Lorquian lunar imagery. And then there is the Sevillan-orange sunset

Merche Esmeralda dances a guajira in *Flamenco* (Carlos Saura, 1995)

behind Mario Maya, the blood-red afterglow around Joaquín Cortés and the low, full moon that makes Enrique Morente's cry seem positively lycan-thropic. Saura and cinematographer Vittorio Storaro's minimalist aesthetic indicates an awareness of the historical and social contexts that have com-peted to repress, honour or appropriate the mythology of flamenco for disparate reasons, while their playful but committed reinvention of the film studio as performing space would continue with *Tango* (1998) and *Goya en Burdeos* (Goya in Bordeaux, 1999).

Saura's move towards non-narrative cinema also signalled his purposeful distancing from the ideology of the commercial cinema and the beginning of a more personal and introspective exploration of his relationship with the cinema that became apparent in the increasingly intimate works that resulted: the semi-autobiographical *Pajarico* (1998) and the autobiographical *Tango* – 'I thought it was a chance for me to tell my own story at last, as a film within a film.' With a similar narrative to *Carmen*, *Tango* was a melancholic but edgy dissertation on the creative struggle of an ageing artist that Saura would continue to explore in *Goya en Burdeos* and *Buñuel y la mesa del rey Salomón* (Búnuel and King Solomon's Table, 2001), a homage to his great friend Buñuel. Thirty years on, with Franco confined to what he calls 'pre-history', Saura is keener than ever to celebrate his personal and creative freedom:

It's one thing to be against many things in contemporary society, but, inevitably, I have to compare it with another age. And compared to what happened in Spain under Franco, what's happening now is extraordinary. To be able to express yourself freely, to speak, to do what you like, it's all a miracle to me. I've made thirty-something films and every time I make one it seems like another miracle.

Notes

1. All quotes from Carlos Saura, unless otherwise stated, are from an interview with the author, June 1999.
2. Antonio Saura's abstract of Brigitte Bardot hangs in the Museum of Modern Art in Cuenca and is prominently featured in Saura's *Peppermint Frappé*.
3. Peter Besas suggests that this was because 'it was the first time the Cannes entry was chosen by a group of Spanish film professionals rather than by bureaucrats' (1985, p.48).
4. This script, titled *La boda* (The Wedding), was based upon Miguel de Unamuno's *Abel Sánchez*.
5. Francisco Rabal had already provided the commentary for Saura's documentary on Cuenca. He combined matinee-idol looks with a powerful screen presence and a magnificently virile voice and would be an important figure in Spanish

cinema, appearing in Buñuel's *Viridiana* (1961) and, most recently, Saura's *Pajarico* (1998) and *Goya en Burdeos* (Goya in Bordeaux, 1999).

6. The garrotte (in which the victim is slowly strangled by an iron collar) was an infamous means of execution employed by the Francoist authorities. Amongst other artists in the cast, the playwright Antonio Buero Vallejo appears as a town crier.

7. There is particular resonance from the casting of Mayo, who had been a pilot in Franco's air force before becoming an Errol Flynn-like champion in propagandist war films and melodramas including the emblematic *Raza* (Race, 1941).

8. Long before the climax, violent impulses that emerge from this powder-keg of machismo are repeatedly directed against representations of women in such scenes as the burning of a girlie magazine, the use of a shapely mannequin for target practice, and the rabbit hunt itself (rabbit is *conejo* in Spanish, slang for the female pubic area).

9. 'Peckinpah once told Saura that seeing *La caza* had changed his life' (Hopewell, 1986, p.76).

10. Saura met Chaplin, daughter of Charlie, when she was on location in Spain filming David Lean's *Doctor Zhivago* (1965). She also appears in Robert Altman's *Nashville* (1975), Alan Rudolph's *Remember My Name* (1978) and *The Moderns* (1988) and Martin Scorsese's *The Age of Innocence* (1993).

11. The young girl is a homage to Luis Buñuel, to whom *Peppermint Frappé* is dedicated, and is based upon Saura's memory of a relative of Buñuel who took part in the festival of the beating of the drums in Buñuel's hometown of Calanda.

12. Marsha Kinder notes that 'his greatest violence is committed against fetishized objects' such as the accoutrements of make-up and the gleaming red Corvette sports car that he pushes over a cliff with the bodies inside (1993, p.170).

13. Other examples include Goya (*Llanto por un bandido* (Lament for a Bandit), *Goya en Burdeos*), Calderón de la Barca and Garcilaso de la Vega (*Elisa, vida mía*) and Federico García Lorca (*Bodas de sangre*) as well as the more generic influence of the *esperpento*, a theatrical genre created by Ramón del Valle-Inclán in which reality is transformed into something grotesque and absurd.

14. Other films that trade on the eyes of Torrent are Víctor Erice's *El espíritu de la colmena* (Spirit of the Beehive, 1973), Jaime de Armiñan's *El nido* (The Nest, 1980), Alejandro Amenabar's *Tesis* (Thesis, 1996) and Helena Taberna's *Yoyes* (2000).

15. For an analysis of *Cría cuervos* see the following chapter on the theme of childhood in Spanish cinema.

16. The morality play or *auto-sacramental* was a medieval morality play performed during Corpus Christi as a medium for the expression of religous doctrine, in which God gives archetypical roles to humans who then have to find their way in the world though a series of temptations, trials and choices. Other examples of intertextuality include the film's title (from a poem by Garcilaso de la Vega) and Luis' vision of death as an accumulation of skinned horses' heads in an abattoir (a Buñuellian image of putrefaction that relates most specifically to *Un chien andalou*).

17. Fernando Trueba, *Guía del ocio de Madrid*, n.75, 23/5/1977 (quoted in Sánchez Vidal, 1988, pp.169–70). Trueba is the director of *Ópera prima* (1980), *Belle epoque* (1992) and *La niña de tus ojos* (The Girl of your Dreams, 1999).

18. Saura denied the accusation, saying that his cast of real-life delinquents (including one, Jesus Arias, who was on day release from prison) had a much better idea than he of where to get drugs. The film's success was partly due to its bestselling soundtrack of rock flamenco by Los Chunguitos.

19. Saura had been viscerally attracted to flamenco in his work as photographer and film-maker before a deeper understanding of the metonymy inherent in its performance system revealed the mythology and philosophy upon which flamenco culture is based. Saura was official photographer for the Festivales de Música de Granada y Santander. In 1955 he produced an eight-minute film on 16 mm entitled *Flamenco*, which documented his artist brother Antonio's attempts to create an action painting, and in 1958 he went on to produce a documentary feature on the dancer La Chunga.

20. Francesco Rosi's *Carmen* (1984) starred Placido Domingo and Julia Migenes-Johnson and was choreographed by Antonio Gades.

21. Molina was a trained dancer who had performed flamenco (naked) in Buñuel's *That Obscure Object of Desire* (1977).

CHAPTER FIVE

Spirits and secrets

Four films about childhood

Children, so the dictum goes, should be seen and not heard; but the problem with rendering them mute witnesses is that the adult world forgets they are there, watching. Perhaps for that reason Spanish film-makers have frequently couched their dissidence through the alternative viewpoint of children, often ignored and frequently frightened, but always observing, always questioning and aware. Far from wallowing in Hollywood-style condescension and sentiment, the four films that are discussed in this chapter have shown how the natural wonderment of childhood was transformed into a distressful fear of the unknown and the unknowable: a parent's past and a child's own future. Víctor Erice's *El espíritu de la colmena* (The Spirit of the Beehive, 1973) relates the trauma of a childhood in post-Civil War Spain – the vulnerability of little Ana, growing up on the losing side in a world in which communication is impossible; while the same director's *El sur* (The South, 1983) continues the theme into adolescence, with the young girl struggling to understand the complexity of her relationship with her parents, who, during the long years of the dictatorship, are barely able to reciprocate her tentative gestures of affection. But there is also evidence of hope for the future in Carlos Saura's *Cría cuervos* (Raise Ravens, 1975), which follows the child through the political transition of the 1970s, and especially in Montxo Armendáriz's *Secretos del corazón* (Secrets of the Heart, 1997), in which a nostalgic view of childhood in the 1960s identifies an optimism that was ignored by adults, but which came to define the generation that would be responsible for reconstructing Spain in the 1980s.

In contrast, the Francoist musicals of the 1950s and 1960s would have had you believe that childhood wasn't always so traumatic, with no end of precocious, happy-go-lucky clones singing their little hearts out to the glory of the state that sanctioned their overacting. There was Pablito Calvo, for example, the pint-sized star of *Marcelino, pan y vino* (Marcelino, Bread and

SPANISH CINEMA

Wine, 1954), whose alternately cheeky and teary-eyed portrayal of the titular orphan boy would occasion the greatest international success for a Spanish film of that time. Marcelino, it is recounted in flashback, was discovered by Franciscan monks in the ruins of a convent following the Napoleonic wars of the nineteenth century, and was brought up to be grateful and devout. One day he sneaks into the monks' forbidden attic and finds a massive crucifix that comes to life in his presence. Innocently unaware of the miraculous nature of this occurrence, Marcelino takes Christ bread and wine and, in return, is granted his wish to see his mother, by dying. The film may have been set in post-Napoleonic Spain, but the fable was clearly emblematic of the convergence of Catholic and Francoist doctrine in the years after the Civil War. Marcelino was a fabricated saint for all good Spaniards, especially those who might surrender to the sentimentality of this film rather more willingly than they had surrendered to Franco's army just a few years earlier. Pablito Calvo would go on to star in similar films until puberty brought on early retirement, but his success inspired producers to the regular discovery of fresh successors. Miguelito Gil, who had been runner-up in the auditions for *Marcelino, pan y vino*, appeared in a few imitations of that film, while Joselito, with a voice that was bigger than he was, was the sensation of *El pequeño ruiseñor* (The Little Nightingale, 1956) and similar films in which he performed variations on the theme of the warbling orphan boy in a rural and religious context that celebrated his desire for a family (a precept of Francoism) as the holiest of virtues.

In the 1960s one might have expected audiences to crave more sophisticated fare, but this was Spain and the decade of Marisol: a blonde and blue-eyed (but nevertheless Andalusian) Hayley Mills or Judy Garland-type whose sparky renditions of popular songs made her Franco's favourite actress. Marisol was eleven-year old Pepa Flores when producer Manuel J. Goyanes discovered her on a television show in 1959, but films such as *Ha llegado un ángel* (An Angel has Arrived, 1961) and *Tómbola* (1962) were a sensation that condemned the actress to an exploitative workload and the trauma of a tightly bandaged physique in order to prolong her wholesome image well into adolescence. In retrospect, her films did let slip an occasionally subversive attitude in the way her characters often triumphed over adults in admittedly hackneyed plots, but such hints of female independence were clearly irrelevant to the marketing phenomenon that surrounded her films, with dolls, novels and sticker-books making fortunes for her promoters.[1] Nevertheless her bonny face of innocence and carefree salubrity could not be maintained forever. It wasn't just her own ageing: by the late 1960s alternative perspectives on society had appeared in the work of film-makers whose experiences of childhood in post-Civil War Spain had given them little cause to sing. Film-makers such as Saura, Erice and Armendáriz had grown up on the losing side

86

and, as adults, they were considerably less grateful or forgiving of a state that had largely disowned them.[2]

El espíritu de la colmena

Víctor Erice was born in the Basque province of Vizcaya in 1940 and graduated from Madrid's Official Film School in 1963 (after studying under Saura) with a short film entitled *Los días perdidos* (The Lost Days). Almost immediately he would find himself labelled as part of 'the San Sebastian group' of film-makers that included Antxon Eceiza, José Luis Egea and Santiago San Miguel. However, rather than launch into film-making, Erice focused on the theory of the art, writing in the magazine *Nuestro Cine* (Our Cinema) as well as in the more academic *Cuadernos de arte y pensamiento* (Journal of Art and Knowledge). His first opportunity to put his beliefs into practice came, as it did to many film-makers of the time, from the producer Elías Querejeta, who invited Erice (an old friend from the film clubs of San Sebastian) to direct an episode of the three-part *Los desafíos* (The Challenges, 1969).[3] Erice's segment represented a peculiar clash of film styles and ideologies in its tale of liberal Spanish youths and their encounter with a homicidal G.I. who personifies the decadence of the American dream. A senseless contest of machismo escalates into a final cataclysm from which only Pinky will survive – Pinky being a pet chimpanzee (with a suspiciously communist-sounding name) whose survival is testament to this journey backwards in evolution.[4] The film won the Silver Shell award at that year's San Sebastian Film Festival, but Erice would have to work in advertising for a few more years until a script that he had written in collaboration with Ángel Fernández Santos convinced Querejeta to back him once more. 'It was a risk,' Querejeta has admitted of *El espíritu de la colmena*, 'but totally shared and accepted by all. I never felt alone, but completely supported by the people I worked with.'[5]

El espíritu de la colmena (The Spirit of the Beehive, 1973) is the undisputed masterpiece of Spanish cinema. Appreciated worldwide for its poetic sensibility and profound investigation into the mind and imagination of its child protagonist, the film originated in a conversation with Querejeta in which Erice discovered that the producer shared his fascination for James Whale's *Frankenstein* (1931). In particular, Erice's obsession centred on a still from the horror classic, in which the monster comes across a little girl by a riverbank. The scene, which was cut from many commercial prints including those available in Spain, showed the girl befriending the monster and teaching him to play by throwing flowers into the stream. The childlike innocence of the monster comes to the fore but, having run out of flowers, he throws in the next prettiest thing he can lay his massive hands on: the girl, whose drowning will occasion the hunting down of the monster by the people of her village. Erice's original idea was to emulate Whale's feature and make a genre film that would enjoy an easy and profitable distribution, but budget limitations caused a rethink. It changed into a story of reconciliation with an ageing monster, as thirty-two-year-old Ana, a maths teacher in Madrid, receives a telegram saying that her father is dying and resolves to return to her village by train. Her journey would have been the conduit for a long flashback in which her childhood experiences were recounted, until Ángel Fernández Santos realised that this journey was properly that of the cinema audience and that the film should begin with Ana (Ana Torrent) as an infant and be seen wholly from her perspective.[6]

Like light through a prism this perspective emerges from Ana's fragmented perception of the world. Her imaginative reinterpretation of events is evident from the drawings that form the background to the credits. Mostly made by Torrent herself, these drawings depict objects that appear prominently in the tale – train, cat, bonfire, school, mushroom, cinema and watch – and suggest chapter headings for the scenes which follow at the same time as they indicate the limited, two-dimensional perspective of Ana, which Erice will appropriate for his own frontal shots of the objects when they appear. 'Once upon a time . . .' says the intertitle, but instead of fairy-tale colours the film opens on an overcast landscape and a long road that stretches through the barren wheatfields around Segovia in Central Spain. 'A place on the Castilian plain around 1940' is the next title, thereby echoing the beginning of Cervantes' *Don Quixote*, at the same time as the bleakness and use of titles anchors Erice's personal vision to the aesthetic of silent films: 'I conceived the film in black and white,' he says, 'I thought of it in terms of the aesthetic of silent films, particularly those of Murnau.'[7] Most immediately, however, the legend situates the action in the post-war period – a fact emphasised in the shot of a Falangist symbol painted on a wall.[8] This is Hoyuelos, an occupied and vanquished town, dusty and colourless, population 338 in 1942. And then something wonderful happens: into the dormant village comes the truck of the travelling filmshow, bringing what is proudly heralded as 'the most beautiful film ever made.' Admission: 1 peseta.

The realism of the social context is emphasised by Erice's use of the actual town crier of Hoyuelos to announce the screening of *Frankenstein*, before the villagers of Hoyuelos take up their positions in front of the makeshift cinema screen in the village hall. Children bring in chairs and the space in front of the screen fills up as Erice cuts back and forth between a frontal shot of the audience and a gradual zoom-in to the screen from their perspective. This zoom breaks down the distance between the audience and the film and thereby anticipates the central quandary of Ana: her inabilty to distinguish between reality and fantasy. Ana is the last to find her seat. She wears a hooded cape, which immediately suggests her kinship with the protagonist of a fairy tale, and pushes through to place her chair beside her sister just as the lights go down. The narrator of the scratchy, black and white film steps out from behind theatre curtains and warns the audience of the moral complexity of what they are about to see. Then he introduces Doctor Frankenstein and a close-up of a masked and hooded scientist fills the screen: but a switch to colour is jarring and it is only a wide shot which reveals that the audience is now split between the intrinsic (those watching *Frankenstein*) and the extrinsic (us watching Ana's father, Fernando (Fernando Fernán Gómez), tending his beehives with the dedication of a similarly obsessed scientist). Fernando was a respected academic before the Civil War, now redundant in defeat and banished to the anonymity of this nowhere village.[9] Broken and insular, he has diverted his intellect on to a treatise on apiarian matters, and it is in this complex metaphor of the beehive that the meaning of the film is found.

The title of the film, and indeed the model for Fernando's thesis, comes from a 1901 work entitled *The Life of the Bee* by Maurice Maeterlinck, in which the author recounts his observations of the beehive in dramatic and poetic prose that recognises a keen philosophical metaphor for the human condition: 'From the crowd, from the city [the bee] derives an invisible aliment that is as necessary to her as honey. This craving will help to explain *the spirit of the laws of the hive*' (1901, p.31). In appropriating this text Erice applies the teachings of Maeterlinck to the destruction of the Second Republic that existed before the Civil War, but which, as in the 'pitiless society' of Maeterlinck's bees, was 'invariably sacrificed to the abstract and immortal city of the future' (1901, p.32). The dulling of the bees with smoke therefore suggests an analogy with the suppression of free thought and will by means of intimidation and the propaganda of the dictatorship. 'Let but a little smoke be deftly applied', writes Maeterlinck,

> and our well-armed workers will suffer themselves to be despoiled without dreaming of drawing their sting. It is not the fact, as some have maintained, that the bees recognise their master; nor have they any fear of man; but at the smell of the smoke . . . they imagine that this is not the attack of an enemy against whom defence is possible, but that it is a force or a natural catastrophe whereto they do well to submit.
>
> (1901, pp.25–6)

The spirit, however, this dormant but vital lifeforce, is clearly present in Ana, and it is her awakening that forms the dramatic odyssey of Erice's film.

Erice discovered Ana Torrent by chance. The go-ahead from Querejeta to make *El espíritu de la colmena* had suddenly filled him with panic at having to construct his film around the performance of a five-year-old girl and he immediately set out from his office to a local school, arriving at morning break to be confronted with a playground full of distressingly ebullient infants. But then his eye was drawn to Torrent, by herself in a corner and talking to imaginary friends: the confused and lonely Ana of his tale (Besas, 1985, p.131). 'I was confused between reality and fantasy,' Torrent has admitted of the actual filming, 'I'd seen some films, but everything gets confused, although you know it's not true.'[10] Tiny and troubled, Torrent is a magnetic presence. Her large eyes are illuminated by the flickering images of the film; she reacts to the plight of the monster with natural wonderment and fear. Her sustained close-up is the only handheld shot in the film, and was shot by cinematographer Luis Cuadrado sitting on the floor with Erice supporting him from behind. The moment when Ana raises her head, open-mouthed at the monster onscreen approaching the girl by the riverbank, is, says Erice,

> *an unrepeatable instance; the most extraordinary and paradoxical of the film. The film was wholly premeditated, but the most essential moment was when all this formal premeditation was wiped out by this moment. I think it's the fissure through which the documentary side of the film comes through the fiction. It's the moment I've always remembered. It moves me. It's the best thing I've ever filmed.*

Frankenstein fills Ana with questions that her sister, Isabel, answers with bluffs and supposedly withheld secrets ('We're going to tell lies' is the children's rhyme that plays several times on the soundtrack). Why did the monster kill the girl and why did the villagers kill him? Isabel tells her that the monster isn't dead, that she's seen him near the village: 'Is it a ghost?' 'No, it's a spirit. If you're his friend, you can speak with him anytime. Just close your eyes.' But it's the sound of their father, pacing in his upstairs study, that diverts the imagination of Ana on to an idea of him as a misunderstood creature and monster. Indeed Isabel's definition of the monster as a shape-changing spirit allows for multiple readings of the film, in which, in different scenes, the monster is variously personified as Fernando, the fugitive *maqui*,[11] the train, and even Ana herself. Such scenes are self-contained units that fit together like the cells in a hive – hexagons which are themselves echoed in the windows of the mansion of the Marquis of Lozoya in Hoyuelos that serves as Ana's home. 'Instead of scenes, I call them emotional areas [*ámbitos emocionales*],' explains Ángel Fernández Santos, *and Víctor Erice called them poetic units [unidades poéticas]. In fact, it's better to call them 'chords' because the script has the form of a circular music score [partitura] that begins exactly where it ends, and its circularity is made of a series of circles that touch each other but are autonomous.*

In each of these 'chords' the lighting offers exquisite variations on the honey colour that was invented by Luis Cuadrado and complemented by the pre-existing windows of the mansion, whose tinted panes were made especially for the film by Cuadrado's father. The Dutch master Jan Vermeer was the major inspiration on the colour and light of the film, while the Spanish Baroque painter, Francisco de Zurbarán, was the model for its framing. The windows act as portals through which the sounds of the outside world (the soundtrack of *Frankenstein* and the train) reach Fernando and his estranged wife Teresa (Teresa Gimpera). Indeed, in one eloquent match shot (which recalls the opening sequence of Orson Welles' *Citizen Kane*) the notion of the windows as portals between the exterior and interior worlds of the protagonists is expressed in a shot of the window from outside that dissolves into a match shot of the window from inside without any movement of the frame.

No more than a brief exchange of words occurs between Ana's parents during the film, and it is clear from the sequence of Fernando preparing for bed that his identification as the monster is not confined to the imagination of Ana. Erice films Teresa pretending to sleep under the shadows of the bars of the bedstead, while the lumbering shadow of an unseen Fernando is thrown on to the wall above her.[12] The isolation of these characters is made apparent in a protracted silence that expresses the pain of each one's internal testimony. Both parents bear emotional scars that prevent them from opening up: 'we have lost our perception of the essence of life', writes Teresa. Cut off from the outside world and each other, they can hardly comprehend the flowering wonderment of Ana (though at least Fernando does stop outside the cinema to listen in; Teresa just cycles past). Instead, Fernando's thesis and Teresa's unanswered letters to a mysterious, possibly romantic aquaintance from before the war are the source of self-censoring monologues that are delivered in voiceover; for, in a world in which communication is impossible, these characters have no recourse but to talk to themselves.

Ana also seeks to communicate but finds her primary school classes an unrewarding medium for discourse. The village children are shown hurrying to school in a series of dissolves that effect temporal shifts which only exacerbate the monotony. When not chanting multiplication tables the children are made to recite poems, including one by Rosalía de Castro that Ana mouths wordlessly in Castilian Spanish, but which, as John Hopewell has pointed out, was originally written in Galician – one of the various regional languages that were forbidden during the dictatorship (1986, p.207). In response to such circumscription of personal expression Ana, like her parents, turns inwards. She seeks answers in her imagination, but suffers from an inability to distinguish between fantasy and reality and is confused by mixed emotions of love and fear. In one gentle but chilling scene, for example, she stands in the middle of railway tracks and summons the train as she might the monster, then faces it down and is only moved to save herself by the screaming of her sister. The train, a potent symbol of progress in the outside world, then hurtles past Ana, thereby compounding her isolation and ignorance. 'Ana,' says Erice, 'is a child who does not yet have the use of reason, so what's evident is that we tried to avoid psychology because that's not how children observe the world and judge it.'[13] Judgement, it seems, is only apparent in the teaching of adults, where it is hopelessly bound up in the wisdom gained from their particular experiences. The initially playful sequence of Fernando leading his daughters on a mushroom hunt, for instance, culminates in his violent stamping of a poisonous fungi that, in the colour of its cap and black bands, provokes his recognition of Falangist insignia and thereby stirs his didacticism: 'A real devil. It seems nice when it's young, but it isn't when it grows up.' Back in school the biology lesson is enlivened by the teacher's use of Don José, a life-sized, cut-out man with peg-on organs. The children are prompted to imaginatively endow the figure with life ('Shush, Don José's going to get mad!'), and Ana's placing of the model's eyes relates to both the primacy of vision in this film and the fact that she, like Doctor Frankenstein, is making a monster in her own image and thereby revealing her own monster within. In addition the assonance of Franco and Frankenstein only deepens the allusion to the unnatural consequences of playing God.

In following her sister's instructions for contacting the monster, Ana's closed eyes and incantation, 'I'm Ana,'[14] is answered by the appearance in Hoyuelos of a fugitive *maqui*, whom she discovers and befriends, indentifying him as her monster. The character of the *maqui* originates in the childhood of Ángel Fernández Santos, whose parents had sheltered a fugitive, whom he recalls 'smiling and holding a pistol', in their hayloft during the war.[15] The scene of Ana taking him food is reminiscent of the boy feeding Christ in *Marcelino, pan y vino*, but the union of Ana and the *maqui* is based on their exclusion from society rather than their obeisance to its laws and beliefs. There is magic here, but it is clearly not in any Christian context; the subsequent hunting down and killing of the *maqui* by the Civil Guard will stretch to breaking point Ana's already tenuous hold on reality. She returns to the abandoned stable where she had befriended him, but finds only bloodied earth and her father. Believing him to be the killer she flees and, in direct imitation of the scene in Whale's *Frankenstein*, is herself hunted through the

'Soy Ana'. Ana Torrent in *El espíritu de la colmena* (Víctor Erice, 1973)

woods at night by the villagers and Civil Guard. Lost in a nightmare world, Ana crouches by a riverbank and makes manifest her monster – a faithful copy of Boris Karloff in the original *Frankenstein*. 'Ana earns the right to see the monster,' says Erice, 'because, fundamentally, what Ana has is faith, extraordinary faith.'[16] Her experience dislocates her completely from reality and leaves her traumatised, though she is found a few days later by her father and taken home to a doctor who expresses the key note of optimism in the film, 'little by little, she will forget', before quietly echoing the infamous cry of Doctor Frankenstein in his considered advice to Teresa, 'the important thing is that your daughter is alive. Alive!' Shortly thereafter Teresa is seen covering Fernando in a blanket and removing his glasses as he sleeps at his desk. There is, after all, a reawakening of her nurturing instinct that suggests a tentative but pragmatic return to reality. And thus there is hope that the sacrifice of Ana is not in vain; for, as Maeterlinck declares in his description of the bee that is both the model for Ana's physical and imaginative flight and the key to an unravelling of the film's symbolism,

> when she leaves the hive she will dive for an instant into flower-filled space,
> as the swimmer will dive into the sea that is filled with pearls. But isolate
> her . . . and she will expire in a few days not of hunger or cold, but of

loneliness . . . The individual is nothing, her existence conditional only, and herself, for one indifferent moment, a winged organ of the race. Her whole life is an entire sacrifice to the manifold, everlasting being whereof she forms part.

(1901, pp.30–1)

El sur

Erice, like Carlos Saura before him, appealed to an international audience seeking Spanish *auteurs* in order to focus their criticism of the Francoist regime. The Spanish censor, meanwhile, had wanted to prohibit *El espíritu de la colmena* but had found the ambiguity of the film too elusive a target for reasoned censure. Its initial reception in Spain was mixed; at the San Sebastian Film Festival in 1973 it both won the Golden Shell and was roundly booed by a considerable part of the public. It would be an entire decade before Erice returned to film-making with *El sur* (The South, 1983), having spent those years working in advertising. For *El sur* Erice adapted the novel of the same name by Adelaida García Morales for Elías Querejeta with a view to a series on Spanish Television (TVE). More linear than *El espíritu de la colmena*, it became obscure by default. There were to have been three episodes tracing the growth of Estrella from infancy to adolescence and then womanhood in the post-war Spain of the dictatorship. But Querejeta was obliged to suspend production, with two hundred and twenty-four pages of the script left to film, when a change in the management of TVE spoiled the agreement and prompted Querejeta to hurry this first part to a close in order to take it to the Cannes Film Festival in the hope of drumming up foreign investment that would refloat the project. It should have been easy; in the ten years since *El espíritu de la colmena* Querejeta had been pestered constantly about what might be Erice's next project: but it wasn't necessary. The missing half weighs heavily, but this absence is exactly as it should be: the sense of loss is wholly appropriate to the mood and meaning of the film. The second half was to have taken place in the south, in Seville, but its absence evokes a palpable sense of a divided Spain and, indeed, the invisible half of Spanish society during the dictatorship: those who fought on the losing side, the exiled, the poor and the dissident.

The story takes place in northern Spain, in an isolated house called The Seagull at the side of a road called 'the frontier'. Like Ana in *El espíritu de la colmena*, Estrella (Sonsoles Araguren) is the daughter of exiled Republican parents, though her father, Agustín (Omero Antoniutti), is more sorcerer than scientist. 'My father was able to do things other people thought were miracles,' she explains in voiceover; and, indeed, the first image of this mysterious man is of him using a magical pendulum over the engorged belly of his wife in order to divine the sex of their forthcoming child. It is a tender but slightly sinister scene, framed like a Zurburán, coloured in the dark, warm tones of a Dutch master, and recalled in flashback by Estrella, the unborn subject of the experiment and therefore clearly gifted with the magical powers of her father. 'That's the first thing I remember,' she says, 'a powerful image which, in truth, I invented.' Such invention echoes the cultural reinscription of the past that was the prerogative of Francoist propaganda, but it also arises because Estrella is clearly bored by life in the false-hearted and inhospitable land which is its result. Indeed her condition is exacerbated by a collection of tinted postcards of Andalusia and her mother's longing for an idealised Spain ('it never rains') that is personified in the lost paradise of this 'south'. 'That story was always ripe for fantasy,' admits Estrella, 'I filled it with images that I carried every-where'; but her natural curiosity is otherwise rebuffed because, in the dark days of the dictatorship, even the simplest of answers are prey to political inference and fear. 'My father's origins were always a mystery to me,' she bemoans, 'I knew nothing about his past.'

Instead of teaching her to deal with the reality of their situation the reserved and distant Agustín tutors Estrella in the use of his magic pendulum. And it is by means of this apprenticeship that Estrella manages the greatest trick of all: her parents' past becomes her future in her determination to visit the south and discover the meaning of so many mysteries for herself. In this she is aided by the arrival from Seville of Milagros (Rafaela Aparicio), a plump and elfin chatterbox, whose energy and matter-of-fact impatience inspires Estrella to strive for a life beyond the trivial and shameful existence that constitutes the life sentence of her parents. 'Too many things have happened,' says Milagros. 'Too many deaths. And all for ideals!' The ideological conflict that occasioned the Civil War and the concept of the 'two Spains' (*las dos Españas*[17]) has clearly been ratified in a rift between Agustín and his supposedly Francoist father, but Estrella struggles to understand the conflict in her own terms ('Grandad was with the baddies, wasn't he?') and finally finds some answers in the childspeak of Milagros:

> Listen to me. During the Republic . . . well, before the war . . . your grandad was a baddy and your daddy was a goody. But after Franco won, your grandad became a saint and your dad a demon. Such is life. Words, nothing but words.

In 1983, of course, there was no fear of such a dialogue being cut, but this even-handed ridicule of political propaganda is still a remarkably blunt summa-tion of the origins of the dictatorship. Its world-weary wisdom recognises a demarcation in the evolution of modern Spain that is transcended by the maturity of Estrella which is subsequently celebrated by her first communion.

El sur is a film that uses the ebb and flow of light and shadow to illustrate similar shifts in the self-awareness of its protagonist. Prolonged dissolves and fade-ins (which recall the films of Andrei Tarkovsky) imitate the natural tenure of daylight and suggest a monotony and timelessness in which Estrella's parents are as frozen as the weather vane that perpetually directs Estrella's thoughts towards the south. Only Estrella's white communion dress effects a contrast with the darkness of her surroundings and signals her move out of the shadows that claim her father. This partial awakening is developed in the celebratory dinner at which Estrella dances a paso doble called 'Into the World' with Agustín, while the Electra complex, in which a female child is sexually attracted to her father, is highlighted in Erice's slow zoom on to the veil that hangs on the back of Estrella's chair. But this psychological union is immediately soured by Estrella's discovery in her father's desk of letters from an unknown woman, Irene Ríos. The mystery unravels but also deepens. One night Estrella watches her father enter the Arcadia cinema (a reference to an idealised land that is similar to 'the south') and discovers that the woman is an actress in a Dietrich-type melodrama. But, just as adults keep their secrets from Estrella, so too is she disallowed entry into the adult-rated film. Later, she spies on Agustín as he writes a forlorn letter to the actress that reveals his idealisation of the past: 'I'd like to know you are still here on earth.' However, this fantasy of a pre-Civil War utopia comes crashing down when Agustín receives a letter by return in which the actress explains, 'The past no longer moves me. I want to look forward and I fear that I've grown up.' The adage also applies to Estrella, who, in a reversal of the dilemma of Ana in *El espíritu de la colmena*, locates herself in reality while her parents, like the onscreen Irene Ríos, linger in a world of make-believe.

Destroyed by contact with reality Agustín loses his magic powers and leaves home, leaving Estrella's idealisation of him in tatters. 'From that day on, my father never used the pendulum,' recounts Estrella, who resolves to break out of her parents' cocoon of denial by refusing to participate in their routine. She hides under the bed: her head on a pillow is like a still-life by Zurbarán. 'I challenged them with my silence,' she explains, but her father is equal to her precocious contest: 'He answered my silence with silence. And then I understood that he was playing my game, accepting my challenge, to show me that his pain was far greater than my own.' Her loss of the contest is liberating, for it is clear that the guilt and suffering she feels is, in reality, not her own. Emerging from her hiding-place she resolves 'to grow up suddenly': a wish that Erice answers in a masterful ellipsis created by means of a dissolve between a shot of the child Estrella cycling into the distance with a puppy at her wheels and a match shot of her returning as a young woman (Icíar Bollaín) with a similarly full-grown dog bounding out to greet her. Time has passed and Spain, like Estrella, is growing up ('the television will arrive soon'

Icíar Bollaín as Estrella in *El sur* (Víctor Erice, 1983)

sings her bedridden mother's maid). An invitation from Milagros to visit her in the south promises to be the catalyst for the flowering of her independence and Estrella prepares for the trip with more care than she had ever invested in her first communion. Before she leaves, however, a final meeting between the generations takes place; but, with Agustín lost to thoughts of what might have been and Estrella set firmly on her future, there is very little potential for their reconciliation.

Agustín's lonely suicide returns us to the opening shot of the film: a slow fade up to Estrella in the bed she was born in, listening to her mother's distress at her father's disappearance. She finds the answer in the magic pendulum that her father has left under her pillow, just one of the objects that Agustín had emptied out of his pockets before he killed himself in testament to his fragmentation. Estrella selects the receipt for a telephone call and packs it in her suitcase with the objects that make up her own sense of self; and that's where this film ends. The second part was to have followed Estrella south, to a romance with a lad who would turn out to be the result of her father's union with the actress.[18] Despite issues of incest and the extension of the Electra complex into Estrella's attraction for a younger version of her own father, this part, avers Erice, would have been unlike the first: 'the second part is not sad. It was to have been the first time that the north and south of Spain were truly united' (Besas, 1985, p.23). However, the union was not to be and

Erice, with one-third, one whole and one-half films to his credit, returned to advertising for almost another decade until the ideological purity and complex aesthetic of the semi-documentary *El sol del membrillo* (The Quince Tree Sun, 1992) reminded the world of cinema what it was sorely, sadly missing. By his own reticence Erice has avoided the label of *auteur*, suffering instead the kind of mystery and its attendant rumours that plagued the American director Terence Malick, with whom Erice shares not just a flickering career as film-maker but also a comparable aesthetic.[19] In recent years Erice had dedicated himself to an adaptation of the novel *El embrujo de Shanghai* (The Spell of Shanghai) by Juan Marsé, in which a boy falls in love with a bedridden girl, whose father, a fugitive anarchist, is supposedly on a mission in China. Erice's script revived the themes and imaginative sensibility of *El sur*, for, in the film he had in mind, the mythologised 'far east', like 'the south', appeared only in a postcard. Then the news came in June 2000 that, after three years of pre-production, the film's producer had taken the project away from Erice and handed it over to Fernando Trueba.[20]

Cría cuervos

'I think there's nothing to enjoy about childhood. It's your memory that tells you your childhood was a wonderful time but that's only because you don't remember things.'[21] Carlos Saura's views on childhood are inevitably preju- diced by his own experiences of growing up in Madrid during the Civil War. To Enrique Brasó, he reflected:

> *I suppose that for Proust his childhood was a series of details more or less poetic of his family and surroundings; for me those memories are much more violent: it's a bomb that falls on my school and a little girl bloodied with shards of glass in her face. And that's no literary invention, it's a fact.*
>
> (1974, p.23)

Saura recreated this image of a bomb falling on his school as the prologue to *La prima Angélica* (1973), a film that, he says, 'dealt with the memories of a certain period of infancy as a period of conflict that marks you for the rest of your life.'[22] It was the tale of an infantile adult and his attempt to try and recover those memories by returning to the town where he grew up, only to find himself shifting between the past and present with dire consequences for his psyche. Yet this was clearly a film about the malformation of adults who had grown up on the losing side during the dictatorship; it was his next film, *Cría cuervos* (Raise Ravens, 1975), that investigated the infancy of those who might grow up as winners, those who were likely to live in a Spain beyond fascism. In fact the dictatorship had been moribund since 1973, when Carrero Blanco, Franco's hardline successor-in-waiting, was assassinated by ETA, but Franco's death on 20 November 1975 pushed Spain into a surprisingly ordered transition to democracy that would rally campaigns for liberalism, feminism, gay rights and a new, pluralist identity for Spain. Similarly, the death of nine-year-old Ana's father, which occurs at the start of *Cría cuervos*, obliges her to face up to a world beyond patriarchy, a challenge which is complicated by her conviction that she has killed him.

Cría cuervos begins with photographs from a family album that traces the life of Ana's mother (Geraldine Chaplin) from black and white prints to Kodachrome, through dance and piano lessons, her marriage to a proud military officer in Franco's army, and the apparently happy circumscription of her own ambitions as the mother of Ana (Ana Torrent) and her two sisters. Yet within this celebration of social and familial harmony there exists a spark of dissent in the eyes of Torrent. Deep and black, they are clearly recognisable as the eyes of Ana in *El espíritu de la colmena* and they carry the look of a frightened witness, for, at various moments in her short life, Ana has observed the frequent infidelities of her father (Héctor Alterio), his rows with her

Like mother, like daughter? Ana Torrent and Geraldine Chaplin in *Cría cuervos* (Carlos Saura, 1975)

mother and the agonising death of the latter. Thus there is nothing playful about her attempt to kill her father with what she believes is a vicious poison (actually bicarbonate of soda), there is only a lucky coincidence that he should shortly thereafter suffer a heart attack.[23]

A few mornings later Ana is being dressed and combed by the maid of the house, Rosa (Florinda Chico), when her little sister, Maite, pronouncing the words from a comic in a dirge that sounds like a Latin chant, appears to conjure up their mother, who takes over the combing and nuzzles at Ana's neck, causing giggles that are stopped by Rosa.[24] Ana has been daydreaming of a reunion with her dead mother that is facilitated by Saura's emblematic play with mirrors; but her comforting hallucination is challenged by her older sister, Irene, who reminds her that their parents are both dead. However Ana is not yet willing to let go of her mother's spirit, and will persist with its invocation by means of what, for her, have become ritualised actions, such as combing her hair, listening to music and opening the fridge to check on a plate of chicken's feet. According to Saura:

> My mother always had plates of chicken's feet in the fridge, she made broth [caldo] with them. Chicken's feet are used for witchcraft, making spells, but the first idea was simple. I'd open the fridge and there was a plate of chicken's feet.[25]

On the other hand Ana is keen to complete the ritual of mourning for her father, whose corpse she refuses to kiss, and once his solemn and silent 'lying in state' is over she heads out to play in the garden. There she imagines herself leaping from the roof of an opposite building and, in a reading that accords with the point of view and movement of the camera, floating to earth like a feather. The death of the patriarch is liberating and this celebratory fantasy, with its soundtrack of blaring traffic, is wonderfully noisy and alive.[26]

Nevertheless the observance of mourning continues in a house that, with its all-female inhabitants, resembles that of Lorca's *La casa de Bernarda Alba* (The House of Bernarda Alba, 1936). Ana takes refuge in the basement, where she keeps her 'lethal' tin of bicarbonate, and where she is watched by an apparition of herself from twenty years in the future. This dramatic twist creates an abrupt shift in the perspective of the film to that of the adult Ana looking back on the events of the film from 1995. Previously the child's version of events has been signified as reality by Saura, who shot the film from her perspective, but the adult Ana's direct address to the camera/audience is a counterclaim on narrative authorship that casts doubt upon the veracity of these events (in particular the child Ana's demarcation of her parents into good and bad stereotypes). 'I don't believe in childhood paradise, or in innocence, or the natural goodness of children. I remember my childhood as a long period of time, interminable, sad, full of fear, fear of the unknown,' says Ana in an echo of the beliefs that are expressed in the initial quote from Saura (whose first script alone this was after a long collaboration with Rafael Azcona). The adult Ana is, like her mother, played by Geraldine Chaplin but, rather than illustrate cyclical victimhood, her appearance here (despite being dubbed by Julieta Serrano) offers a warm and delicate portrait of a lovely and confident woman.[27] The suggestion is that Ana will come of age in a world where self-determination is possible, even though she was born into one where the female role and her own childhood imaginings were circumscribed by Catholic doctrine and the culture of state-sanctioned machismo: 'Your father was disgusted when you were born,' Rosa tells her, 'God had punished him. Three daughters!'[28] As the saying goes from which the film takes its title, 'raise ravens and they'll pluck out your eyes' – a refrain that Spaniards use to warn against those who might repay favours with betrayal, but which is here given a bitterly ironic spin that recognises how rebellion against the patriarch might be seen as ingratitude by some.[29]

Into Ana's mother's place comes Aunt Paulina (Mónica Randall), who nags her nieces but is clearly sacrificing her own young life to the care of these three orphans. And life goes on. With the summer holidays just beginning, Saura lets his actresses play and captures moments of spontaneity and realism that he, like Erice, cherished. Music and make-up, dressing-up games and dances provide ample occasion for such moments, but, as in common psychotherapeutic practice, the girls' role-playing offers evidence of their working through the trauma of their parents' deaths. One scene has Irene dressed up in her father's cap and Ana playing the wife, with their dialogue obviously based on overheard arguments about late nights and accusations of adultery that occurred between their parents: except that Ana is far more assertive here than her mother ever was in an earlier flashback to a similar confrontation with her father. Instead of threats and violence this row ends in giggles. Exhilarated by such make-believe, Ana continues to avoid reality in similar games and fantasies, in which music is a vital catalyst and no distinction is made between prayer and rhyme, between religion and superstition. Her mother, for example, is resuscitated by piano music,[30] while Ana's somewhat sadistic game of hide-and-seek with her sisters ends with their play-death and revival by Ana's rapid recital of the 'Our Father' – a prayer that is an ironic precedent to Ana's subsequent resuscitation of their father in a memory of his injurious philandering: 'Our father, who art in Heaven, hallowed be thy name . . .'

Increasingly, if Ana wants something, she gets it by means of such ritual. 'I'll close my eyes and count to five,' she declares to Rosa, when the maid refuses to show Ana her bosom, and five seconds later – '¡Qué grande!' Most memorably, Ana plays the pop song *¿Por qué te vas?* (Why are you going?) by Jeanette, an English singer, singing in Spanish, whose accented voice surely reminds Ana of her mother, who, as played by Chaplin, has her own English-accented voice. Despite an infectious rhythm the song has sad and poignant lyrics: 'Why are you going? / All the promises of love will go with you / you'll forget me . . .' The song expresses the fact that Ana has no understanding of death, only of absence. Her father's death means little because he was absent in life anyway, but the worrying absence of her mother is confounded by Ana's last sight of her writhing in agony and refuting all the teachings of her faith – 'It's all lies. There's nothing. They've deceived me. I'm afraid. I don't want to die' – before Rosa shuts her out of the room. Indeed it is only with her actual witnessing of the death of Roni, her guinea pig, that Ana expresses a healthy compulsion to grieve by burying the animal herself and then smearing her face with black earth.

When asked to elucidate on the nature of Ana's suffering, Saura replied:

> Cría cuervos *is a sad film, yes. But that's part of my belief that childhood is one of the most terrible parts in the life of a human being. What I'm trying to say is that at that age you've no idea where it is you're going, only that people are taking you somewhere, leading you, pulling you and you're frightened. You don't know where you're going or who you are or what you're going to do. It's a time of terrible indecision.*

Indeed it is Aunt Paulina, with her constant reminders of decorum and responsibilities, that grounds Ana in the real world – a 'crime' for which Ana targets her as her next victim.[31] Paulina's fate is apparently decided by the choice between fantasy and reality that she unwittingly enforces upon Ana in the sequence where Ana lies awake in bed and summons up her mother by closing her eyes (a trick that works equally well in *El espíritu de la colmena*). Her mother sits on the bed and tells her the story of Almendrita (Thumbelina) and a contented Ana falls asleep, only to wake screaming and be answered not by her ethereal mother but by this down-to-earth intruder, Aunt Paulina, whose attempts to comfort her with the same story are met by Ana's demands that she die. A would-be murderer once more, Ana 'poisons' Paulina, but is astounded by her aunt's buoyant appearance the next morning, the first day of the new school term. Saura's 'time of terrible indecision' appears over, and Ana faces up to the future with some of the optimistic pragmatism with which her aunt has faced up to hers. Irene spends breakfast telling Ana of a dream about their parents, but this time it is Ana who corrects her, explaining that their mum and dad are dead.[32]

They troop off for school as the pop song plays over the cacophony of the traffic, passing bright billboards and painted-over graffiti (though the Spanish word for freedom – *libertad* – still comes through), and are lost within a swarm of uniformed schoolgirls, all heading for a religious school. It is an ambiguous ending that reflects the time of the film's making: the dictatorship was ending, but the film still angered the censor, who only relented after deciding that the film's prohibition would reflect badly on the new government's proposed move towards openness. Spain could have gone either way: on the one hand there is the light and the music and a certain solidarity in the coming together of the children; but there is also a final blurring of their individual identities both in the symbolism of their uniforms and, more literally, in the zoom in towards abstraction of Saura's camera. The final panorama of Madrid, with its traffic noise and building sites, could either be seen as lively and progressive or, in the opinion of Agustín Sánchez Vidal, as 'inhospitable' (1988, p.103). It should be remembered, however, that this is a nostalgic view of the city, just a distant memory for the adult Ana of 1995, looking back from the other-worldly perspective that Saura imagines on her behalf.

Secretos del corazón

If Ana is Almendrita (Thumbelina), adrift in a world of giants, then Javi, in Montxo Armendáriz's *Secretos del corazón* (Secrets of the Heart, 1997), is quite literally her male equivalent; for Garbanzito (Tom Thumb) is both his lead role in the school pantomime and a fitting extension of his persona. Because it's a big world that nine-year-old Javi inhabits, back and forth between the Pyrenean mountain village of his widowed mother and the city of his two aunts during term. Armendáriz's sincere and touching recreation of growing up in Navarre during the early 1960s is both semi-autobiographical and universal, in which the child protagonist is relieved of his function as catalyst for the development of a political analogy and becomes instead an observer, a listener with his own problems to concern him.[33] And at last, at least, they are problems befitting a child, whose questions are designed solely to make sense of an empirical world rather than the abstract, adult one: 'If father was so good with the rifle, how come he shot himself?'; 'Where do you keep a really big secret?' and 'What does *chingar* mean?' Because *Secretos del corazón* is not so much about inhibition as it is about growth: it may revisit the fears and darkness of the dictatorship in the rites of passage of its young hero, but such simple, universal metaphors as his terror of the space between stepping stones and the spider in the cellar are surmounted with reasoning and guts. Gone are the multiple deaths, sexual menace and trauma of *Cría cuervos*, *El espíritu de la colmena* and *El sur*: Javi's eventual crossing of the river, his triumphant breaking of the cobweb, are signs that his new generation would beat its irrational fears and soon substitute a progressive, liberal Spain for the terror of an annihilation that never happened.

There had been other films that used the child's rite of passage as a metaphor for changes in Spain, particularly in the Basque Country, where the troubled coming of age of adolescents held an emotive resonance for the similarly struggling region. Juanma Bajo Ulloa's *Alas de mariposa* (Butterfly Wings, 1991) was a mood piece that explored the plight of six-year-old Ami, who suffers from her mother's obsession with producing a male heir for her largely indifferent husband. *Alas de mariposa* displays the minimalism and visual impact of a very good short film, but it has an over-extended narrative and pretensions to gothic horror that effectively demonise the child. Arantxa Lazcano's *Los años oscuros* (The Dark Years, 1993) was a more thoughtful work, which observed post-war life in a Basque village through the eyes of a schoolgirl and provided original insights into notions of linguistic identity and religious education. More recently the Basque–Cuban co-production *Maité* (1995) delighted in the mischievous matchmaking of its infant star and used its gentle humour to celebrate links between the otherwise culturally isolated nations. Meanwhile adventures of childhood in other regions of Spain were explored in Carlos Saura's *Pajarico* (1997) and José Luis Cuerda's *La lengua de las mariposas* (Butterfly's Tongue, 1999). The first was a light, episodic tale of boyhood from the director of *Cría cuervos*, who relocated incidents and characters from his own childhood to present-day Murcia in order to effect the contrast of 'a different time, for a warmer experience, more Mediterannean, more modern.'[34] But, in reflecting the relaxed attitudes of contemporary Spain, it is a film without conflict, in which even the child's spying on homosexual lovers, for example, is inconsequential: the final voiceover affirming life changes and enlightenment appears trite. *La lengua de las mariposas* was similarly episodic and nostalgic, but was set in a pre-Civil War utopia of the Galician countryside that was too good to be true, even if its climax was appropriately grim.[35]

In contrast, Armendáriz's *Secretos del corazón* succeeds because of its authenticity and optimism, plus a fine array of performances from a gifted and well-chosen cast. In its making Armendáriz aimed to

> *vindicate the enthusiasm [afán] for discovery that is being lost. In this world and time in which we live, television, video games and the media force children into sexual initiation and the adult world in a different and hurried way. Because of this I set the film in a time and place [1962] which were not yet contaminated by television.*

> (Roma, 1998, p.34)

Ironically, the lead role of Javi was cast after the young Andoni Erburu's spirited scene-by-scene recital of Spielberg's *Jaws*, but, as Armendáriz recalls,

104

only ratified when he agreed to the wishes of Erburu's parents that 'we would not treat the boy like a film star, and that we would make it clear that his opportunity to make the film was a learning experience that was beyond other children' (Roma, 1998, p.34). Correlatively, *Secretos del corazón* describes the awakening of Javi in a naturally hesitant but enthusiastic way that expresses encouragement for a generation that would reach adulthood at the same time as Spain became a democracy. Saura and Erice's Ana is wide-eyed from shock, but Javi is all ears from curiosity. Unfortunately, like Saura's Ana, Javi maintains a fearful relationship with his dead father while, like Erice's Ana, he also has an older sibling who covers up his ignorance with lies and bluffs of maturity. Nevertheless, unlike either, Javi's capacity for affection finds ample reciprocation in the people who surround him.

The film begins with Javi and his best friend Carlos (Íñigo Garcés) investigating an abandoned house, whose gates echo the cobweb that similarly fascinates and scares him, where a passionate crime is reputed to have occurred. Amongst the cat-cries and banging shutters Javi tells Carlos that you can hear 'the voices of the dead' (the film's original title) screaming to free themselves from secrets. 'What do they say?' 'I don't know, you can't understand them,' answers Javi. But there are secrets for sure, just as there are in the forbidden room in his mother's house, with its faded photos and blood-stained armchair; for the truth is that Javi's father had killed himself after discovering Javi was his brother's son. Since then the family has been wrapped up in shame and recriminations, with Javi's gruff grandfather (Joan Valles) consumed by his various grudges (not the least of which is his memory of losing the Civil War) and his God-fearing Aunt Rosa (Vicky Peña) doing penance for all. But, on the other hand, there is the optimism and gregariousness of Javi's mother (Silvia Munt), his tipsy but sensual Aunt María (Charo López) and his uncle/father (Carmelo Gómez), whose delight in the child is just one facet of a generous, affable nature. Moreover, *Secretos del corazón* scares away the quiet and sombre stillness of *El espíritu de la colmena* and *Cría cuervos* with its movement, light and noise. The weight of the past is lifted, for example, in the Good Friday festivities, in which the lights of the church are dimmed in silence but brought back up again by the almighty racket of the congregation whose cacophony symbolises the screaming of the dead. There are big secrets that are 'best kept in the heart' says Javi's mother, but when Javi creeps into the forbidden room to commune with his dead father, they are his mother's groans he hears as she makes love with his uncle in the next room. Instead of the cries of the dead Javi hears those of the living. Voices, noises, sounds of any kind are all indications of life: where once there was only fearful silence now there is singing, foreign voices on the radio, hordes of shouting children and celebratory shotgun blasts at the final wedding of Javi's mother and uncle.

Silence also disappears in the telling of secrets and the noisy reconciliations that follow. Juan says that people get married to *chingar* without sinning, so Javi's concern for the ungodly actions of his mother and uncle soon escalates into an unbearable secret that he blurts out at the dinner table. His uncle slaps him, but it's the grandfather who recognises a need that the other adults ignore: 'That's right,' he sneers, 'hit the kid for telling the truth, that way he'll learn not to.' But Javi's need for answers is invariably complicated by the fact that he's the only one telling truth. Why does his grandfather wear his slippers on the wrong feet on alternate days? Because that way the sole gets worn on both sides and the slipper lasts longer. 'But you hardly walk,' says Javi. What does a girl conceal beneath her skirt? Not much it seems, learns Javi, after being diddled out of his pocket money by a young strumpet who barely reveals her knees. And it's Armendáriz's pleasure to involve us in these misadventures: when she pulls her skirt up an inch, we see it from the point of view of Javi and Carlos, the camera's double-take coinciding with that which passes between the boys. Similarly, when the boys run up to the abandoned house, the handheld camera jogs along behind. Like most of their sights and sounds of adult doings, the boys' view of Aunt María and the resident of the house in the throes of passion comes through a slightly ajar doorway that conceals as much as it reveals, but then truths do tend to slip out in whispers rather than screams. 'Aunt María hasn't gone away on a trip,' Javi tells his supposedly wiser brother. 'It's a lie. She's escaped with the man from the house.' Then later: 'Mother is going to have a baby,' an event that prompts her marriage to their uncle and so unites Javi with his rightful father.

The wedding is followed by a family dinner that is capped by a raucous toast in the forbidden Basque language of Euskera that is 'an anarchic Republican type of ritual' which gratifies and reconciles the grandfather with his kin and their celebration of life.[36] 'I'm an old man now,' he explains, 'I know I'm a nuisance. However, I still want to live.' Thus *Secretos del corazón* looks forward to a time and a country in which the potential of Javi, whatever it might be, will be realised. Armendáriz replaces Ana, the mute, female witness of Erice and Saura, with a boy whose voice is as authentic as the details of his film: chocolate sandwiches, the fumes of a bus station, thick Duralex cups and plates and the sound of rain falling on a patio. '*Secretos del corazón* comes out of Navarre', says Armendáriz, 'because it comes out of my own memories about the place, about the light, the atmosphere, a street, a room' (Roma, 1998, p.34). Coming after the grim depiction of drug-addled Spanish youth in the same director's *27 horas* (27 Hours, 1986) and *Historias del Kronen* (Stories from the Kronen, 1994), it is tempting to read *Secretos del corazón* as golden-hued nostalgia for childhood, were it not for the chronology which identifies Javi, who would be 21 at the time of Franco's death, with the generation that came of age in the political transition. When Javi crosses

Charo López embraces Andoni Erburu as Javi in *Secretos del corazón* (Montxo
Armendáriz, 1997)

the stepping-stones in his bid to catch up with Aunt María there is a tangible
besting of fear. No longer a child of the dictatorship, Javi is destined to be a
champion of its passing. The first moral lesson that he receives from his new
and rightful father is to be good and to never miss school, shortly after which
he is expelled. 'My father says we'll find another school for next year,'
concludes Javi with pride and satisfaction; because, more than anything else,
Secretos del corazón recuperates the figure of the father from a cinematic
tradition that suffered and reflected the patriarchal state of the dictatorship.
It is the first time in these films about childhood that the word is said with
love.

Notes

1. In time, Pepa Flores would escape her image with an infamous nude layout in
    the magazine *Interviu* and a professional, political and personal collaboration
    with the dancer Antonio Gades, whom she married, which would lead to
    memorable appearances in Carlos Saura's *Bodas de sangre* (1981) and *Carmen*
    (1983).
2. Montxo Armendáriz spent his formative years in the vanquished and sub-
    sequently punished Republican area of Navarre. Carlos Saura grew up in the
    besieged Republican sector of Madrid.

3. The script was co-written by Rafael Azcona and the directors, the other two being Claudio Guerin and José Luis Egea.
4. For an analysis of *Los desafíos*, see Marsha Kinder (1993, pp.172–83).
5. *Huellas de un espíritu*, documentary feature shown on Spain's Canal Plus, 1988.
6. The initial idea wasn't wasted. Querejeta kept it for Carlos Saura's *Elisa, vida mía* (Elisa, My Life, 1977).
7. *Huellas de un espíritu*, op. cit.
8. The Falangists were founded in Spain in 1933 and were the one legal party during the Franco regime.
9. A photograph reveals Luis as an acquaintance of philosopher and writer Miguel de Unamuno, rector of the University of Salamanca, who was famously shouted down by Fascists chanting 'Death to intelligence!'
10. *Huellas de un espíritu*, op. cit.
11. The *maquis* were anarchists turned fugitives after the Civil War. Many attempted to continue the struggle with guerrilla warfare, but most were forced to flee to the Pyrenees and beyond.
12. Ana and Isabel also pretend to sleep in the presence of their father.
13. *Huellas de un espíritu*, op. cit.
14. Many critics and, indeed, the subtitler of the version of the film that is currently available on video have translated this phrase ('*Soy Ana*') as 'It's Ana.' However, the literal translation 'I'm Ana' implies an act of self-affirmation that is otherwise lost.
15. The original Don José was a tailor's mannequin from Fernández Santos' schooldays.
16. Nevertheless, Fernández Santos has argued (then and since) that the monster should never have been shown on camera.
17. *Las dos Españas* is a phrase that describes the ideological divide between Republicans and Nationalists.
18. Vicente Molina Foix (1984) interview with Víctor Erice, *Positif*, 278, Paris, April 1984.
19. Malick is the director of *Badlands* (1974), *Days of Heaven* (1978) and *The Thin Red Line* (1999).
20. *Cinemanía*, 57, June 2000, p.40.
21. Author's interview, June 1999.
22. Ibid.
23. The fact that Ana believes that she kills her father on a night when he is making love to Amelia, the wife of Aunt Paulina's future lover, inspires Agustín Sánchez Vidal to identify the secret relationship between two taboos that are usually hidden from children, eroticism and death (1988, pp.97–103).
24. The combing of Ana's hair is but one of the most obvious echoes of *El espíritu de la colmena* (and will be further echoed in that of Javi in *Secretos del corazón*).
25. Author's interview, June 1999.
26. The building she leaps from was actually that of the flat on Madrid's María de Molina street, where Saura lived with Geraldine Chaplin. The increasing sound of the traffic was a particularly intense example of the personal experiences that Saura included in Ana's story (Besas, 1985, p.128).
27. Chaplin was Saura's common-law wife and muse and appeared in ten of his films.
28. The father-daughter tensions of *Cría cuervos* are revisited in Jaime de Armiñán's *El nido* (The Nest, 1980) in which Ana Torrent plays thirteen-year-old Goyita, who

enjoys an innocent but manipulative romance with an old Republican played by Héctor Alterio, who plays her father in *Cría cuervos*.

29. The phrase '*cría cuervos y te sacarán los ojos*' is said to originate with Don Álvaro de Luna of Castile during a hunting expedition. In the course of the hunt his party came across a beggar with terrible scarring in place of eyes. The beggar explained that he had raised a raven for three years with affection and great care, but which had one day attacked him, leaving him blind. The *bon mot* was Don Álvaro's reply.

30. Saura: 'My own mother was a pianist, so I've always listened to music at home and it's opened me up a lot, kept me more sensitive to things.' Author's interview, June 1999.

31. It is Aunt Paulina, for example, who charges the girls with the care of their stroke-victim grandmother – a task which Ana dutifully takes for herself. Virginia Higginbotham, incidentally, sees the grandmother as a 'mute testament to the fact that women in a paternalistic society are not only confined as the grandmother is to her wheelchair . . . but are without voice in the Franco dictatorship' (1988, p.94).

32. John Hopewell reads this scene as the 'capitulation' of Ana, which shows her 'drawing a line between what she thinks and what she says' (1986, p.139).

33. For a description of Armendáriz's life and career see Chapter 7.

34. Author's interview, June 1999.

35. *La lengua de las mariposas* was adapted from the short story by Galician writer Manuel Rivas, and starred Fernando Fernán Gómez in a role that echoes his portrayal of Fernando in *El espíritu de la colmena*.

36. *Secretos del corazón* Pressbook, courtesy of Ana Blásquez Blanco of Aiete and Ariane Films.

CHAPTER SIX

Over Franco

Spanish cinema in transition

Old soldiers do die. Franco went in 1975, Buñuel in 1983. In between, the fascist regime of the first was supplanted by the decadent dream of the latter. Four decades of repression had ended, and in its stead came a new age of political and personal freedom that would revitalise Spanish cinema. Democracy was the result of a gradual process, but liberalism, experimentation and explicitness seemed to happen all at once. Film-makers found themselves in an unsupervised candy store of previously forbidden treats, and either stood there gawping at all the bare flesh and blasphemy or gorged themselves sick on the new permissiveness. From Madrid came films that expressed the bleary-eyed bemusement of the first generation to come of age in the democracy, alongside those which reflected the soul-searching of thirty-somethings, for whom the transition was the impetus for reflections on their own lost youth. Meanwhile, from Barcelona, came Vicente Aranda, whose explorations of sexuality offered incisive commentaries on the contemporary socio-political context. Some Spanish film-makers found that commercial pressures were a greater challenge to their creativity than censorship. Others, such as Pedro Almodóvar, simply revelled in their time. Camp, kitsch and cosy, his films were playful, rude and fun. And then, when the party ended, and the moral hangover was added to the whiplash of accelerated change, popular disillusionment with democracy was either treated with honesty and imagination, as in Almodóvar's ever more sophisticated features, or assuaged by a panacea of nostalgia in films that propounded a recreation of Spain from long before the burden of democracy.

In the final years of the dictatorship film-makers had known only intimidation and censure as the moribund Franco strived to leave everything *'atado y bien atado'* (all tied up). Buñuel had remained in exile after his *Tristana* (1970) fell foul of the regime, but Carlos Saura's *La prima Angélica* (1973) had barged through the state censor with international backing and emerged bloodied, bombed and blacklisted, but as a symbol of changing times. Most film-makers, however, were incapacitated by economic and political restrictions. Indeed, the key films of the transition exhibited a brutality that seemed to reflect the anger that their makers felt as the result of ideological and creative limitations. José Luis Borau's *Furtivos* (Poachers, 1975) was a remorseless tale of incest and killing, whose protagonists reacted to deprivation by raging against animals and each other. Similarly Ricardo Franco's *Pascual Duarte* (1976) observed the poverty of pre-Civil War Spain with a murderous eye. Although based on Camilo José Cela's novel the film (from a script by Ricardo Franco, Emilio Martínez-Lázaro and Elías Querejeta) exhibits no discourse, only violence. Pascual (José Luis Gómez) pets his dog, then shoots it, and, as with the killing of a wolf in *Furtivos*, there is no fakery here: the dog is simply blasted away onscreen.[1] Neither is there any compassion: Pascual takes to murder and the film ends with his summary garrotting.[2] Even the infant Ana in Carlos Saura's *Cría cuervos* (Raise Ravens, 1975) exhibited all the nerve of a cold-blooded killer. Nevertheless, these films did not condone sadistic impulses but the responses of brutalised persons. The protagonists are all solitary and abused, robbed of their capacity for communication by a regime that derived its strength from an elitist, chauvinist doctrine that proudly withheld compassion. And now that it was ending, what could film-makers do but express their similar lack of pity?

Franco died on 20 November 1975 and it was, perhaps, a begrudging tribute to his dictatorship that, at a time of economic recession for the whole of western Europe, Spain did not slip back into autocracy or even civil war. Instead change came from within the old regime, most remarkably from the progressive and conciliatory actions of the reinstated monarchy led by King Juan Carlos, while those who wished to return to dictatorship were rather dismissively termed nostalgics (*nostálgicos*). The dismantling of the regime began with the pardoning of political prisoners, tacit freedom of assembly and the lifting of restrictions on the press. In 1976 the ex-Secretary-General of the National Movement, Adolfo Suárez, was appointed Prime Minister and Spain's transition to democracy began in earnest.[3] Following the Political Reform Bill in September and a national referendum, the first free elections were held in June 1977.[4] Suárez was Hollywood-handsome and too young to remember (or make others recall) the Spanish Civil War. Moreover he had served as head of the state television service, was acutely aware of the potential of the medium, and similarly mindful of the role that Spanish cinema might play in the reconstruction of democracy. Censorship was revoked by royal decree the following November.

As expected, the old guard were first into the undefended breach. Luis García Berlanga, the eloquent chronicler of working-class misfits and middle-class mediocrity under Franco, now turned his sights on the ruling classes in

La escopeta nacional (The National Shotgun, 1978). The raucous, scattershot farce was inspired by a true incident when Franco's daughter was shot in the bottom by accident during one of the frequent hunting parties that were the main indulgence of her father, but here the hunting party functioned as a microcosm of the battle that flared between aristocrats and technocrats in the final years of the dictatorship as they each sought to reap a final harvest from corruption. 'My film,' remarked Berlanga, 'is the chronicle of the extinction of the aristocratic race.'[5] A masturbating marquis with his collection of pubic hair, rabid priests, wide-boy ministers, floozies and assorted hangers-on are just a few of the caricatures from Berlanga's habitually brilliant roster of supporting actors that bedevil José Sazatornil's obsequious Catalan business-man. His befuddlement at this parade of grotesques allowed Spanish audiences to laugh loudest and last, and obliged Berlanga to deliver two sequels of equal amusement but far less bite: *Patrimonio Nacional* (National Heritage, 1980), in which members of the ruling class attempt to maintain traditions in an increasingly disrespectful Madrid, and *Nacional III* (1983), in which they give up the inverted class struggle and retire to Miami. Rather than further the evolution of Berlanga's work, these sequels responded to the new commercial considerations that were to prove more inhibiting to film-makers than the censor. The classification of 'special interest', which had allowed the careers of *auteurs* such as Carlos Saura to flourish under Franco, was withdrawn. Meanwhile a large section of the traditionally rural population relocated to the rapidly sprawling cities on the promise of new wealth. There was simply no way around the burgeoning urban cult of consumerism: either a film made money or its maker looked for work in the lower bastions of popular genres, which at least offered a viable response to lack of resources, limited distribution and competition from television. International co-productions (musicals with South American countries, for example, and horror/sex films with Italy) even prompted the establishment of new genres: the *'paella'* western, the *policíaca* (brutal urban thrillers) and the smutty, softcore genre known as *el destape* (literally 'the undressing'). The late 1970s also saw previously forbidden films reach Spanish screens, including Eisenstein's *Battleship Potemkin* (1925), Chaplin's *The Great Dictator* (1940) and Luis Buñuel's *Viridiana* (1961), but their audiences were largely scholars and film-makers. Once, going to see such films as Berlanga's *El verdugo* (The Executioner, 1963) or Saura's *La prima Angélica* (1974) had been an act of defiance, rebellion and solidarity: could Spanish cinema survive its new role as mere entertainment?

The producer Elías Querejeta typically refused to compromise and continued his support for the *auteurist* trajectories of Saura, Víctor Erice, Jaime Chávarri and Montxo Armendáriz along with several initiatives designed to encourage new film-makers. Meanwhile the Basques recognised film as a potent weapon in the vindication of their beleaguered nation, and directors such as Imanol Uribe dedicated themselves to the realisation of its potential. A few directors whose reputations had been built on their resistance to the demands of the dictatorship also refused to surrender to the greater demands of commercial tastes, and tried an alternative mode of expression as documentarists. Juan Antonio Bardem's *Siete días de enero* (Seven Days in January, 1979) explored the darker side of the transition in its investigation of the week in January 1976 when five labour lawyers were murdered by right-wing vigilantes, while Jaime Chávarri's *El desencanto* (The Disillusion, 1976) deconstructed the pretensions and privileges of the family of conservative poet Leopoldo Panero.[6] Film-makers only other response to commercial disregard for their art was to work within the various hackneyed genres but to stretch the rules with the same ingenuity with which they and their forebears had subverted the dictates of the censor. It wasn't a question of selling out, but of bargaining up, and besides, as with the revaluation of Hollywood genres that inspired the French New Wave, the most popular genres held a definite kitsch-and-cool appeal for the Spanish avant-garde, most of whom were located in Barcelona.

The Barcelona School was a propagandist label that purposefully countered the respect and financial assistance accorded the graduates of the film school in Madrid. Under the aegis of the producer and writer Ricardo Muñoz Suay disaffected members of the Catalonian middle classes such as Vicente Aranda, Gonzalo Suárez and Pere Portabella were promoted as standard bearers of an avant-garde movement named the *gauche divine* that had appeared in Catalonia in the late 1960s and included architects, singers, photographers, models, the film historian Román Gubern and novelists Juan Marsé, José Goytisolo and Gabriel García Márquez, who lived in Barcelona at the time. Catalonia had always aimed to estrange itself from a centralised government and the dictatorship that enforced it. In looking towards Paris as its model the movement's film-makers also sought to emulate the post-modernist chic of their French peers by the reinscription of popular genres as examples of a Catalan sensibility and irony. There was also an element of nationalism in their use of the Catalan language, for this was not just a dissident act but a prerogative of many of the folk singers and writers who had maintained a linguistic and ideological separatism until the declaration of autonomy for Catalonia in 1977 when, unlike the Basque culture that had to be largely rebuilt, Catalan cultural identity was found to be largely intact. Indeed a testament to all these facts was Francesc Bellmunt's Catalan language 1976 documentary *La nova cançó* (The New Song) on the new song movement in Catalonia, as was Bellmunt's clandestine collaboration with the controversial theatre group *Els joglars* that resulted in the libertine *L'orgia* (The Orgy, 1978), which shocked, but served as a showcase for many young Catalan actors. Meanwhile, Antoni Ribas' *La ciutat cremada* (The Burnt City, 1976) was a period film that played up Catalan history and achieved a major commercial success. This multilayered family saga unfolds in Barcelona during the first ten years of the twentieth century and features recreations of many notable events in which numerous key personages are impersonated; but its most encouraging testament to the viability of cinema from the region was that the financing and crew (with the exception of Teo Escamilla as director of cinematography) was self-sufficiently Catalan. Most Catalan film-makers were non-professionals who had kept dear the call to arms made by Román Gubern and others in the Sitges conference of 1967, when demands for an independent, uncensurable cinema were answered by the violent intervention of the Civil Guard.[7] Nevertheless the Catalans would continue to resist the centralisation of the film industry (as with most commerce and all government) in Madrid. More attuned to the French New Wave than New Spanish Cinema, they were inclined to be experimental, mainly because, coming from a wealthy middle class, they could afford to be. In their playfulness, film-makers from the Barcelona School took to the sub-genres of fantasy, horror and sex comedy and revamped them, most notably Vicente Aranda, whose sensitive, sordid films would elevate him to the front rank of Spanish cinema in the democracy.

Aranda was actually born in Huesca in 1937, but his family returned to spend the Civil War in Barcelona. Like many of his contemporaries, he spent his youth in the local fleapit, much against the wishes of his parents, who took to smelling him on his return for traces of the disinfectant that was sprayed in cinemas of the time. He never finished his studies and, instead, tried a multitude of trades before following his brother to Venezuela in 1952. Wealthy and married upon his return in 1959, he fell in with the cultural elite of Catalonia and was encouraged to try his hand at film-making, even after being denied access to Madrid's Official Film School because he lacked a first degree. Working with Román Gubern, he co-directed his first feature *Brillante porvenir* (A Brilliant Future Ahead) in 1964. Loosely adapted from *The Great Gatsby*, the film was naive in its appropriation of the aesthetic of neo-realism for a portrait of the Catalan middle class, but it served to redirect Aranda towards the more fantastic ambit of film-making and the comic spy thriller *Fata Morgana* (1966). Ignored upon release, the film would eventually be recognised for inspiring the particularly kitsch aesthetic of the Barcelona School of film-makers. This and his next two films, *El cadáver exquisito* (The Exquisite Corpse, 1969) and *La novia ensangrentada* (The Bloody Bride, 1972), in which a female vampire seeks revenge against all men, were genre films for the cultural elite, that got around the censor by virtue of their incomprehensibility. By Aranda's own admission he had 'sacrificed conventional coherence for the cinematographic and phenomenological possibilities of each action' (Hopewell, 1986, p.69). Absurdity, it seemed, could be a potent weapon of subversion, or as Joaquín Jordá, the emergent leader of the Barcelona School, famously exclaimed, 'if they won't let us make Victor Hugo, then we'll make Mallarmé.'

Absurdity tends towards extremes, and Aranda's determination led him towards increasingly shocking themes. In *Clara es el precio* (1974) he cast Amparo Muñoz, Spain's future Miss World, as an innocent adrift in a world without taboo: a young virgin bride, whose infantilised husband is impotent with her alone, and who then pursues a career as a pornographic film actress in order to fund a business project. If the film had a meaning it was doubtlessly objectionable, but the censor passed it anyway, thereby missing the point that the film's impudence was also its purpose. Like the Surrealists, Aranda's ability to shock was itself a political statement: 'we have lived in a state of consensus and this is fatal for cinema,' he complained, 'we have become our own censors and all we want to do is forget, be silent, not speak' (Hopewell, 1986, p.228). Post-Franco, Aranda maintained the sordid milieu of his previous films, but, probably as a response to the flood of meaningless porn and horror films that had quickly contaminated the possibilities of their genres, he reintroduced the metaphor of social criticism that had been the mainstay of New Spanish Cinema.

Cambio de sexo (Change of Sex, 1976) posited a trans-gender operation as a metaphor for the political transition and was based on a clipping from a French magazine about a Belgian transexual who had died after undergoing the operation. Aranda's script was written (in collaboration with Joaquín Jordá and Carlos Durán) in 1972 but needed democracy to pass the censor: it wasn't so much the subject matter that offended (the theme had already been explored in 1971 with Jaime de Armiñan's affectionate and humorous *Mi querida señorita*) as the portrait of family life as a morass of stagnating traditions from which the protagonist must escape in order to realise his true identity. 'If I don't cure you, I'll kill you,' shouts the father as he packs José María, his effeminate son, off to hard labour on a country estate and then an acquaintance whore. This is supposedly a model patriarch, who boasts of having already abandoned a pregnant girlfriend by the time he'd reached his son's age, and whose entry into a Barcelona strip club is met with obsequious recognition from the doorman and performers. But his plan backfires, for instead of prompting his son's desire for the performers, José María feels only a wish to become like them. The strip club offers a glimpse of liberalism in which masculinity and femininity are transitive states. The star of the show is Bibi Anderson (who would become a regular presence in the films of Almodóvar) and her stage name of 'The Enigma' relates to her display of all-over femininity that culminates in a show of her male genitalia. Her performance is disruptive, even José María's father is confused; but José María (Victoria Abril[8]) is entranced by this celebration of his own potential. Under

Victoria Abril as the pre-op José María in *Cambio de sexo* (Vicente Aranda, 1976)

threat of punishment for failing to respond to a whore, José María leaves home for Barcelona and becomes María José, wearing dresses and wigs but pretending to be mute in order to meet men. As a woman in a land where machismo rules, she is denied a voice anyway, but it is through the transition from male to female that the character functions as a metaphor for the transition in Spain from the phallocentric, patriarchal autocracy of the past to a liberal and comprehensive future. 'Our film didn't only recount the life of a transsexual,' said Aranda, 'that was just an anecdote, a metaphor in order to discuss something more generic, of personality, of who we are. At heart we were filming the ugly duckling' (Álvares and Frías, 1991, p.104).

Spain as an ugly duckling? The metaphor was so obvious that it hid in plain sight and allowed the film's distributors to change Aranda's original title of *Una historia clínica* (A Clinical History) to *Cambio de sexo* and foist it on the public as a salacious melodrama. Nevertheless the film's growing reputation has been based not only on the career of Victoria Abril, whose first film this was, but of what became of Spain.[9] The Belgian transsexual, on whom the film was based, may have died, but Aranda's María José survives an attempted self-castration to dance a spectacular tango with Bibi Anderson and wake up in hospital a new woman. 'Six months later, María José had her first female orgasm' reads the postscript, but it's the only stilted note in an otherwise shy and formal film.[10] The film's sensibility also responds to notions of language as a determining factor in individual and, by inference, regional identity. 'Estoy cansado (I'm tired)' says María José; but Bibi counters with the feminine version of the adjective: 'Cansada! Say it from the heart!' *Cambio de sexo* may have been made in Castilian Spanish, but its vindication of self-determination and autonomy held a clear message of support for movements in favour of independence. The film could have ended with the death of María José or her degeneration as an hermaphroditic performer in the style of a similarly pre-op Bibi, but it doesn't. Instead she visits a doctor who explains things in careful, considerate detail: this will be a peaceful, ordered transition after all.

An echo of Aranda's reinscription of genres could be found in the shuffle of ideologies that took place in the early years of the democracy, with numerous Francoists reinventing themselves as concerned liberalisers and playing down or denying their previously hardline support of the regime. Indeed, one result of this opportunist scramble was that most changes came not from the pressures of oppositional movements such as the communists but from former Francoist bureacrats such as Adolfo Suárez, whose sleight of hand often embroiled the bastions of the dictatorship in their own undoing. In 1976, for example, Suárez replaced the existing army minister with Lieutenant-General Gutiérrez Mellado, a democrat, whose determination and discipline brought the army under the control of the new, fully elected Parliament. More-over, most liberals and reformers willingly colluded in the tacit social amnesia that allowed the wolves of the dictatorship to don sheep's clothing. This, in effect, was the secret history of the transition that Aranda explored in *La muchacha de las bragas de oro* (The Girl in the Golden Panties, 1979).

Aranda had hoped to adapt Juan Marsé's novel *Si te dicen que caí* (If They Tell You that I Fell), which recounts the morass of perversity that accompanied the birth of the dictatorship, but due to expense this project would have to wait until 1989. Instead Aranda turned to the new novel by Marsé, just out and a controversial winner of the 1979 Premio Planeta (the Spanish Booker[11]). *La muchacha de las bragas de oro* was to be made cheaply in just a few interior settings, but Aranda upped the budget with money from his Venezuelan contacts and added exterior locations to the script, thereby allowing the film to function in terms of a calculated chiaroscuro that alternates light and shadow as an illustration of the truth and lies of the protagonists. It opens with a man walking on the sun-drenched beach at Sitges, with a soundtrack of solemn cello and the voiceover of Luis Forest (Lautaro Murúa): 'I am a furtive searcher for a second identity that has been abandoned in some corner of the past – those arrogant years, obligatorily classified as victorious.' But as he draws nearer it becomes apparent that this is not a voiceover but a monologue, a rehearsal of his memoirs that he declaims to an empty beach: 'I feel nostalgia,' he says, 'for that which is not allowed to live.' Luis is an ageing ex-Falangist, both redundant and retired in democracy, who is in the act of reinventing his past, becoming, in effect, a compassionate ex-soldier and discreet Socialist.[12] In chaotic flashbacks he recreates the past: the stately funeral of his Republican father in 1942, for example, who actually died following torture by Luis' own companions; or the replayed seduction of two sisters by himself and a friend, in which he places them at a piano and swaps their places and affections until the past has been reinvented to his liking. But his indulgence is broken by the arrival of his niece, Mariana (Victoria Abril), a liberal, adolescent beauty who transforms his mansion hideaway into a hippyish squat by taking doors off their hinges ('I hate doors, they're a bourgeois impediment') and cavorting with a series of casual lovers of both sexes. Mariana takes to typing Forest's memoirs and gradually picks at her uncle's new persona: when he claims that he shaved off his military moustache, for instance, she disagrees and works out the dates to prove him wrong. Gradually his alibi crumbles, as does his resistance to the sexual forwardness of Mariana. She tricks him into having his photograph taken with his arm raised in the fascist salute (he thinks he's holding up a pretend fish) and, in one witty moment, she looks up from performing oral sex on him, takes a pubic hair from her tongue ('to not have hairs on the tongue' is a Spanish saying meaning to speak bluntly and truthfully) and calls him a 'renegade fascist.' Just like Luis and his reinvention, Mariana tells him that her father (the friend that snagged the other sister), 'has hidden his medals and now wants to be mayor of Marbella.'[13] Meanwhile, the Falangist symbol is uncovered beneath the loose plaster on the wall around Luis' mansion.

Ultimately, however, Luis' emendation of his fascist past is exposed as a vital element in the birth of the liberal democracy; for Mariana reveals herself to be Forest's daughter and her collusion in the rewriting of his persona is thus symbolic of the mutual social amnesia that both sides deemed necessary in order for democracy to proceed. Indeed the overhaul of the old regime was condoned by the majority of Spaniards who flocked to the voting booths in 1977 and provided a clear endorsement of Suárez's strategy. This was the period of compromise (*consenso*) in which both sides plucked their extremist wings and settled for a process known as 'social concertation' that began with the 1978 constitution. Just as liberal, opportunist Mariana is the product of self-seeking Falangist Luis, so too did democracy emerge from the Francoist regime: 'The time of grand ideals having ended,' reflects Luis, 'came the time of great businesses.' In the film's astute conclusion Forest shoots himself with a gun that he claims to have forgotten was loaded. 'At your age and playing with pistols,' sneers Mariana as she tends his bleeding wound. 'But you're my daughter.' 'So what' is the reply from Mariana, with his blood all over her hands. 'It's as if she's telling him not to worry', says Aranda, 'that they're all part of the same family' (Álvarez and Frías, 1991, p.124).

Aranda would return to genre and his collaboration with Abril in *Asesinato en el Comité Central* (Murder in the Central Committee, 1982), a *policíaca* in which a power cut interrupts the proceedings of the Communist Congress and, when the lights come back on, the leader is found dead, murdered. The film was based on one of a series of novels by Manuel Vázquez Montalbán that featured a hard-boiled detective called Carvalho, but the intrigue runs a poor second to Aranda's commentary on the transition. 'The truth is that I can't think of another film that deals with this fascinating period', he stated, 'there's a kind of collective amnesia about the time' (Álvares and Frías, 1991, p.130). Thus much of the film's action is filtered through headlines and television reports in imitation of the way in which the Spanish public lived the transition. The killing of the Communist leader is clearly an attack on democracy, but Aranda is a droll subversive who knows how to wage a fair fight: the televised funeral of the Communist leader, for example, is a sly montage of mourners at the funeral of Franco, while La Pasionaria (the legendary Spanish Communist leader who passed the dictatorship in exile in the Soviet Union) appears as a senile old dear who sits next to the victim but doesn't even realise he's dead. Like *La muchacha de las bragas de oro*, this was a film about extremists coming together in a democracy, in this case in order to solve a crime. Whodunnit? It doesn't matter. As the interior minister (played by José Carlos Plaza) exclaims: 'In the same way that we've had to forget everything, you should do the same.'[14]

Aranda's ambivalent attitude to the transition met with a cold commercial response. Perhaps the first victim of liberalism was irony: Spaniards were determined to take democracy at face value and so feared ambiguity. Aranda continued making thrillers, often adapting novels that allowed for a subversive twist on genres, and nurtured a roster of faithful actors (Victoria Abril, Imanol Arias, Jorge Sanz) alongside a personal aesthetic that centred on an examination of the baser instincts of his characters as motors for the hybridisation of these genres. Two films on Eleuterio Sánchez 'el Lute' (Spain's most wanted criminal of the 1960s, played winningly by Imanol Arias) were based on the subject's autobiographies; but if *El Lute: camina o revienta* (Walk or Die, 1987) played up the Robin Hood myth, its sequel *El Lute: mañana seré libre* (Tomorrow I'll Be Free, 1988) deconstructed the legend with comedy. This twisting of genre would reach its peak with *Amantes* (Lovers, 1990) in which film noir claustrophobia seeps into a realistic recreation of post-war Madrid, producing a brutal but beautiful thriller that maximises the erotic potential of its leads.[15] More recently, the sordidness of his plots for *Intruso* (Intruder) and *El amante bilingüe* (The Bilingual Lover) (both 1993), *La pasión turca* (The Turkish Passion, 1994) and *Libertarias* (1996) has tended to over-power the credibility of his characters. Nevertheless Aranda has maintained an ironic perspective on the passionate Spanish character and continues to provide an alternative to a preponderance of lightweight comedies – a much-needed tug back into the shadows.

On the other hand, comedies could occasionally be an effective vehicle for social criticism. Berlanga's *La vaquilla* (The Little Bull, 1984) was a popular farce that saw the Civil War as a bull-napping contest between two teams of equally incompetent buffoons, while, in the 1990s, Manuel Gómez Pereira's *¿Por qué lo llaman amor cuando quieren decir sexo?* (Why Do They Call It Love When They Mean Sex?, 1992) and *Todos los hombres sois iguales* (All You Men Are The Same, 1993) would offer amusing deconstructions of machismo that left no doubt as to how far Spain's transition from a patriarchal state had resulted in the emasculation of its previously dominant males. Back in the mid-1970s male desire for fleshy farces had been well served by a variety of opportunist producers, who invested in pretty girls and punchlines and made fortunes in providing vulgar comedies (*comedias zafias*) to the newly consumerist and liberalised, but still male-dominated, society. Many of these producers were businessmen fulfilling dreams of moguldom, who ploughed little back into the industry, but a few were film-makers themselves, turned producers to maximise their profits. One such beneficiary of this demand was Luis Dibildos, whose contribution to Spanish cinema had been the design and implementation, as writer and producer, of the *tercera vía* (third way) films of the early 1970s, so-called because, at a time when the Spanish cinema-goer had little to choose from besides the complex metaphors of Saura and his like, or the relaxing mindlessness of farces, Dibildos had offered an alternative, a 'third way' to make films: comedies with added social criticism and a fair few satirical barbs. Post-Franco his satire softened, but the innovation of the *tercera vía* inspired a genre of contemporary social comedies in which the keys to a film's success were audience identification and the frisson with which such previously forbidden themes as adultery, abortion and impotence were featured. A typical product was Roberto Bodegas' *Vida conyugal sana* (A Healthy Married Life, 1973), in which a Spanish husband (José Sacristán) is disoriented by liberalising ideas of sex and is told by his doctor to stop reading, or watching any films except Spanish ones. Much of the film's humour arises from an ironic contemplation of Spain as a refuge of healthy sinlessness; but the genre's ridiculing of innocence could not possibly last in changing Spain with its emergent movements in favour of women's rights, feminism, divorce, homosexuality, abortion and contraception. Nevertheless, in a clear instance of cinematic evolution, a number of film-makers in this genre attempted to reflect the transition with cheaply made and independent but sophisticated comedies of manners that acquired the title of *comedias madrileñas* – the Madrid comedies.

Chief amongst these would-be *auteurs* were Fernando Colomo and Jose Luis Garci. Colomo's *Tigres de papel* (Paper Tigers, 1977) was a snapshot of a

Carmen Maura in *Tigres de papel* (Fernando Colomo, 1977)

generation, in which Carmen (Carmen Maura) rattled on about sex and politics in dialogue that was often so colloquial it would baffle any spectator over a certain age – and purposefully so, for hers was the authentic voice of a new generation that had quickly estranged itself from the dictatorship which had raised it. Indeed, in addition to the linguistic distinctions, the *comedia madrileña* involved the reinvention of a filmic language. The metaphors and analogies of films by Saura and his peers (most of whom had been raised on the exemplary parables of their religious education) were replaced by films that presented a confluence of thought and action, where characters' free speech, with all its spontaneity and sincerity, was mirrored in the rawness of the film-making. Colomo shot on a budget of only 9 million pesetas and made a virtue of his technical limitations by filming long takes in a few interior settings with direct sound and allowances for improvisation. Not much happens anyway: against a background of the first democratic elections Carmen and Juan debate their crumbling marriage while Alberto tries to come between them. But notions of equality, liberty and responsibility are discussed in a way that personalises the larger political context and converts the three protagonists into representatives of their generation. Unsurprisingly, this ragged, sincere and tender film was recognised as a precise reflection of its audience: more Cassavetes than Rohmer, *Tigres de papel* celebrated the replacement of an archaic bourgeois morality with youthful liberalism and became one of the first major successes of the democracy.[16]

José Luis Garci, meanwhile, had used the experience gained as scriptwriter of many films of the *tercera vía* (including *Vida conyugal sana*) to write and direct films that played up heart-on-sleeve debts to Hollywood as an ironic counterpoint to the disillusionment of its protagonists. *Asignatura pendiente* (Subject Pending, 1977) is, like Colomo's *Tigres de papel*, a defining snapshot of a generation, though its protagonists are older and less concerned about the future than the youth they've left behind. José (José Sacristán) is a left-wing lawyer and Elena (Fiorella Faltoyano) is his childhood sweetheart, both equally disillusioned by life. The film opens in October 1975, a few weeks before the death of Franco, on a panorama of Madrid that is accompanied by melancholic music and voiceovers from them both. 'We had so many plans,' reflects José, as the juxtaposition of their lifestyles is narrowed down to identical shots of them sitting awake in bed next to dormant spouses and remembering their secret, adolescent romance, when 'we kissed underwater.' Garci wrote the script in collaboration with José María González Sinde by transcribing conversations from improvisations and the film's consideration of lost youth is eloquent and regretful for 'the times that you and I should have made love, and didn't; the books we should have read; the things we should have thought.' José and Elena have become the establishment that a younger generation is suddenly empowered to ignore. Their reunion takes place in one of Madrid's grand cafés, where they must talk over the street noise from a celebratory political rally that impinges on their romantic revival (the pending exam of the title). Clearly the end of the dictatorship will have little effect on their lives: even the news of Franco's death is met with a doleful cigarette, a retreating camera and a slow fade to black. Instead they seek refuge from redundancy in their rekindled affair, but for José, who signs himself Robert Redford, the sex is a regression tactic that identifies him as a similarly infantilised male to that of Saura's *La prima Angélica*. 'You're much younger today than you were yesterday,' José tells her, but it is clearly himself that he is flattering. José's political convictions are rejuvenated by the affair, but he ultimately fails to renounce his hypocrisy and breaks up with Elena when she bores him. The film is dedicated 'to us, who've arrived late for everything, infancy, adolescence, sex, love, politics . . .' and has a sombre, autumnal hue that changes to a wintry cold as the lovers fall victim to the same disillusionment that they were escaping. Its sombre resolution has a drunken José urinating against a billboard that welcomes the union of democracy with consumerism ('35 million political parties vote for Condor socks'), but over which has been scrawled the infamous slogan 'We lived better under Franco' (*Bajo Franco vivíamos mejor*). Old enemies have become the new profiteers of contemporary Spain and José, who describes himself as 'one of the saddest men in western Europe, besides Arias Navarro, of course' is doomed to live long and prosper.[17]

Garci reunited his cast the following year for *Solos en la madrugada* (Alone in the Early Hours, 1978), in which a radio presenter (José Sacristán) spouts what appears to be a stream of consciousness discourse on politics and philosophy but comes to a stagnant end with interminable ponderings on his own mid-life crisis. The film purports to be a tribute to those who worked on Spanish radio, but its bitter ending sees José Miguel belittled and abandoned by the various women in his life. The film's one note of celebration is the recreation of the legalisation of the Communist Party by Adolfo Suárez, who leaked the announcement over national radio at the peak of the Easter holidays, when there was no one in the cities to protest.[18] Garci would later achieve notoriety for winning Spain's first Academy Award for best foreign language film, though his overly sentimental *Volver a empezar* (To Begin Again, 1981) had rather less impact than the photographs of the director raising his Oscar aloft – a sign to the world that Spain had become a fit place for artistic and, by inference, political freedom. The only question that remained was whether Spanish youth had the inclination to exploit it.

The answer came with Fernando Trueba's *Ópera prima* (1980), though it wasn't necessarily the one that was hoped for. 'Since I've stopped being an intellectual, I screw a lot more' Matías' best friend tells him, but it's not much comfort to Matías (Oscar Ladoire, who co-wrote the script with Trueba), a twenty-something would-be author and already has-been hack, who's a slave to his own dry, laconic wit and monologues of free association that inevitably confuse him even more. *Ópera prima* was filmed in four weeks almost entirely in economical mid-shot and long takes, with a ration of slow zooms and pans and characters moving in and out of frame. Like Colomo's *Tigres de papel*, *Ópera prima* makes a virtue of its limitations, but in its affectionate sarcasm delivers another vivid and poignant snapshot of life in Madrid during the early years of the democracy. On a wet day, Matías buys a newspaper and strolls in Madrid's district of Ópera, when a woman creeps up behind and clamps her hands over his eyes: 'Who am I?' 'Rosa?' asks Matías, 'Almudena? Wait, don't tell me. Milagros? Mari Puri? Mari Pili? María Luisa?' on and on until he runs out of fingers and turns to confront his beautiful young cousin, Violeta (Paula Molina).[19] Their matter-of-fact romance becomes a comedy of errors for Matías, who struggles to control feelings of jealousy that are rebuffed by his liberated cousin, but not even the incestuous nature of their affair can add spice to this rather ordinary indulgence in the new spirit of liberalism. The problem facing Spanish youth in the democracy is that there is nothing left to rebel against (Matías even pretends to shoplift so that he can argue with a store detective) and this ennui also affects what in other times would have been his political enemies: 'They used to beat you up for a reason,' he laments, 'now, nothing.' Liberalism begets its own satiety and fashionable aimlessness soon palls, though Matías does ruin everything in the

Oscar Ladoire surprised by Paula Molina in *Ópera prima* (Fernando Trueba, 1980)

film's ludicrously happy ending by telling Violeta he loves her because she makes him want to finish his novel.

The *comedias madrileñas* made aimlessness seem like a political stance and gladly wisecracked about personal liberties with a sarcasm that expressed fearlessness but, in truth, a few things such as the Civil Guard were still sacred, as Pilar Miró found to her cost when she made *El crimen de Cuenca* (The Cuenca Crime) in 1979. Miró had come from a strict, middle-class family in Madrid, had studied law, then film-making under Carlos Saura at the Official Film School.[20] Since graduating in 1967 Miró had also worked in Spanish television on adaptations of classic works, but in 1979 she determined to leave television for the cinema. Unable to find backing for her own projects she accepted the job of directing a script based on a thorough investigation of a judicial error that had occurred in 1910, when two men from the province of Cuenca were accused of the murder of a third and horrifically tortured by the Civil Guard. Despite the lack of a corpse, motive or witnesses, the two men were forced to make confessions and were imprisoned for a crime that, sixteen years later, was solved by the reappearance of the supposed victim, a mental retard who had simply wandered away from his village. At a time when cases of torture against members of ETA were receiving overdue publicity, Miró filled her film with excruciating and protracted recreations of similar torment: a moustache is removed with pliers, fingernails are torn off with scissors. But, to the authorities, the most objectionable element of the film was that the mistreatment of the two men was shown to have originated with the connivance of the army, the Church and Conservative politicians – the same trinity that maintained control of the democracy. The film reached the Berlin Film Festival in 1980 but was confiscated in Spain on the grounds of its affront to the Civil Guard. Two months later Pilar Miró faced a military trial and a possible jail term of one to six years. The case dragged on until March 1981 when, as part of the government's desperate attempts at asserting the steadfastness of its democracy just a few weeks after the attempted coup of Lieutenant-Colonel Antonio Tejero, the case was transferred to the Civil Court and dismissed, thereby allowing the film to be screened to massive audiences in Spain.[21]

Miró would continue making films of an often personal nature, even after she accepted ministerial responsibility for cinema in the newly elected Socialist government of Felipe González in 1982.[22] From this position she would attempt a transformation of the Spanish film industry by the revision of government funding and distribution quotas that came to be known as Miró's Law (*Ley Miró*).[23] In 1986, following much criticism from those who accused her of favouritism in her support of projects, she (technically) left the government to become head of RTVE (Spanish Radio and Television) but would be forced to abandon this position in 1988 over accusations of misappropriation of funds that once more brought her to the courts. The accusations were dismissed, but suspicions were voiced that this was but a second attempt at bringing her to justice for daring to criticise the Civil Guard in *El crimen de Cuenca*. Even more than a decade into democracy, it seems, the forces of the old regime were still scheming to contain the liberalism that surrounded them. In Madrid especially, where the underground cultural movement known as the *movida* had taken hold of the nightlife, its culture of sexual liberalism and drug use was a particularly red flag to an old and angry bull.[24]

However, rather more subversive than Miró's filmic attack was the ribbing of authority that is a singular delight of the films of Pedro Almodóvar, the *movida*'s favourite son, whose films avoided stereotyping the police and Civil Guard as antagonists and, instead, realigned them as often unwitting accomplices in their farce. In Almodóvar's first full-length feature, *Pepi, Luci, Bom y otras chicas del montón* (Pepi, Luci, Bom and Other Girls on the Heap, 1980), for example, a policeman treats his masochist wife Luci with such respect that she takes to life in the *movida* as 'groupie for a band of degenerates', until her fulfilment provokes her jealous husband into beating her senseless, thereby occasioning a happy ending. Similarly, in *¡Qué he hecho yo para merecer esto!* (What Have I Done to Deserve This!, 1984) an impotent detective, both sexually and in the case under investigation, seeks a cure in a potentially romantic encounter with a happy hooker, while in *Tacones lejanos* (High Heels, 1991) the investigating officer works nights as a transvestite diva in a thriving club. Almodóvar's aim was not to antagonise the authorities but to invite them to his party. This was not a matter of vengeance but of reconcilliation; for Almodóvar's genius as a director is for mixing old and new, whether it be songs, styles, genres, cultures or attitudes to Spanishness and Spain. His witty, incongruous juxtapositions of lifestyles may seem anarchic, but as his affectionate satires sharpen they often focus on a surprisingly old-fashioned but updated moral. In *La ley del deseo* (The Law of Desire, 1987), for example, he presents a family unit in which the father figure is a homosexual, the mother is his transexual brother and the child is the daughter of the latter (aptly named Ada, short for Inmaculada, meaning 'immaculate conception'): but the integrity and bonding of these three is as strong as any model family from the propagandist melodramas of the dictatorship.

Indeed this most traditional desire for a family is a defining theme of Almodóvar's films, whether it arises from the ragbag clan of Pepi, Luci and Bom, the wayward nuns of *Entre tinieblas* (Dark Habits, 1983), the mother–daughter conflict of *Tacones lejanos*, the beguiling fantasy of Antonio Banderas' psychopath in *¡Átame!* (Tie Me Up!, Tie Me Down!, 1989), the career-woman broodiness of Pepa (Carmen Maura) in *Mujeres al borde de un ataque de nervios* (Women on the Verge of a Nervous Breakdown, 1988) or the female solidarity in *Todo sobre mi madre* (All About My Mother, 1999). It is a desire that originates in Almodóvar's reflection on his own youthful rebelliousness. Born in the province of La Mancha in 1949, the son of a muleteer, Almodóvar took off for Madrid in 1969 with aspirations to an artistic career:

> *I think I had to go my own way because [my family] was so possessive; the best thing for me was to get as far away as possible. When I left it was an unpleasant, tense situation. After a certain amount of time goes by, you recognise the value of your family and they recognise you as well, they recognise who you are. Things happen. Since then we have established mutual respect. And little by little I've become aware of how important [my mother] has been, not only in my life, but also in my career.*[25]

It could be argued that Almodóvar found a new family in the *movida*, one that stressed solidarity as a response to their marginalisation from society and was supportive of both his homosexuality and interest in film-making; but the apparently incongruous primacy of family in Almodóvar's early films about the marginalised folk of the *movida* also points to his indebtedness to the various theatrical, literary and performing traditions in Spanish culture. In other words the *movida* was not a break from the past, but a newer version of it. Thus, in the feverish fusion of melodrama and film noir that is *La ley del deseo*, for example, the classic, madly romantic bolero 'Lo dudo' by Los Panchos becomes an anthem to homosexuality, while the transvestite Letal (Miguel Bosé) in *Tacones lejanos* performs in front of a mural that features the most traditional elements of Spanish folklore. Meanwhile, in *Pepi, Luci, Bom y otras chicas del montón*, the policeman husband of Luci is roughed up by a band of punks who have disguised themselves in the traditional folk costumes of *chulapos*, a kind of Cockney from turn of the last century Madrid, whose arrogance, slang and intensely urban culture was a predecessor to the clique of the *movida*.[26]

Watching *Pepi, Luci, Bom y otras chicas del montón* now is like opening a time capsule from a particularly schizophrenic period in the history of Spain. It features elements of silent films, porno films, television ads, photo-novels, songs from the music hall, punks, hippies and glam-rockers. It's as if the shock of post-transition liberalism had caused the previous four decades to be thrown forward, tumbling into the 1970s. The satirical collage is more cheeky than anarchic, never more so than in the contest of 'General Erections' in which Almodóvar appears as compère, refereeing a penis-measuring contest that offers a gleeful parody of the general elections of the democracy. Shot intermittently in 16 mm and then blown up to 35 mm for commercial distribution, the film was a *succès de scandale* that was still playing the midnight show at Madrid's Alphaville cinema in the already nostalgic 1990s. This and its follow-up, *Laberinto de pasiones* (Labyrinth of Passions, 1982), offered celebrations of Almodóvar's time in 'that crazy period, the *movida* [when] apart from taking a lot of drugs and going out, etcetera, etcetera, we made a few films together.' Except, by the middle of the 1980s, the *movida*'s head of steam had evaporated, leaving numerous victims of drug abuse in its wake. Perhaps, after sitting out most of the twentieth century, Spain had grown up too fast and was not prepared for the fall-out that accompanied accelerated change. Almodóvar's compassion and increasing maturity as a film-maker would provide an intimate portrait of the people that this time forgot in *¡Qué he hecho yo para merecer esto!*

The film reflected Almodóvar's belief that 'the attention of film-makers is fixed on the past, the post-war, but these are ghosts which half the country doesn't share.'[27] Instead, the contemporary tale of Gloria (Carmen Maura), an illiterate, glue-sniffing housewife, is one of anonymous suffering. Gloria lives and labours in a pokey flat on the outskirts of Madrid with her difficult mother-in-law, her abusive husband and their two adolescent sons, one a drug dealer and the other a promiscuous homosexual who leaves home to live with a pederast. In various moments, Almodóvar films her through a frame of household objects (e.g. oven and washing-machine doors), thereby identifying her as one of the many rural emigrants to Madrid who ended up as prisoners of urban squalor, at the same time as these images attest to the influence of 'housewife culture' on the origins of the director's beloved pop art (e.g. Warhol's soup cans and detergent boxes). The film also hosts a bizarre plot about forging Hitler's diaries, but this barely impinges on the authenticity of Maura's portrayal of beleaguered femininity. Like Maura, the film displays a striking lack of vanity in its portrait of post-Franco Madrid and even goes so far as to posit a return to nature as a response to ineffectual democracy and rampant materialism. The conclusion shows Gloria abandoned by her elder son and mother-in-law, who head back to the simple comforts of an ethically reinscripted village: once a symbol of backwardness, the village has become a refuge from progress. Indeed, this mythic village also provides the nostalgic setting for the bittersweet romantic postscript of *¡Átame!* (Tie Me Up!, Tie Me Down!, 1989) and the spiritual home that Leo (Marisa Paredes) finds herself distressingly estranged from in *La flor de mi secreto* (The Flower of My Secret, 1995). In *¡Qué he hecho yo para merecer esto!*, Gloria is similarly denied the succour of 'the village' as Almodóvar returns her to the cramped and lonely flat. But, like the grandmother who helps her son with a homework exercise in which authors have to be split into realist and romantic canons and proudly gets all of them wrong, Almodóvar is a romantic who won't let reality get him or his characters down: the film's fairy-tale ending is an emotional reunion

Verónica Forqué and Carmen Maura in *¡Qué he hecho yo para merecer esto!* (Pedro Almodóvar, 1984)

between Gloria and her homosexual son. 'This place needs a man,' he tells her, and it's tempting to see this tender reconciliation of mother and gay son, of romanticism and reality, as a particularly poignant example of the many autobiographical touches that appear in the director's films.[28] According to Almodóvar:

> [My mother] fits very well not only in my life but also in my films. This being, at the same time, a woman from whom I had to flee. When I was young ... we didn't have any money and she invented a profession for me. I'd write letters for the neighbours, who were all illiterate and my mother would read the ones they received. I learned something essential at the time: the difference between fiction and reality, and how reality sometimes needs a dash of fiction to work better. Because when she read the letters she used to invent things she knew the neighbours wanted to hear. I was scandalised. Now, years later, I see that this is what we do, we take reality but complete it with something else, which is fiction.

Into the mid-1980s, and many Spaniards began to wonder if the economic marginalisation that they suffered in the new capitalist society was in any way preferable to life under Franco. The new Socialist government of Felipe González was both homespun and trendy, but with that went nepotism and a new celebrity cult around politicians, bankers and businessmen. A new climate of disillusionment (*desencanto*) took hold, and if the fantasy of the Madrileñan nightlife was spurred by drugs, its antidote was the very real effect of drug abuse (and Aids) on its participants.[29] Nowhere is this change of attitude more explicit than in the films of Almodóvar. In *Pepi, Luci, Bom*, drugs are simply fun, and in *Laberinto de pasiones* (Labyrinth of Passions, 1982) they're so cool it's crazy; but by *¡Qué he hecho yo para merecer esto!* Gloria's drug-dealing son, who stays clean himself, is warning her not to dabble. Come *¡Átame!*, and Marina (Victoria Abril) is an ex-addict, whose captor (Antonio Banderas) shows grave concern for her returning need, while in *Todo sobre mi madre* (All About My Mother, 1999) a principal motor of the plot is the efforts of the women to rescue Nina (Candela Peña) from her habit. However, not only is Nina saved and returned to happy housewife duties in the now familiarly mythical village, but the worst side effects of excessive liberalism are also relieved by the birth of a baby whose immune system holds a possible cure for Aids. In this case, Almodóvar's take on reality is subsumed beneath his wish-fulfilment fiction, but it is partly this contradictory nature that spurs the evolution in his work. 'My films will always contradict each other,' he says, 'I don't have any commitment to anybody, not even to the audience ... I think a change is good for everyone at any moment, whatever it is you're doing. Change always revitalises, and demands courage.'[30]

Abstinence and family values are hardly the kind of resolutions that one might expect from Almodóvar but, in part, they reflect a disillusionment that was seen to far more extreme effect in the films of a number of his contemporaries. By the mid-1990s the government of Felipe González was out of its depth in corruption and scandals that included the illegal financing of the Socialist Party (FILESA) and the similarly unlawful running of a secret anti-terrorist hit squad (GAL). The responses of José Luis Garci (*Asignatura pendiente*) and Fernando Trueba (*Ópera prima*) were nostalgic reproductions of Spain from long before the disappointments of democracy. Garci's *Canción de cuna* (Crib Song, 1994) was a solemn and saintly tale of an orphan girl raised (correctly) by nuns, while Trueba's *Belle epoque* (1992), like José Luis Cuerda's *La lengua de las mariposas* (Butterfly's Tongue, 1999) – both of which were written by Rafael Azcona – posited a utopian idea of liberalism that advertised the Second Republic of the 1930s as a true model of progress: an idea of what contemporary Spain might have aspired to. *Belle epoque*'s chocolate-box picture of Spanishness met with huge international acclaim and even won the Oscar for best foreign language film, but a large part of its appeal was that its contrivance extended to the sexual shenanigans of its youthful, attractive cast. An army deserter (Jorge Sanz) happens upon a country mansion where a dotty patriarch (Fernando Fernán Gómez) lives with his four nubile and welcoming daughters. In quick succession the lad is willingly seduced by three sisters who function as stereotypical male fantasies – a frustrated widow, a nymphomaniac and a lesbian – before morality comes to bear and he marries the fourth stereotype: an adoring virgin. Though much of the film's humour resides in the sexual objectification of the young male this was, at times, nonsensical; for, quite apart from ignoring the rather more genuine and forbidding morality of the time, Trueba would have his audience believe that a lesbian would be desirous of a man if he dressed up as a woman.

These films attested to a growing atmosphere of disillusionment with the achievements of socialism that would contribute to the election victory of the right-of-centre People's Party (*Partido Popular*) in 1996. Since then, Spanish film-makers have barely touched on contemporary social issues or even a political theme. A notable exception was Benito Zambrano's *Solas* (Alone, 1999) in which Ana Fernández plays María, a pathetic alcoholic, a victim of familial neglect and social disregard, who relearns the value of commitment. Otherwise the leading young *auteurs* of the moment, Julio Medem and Alejandro Amenábar, have always been too involved in personal issues or were having too much fun with genres to attempt a chronicle of their time. Then, in 2000, came *Sé quien eres* (I Know Who You Are) from first-time director Patricia Ferreira, an effective romantic thriller about a psychiatrist (Ana Fernández) whose patient (Miguel Ángel Solá) professes loss of memory for the last twenty or so years of his life. Her desire to locate the trauma that occasioned his condition prompts her to investigate the secret history of Spain's political transition and discover a history of violent episodes, subterfuge and betrayal. Digging through archives she unearths the convulsions that occasioned the birth of democracy and is stunned by the realisation that an entire population has been able to blot out the past. By confronting her patient with the truth about his role in the transition – 'I know who you are!' – she is able to reawaken his memories of self and country, and thereby revise her own sense of identity and Spain. Thus, in this film's honest look back at recent Spanish history, there is, perhaps, the beginning of a cure for social amnesia and a recognition of its necessity. Wrote Luis Buñuel: 'Life without memory is no life at all, just as intelligence without the possibility of expression is not really intelligence. Our memory is our coherence, our reason, our feeling, even our action. Without it, we are nothing' (1983, p.5).

Notes

1. Later in the film Pascual literally hacks a mule to death with a knife. John Hopewell writes of a 1985 screening in London's National Film Theatre at which a large number of the audience walked out in disgust (1986, p.27). The author, on the other hand, attended a screening in Madrid's Filmoteca, where a post-film discussion was overwhelmingly in support of the slaughter for the purposes of realism and the impact of its symbolism.
2. Virginia Higginbotham sees the garrotte as 'a metaphor for a slowly asphyxiating, repressive culture as well as for stark reality in Spain' (1988, p.111).
3. The National Movement (Movimiento Nacional) was a term adopted by the Franco regime as the official designation of the sole political organisation allowed under its rule. All government employees were required to be members.
4. The elections were won by Suárez's Centre Democratic Union (*Unión de Centro Democrático*, UCD), which garnered 79 per cent of the vote. The UCD was a hastily formed centre party that included both opponents and servants of the Franco regime. Due to internal divisions the party would crumble in a few years and be dissolved after losing the elections of 1982.
5. *Antología del cine español*, Spain: Mundografic, S.A., Vol.I, p.76.
6. A few years later one could add Carlos Saura (*Sevillanas* and *Flamenco*) and Víctor Erice (*El sol del membrillo*, The Quince Tree Sun) to this group.
7. The Sitges congress was outlawed and became, instead, a festival of fantasy and horror films that thrives to this day.
8. The original choice of actress was Ángela Molina (with her younger, near-identical brother playing herself as a boy).
9. Marsha Kinder provides an intriguing description of contemporary attitudes to *Cambio de sexo* (Evans, 1999, pp.128–47).
10. The cinematographer was Néstor Almendros, whose innovative use of fluorescent lighting created a stark, realistic tone. However, Almendros could not finish his labour as he was called to work on Terence Malick's *Days of Heaven*, for which he won an Oscar.

11. Juan Marsé is the author of *Últimas tardes con Teresa* (Last Evenings with Teresa) and *El embrujo de Shanghai*. He claimed that he had written *La muchacha de las bragas de oro* for the express purpose of winning the Premio Planeta.

12. Rosa Álvares and Belen Frías speculate that Luis Forest is based upon the writer Guillermo Díaz Plaja (1991, p.121).

13. Marbella was rapidly transformed into the playground of the Spanish jet set, the so-called *los beautiful*, who made quick profits from democracy and retired to play in the resort that has a consequently right-wing reputation.

14. Okay, it's a militant Communist who fears a softening of the revolution.

15. *Amantes* is analysed in Chapter 9.

16. The title *Tigres de papel* is a contemptuous term for capitalists.

17. Arías Navarro was vice-president of Franco's last government and the person who famously and tearfully announced the death of Franco on Spanish televsion.

18. If Suárez had not legalised the Communist Party any attempt at true democracy would have been effectively annulled.

19. The film's title is a play on words: *Ópera prima* means 'first work' and can also mean 'a cousin in Opera', with *prima* meaning cousin and *Ópera* being the district where she lives.

20. In later years Miró would herself take on teaching duties and be mentor to Imanol Uribe, whose own commitment to film-making, often against all odds, was inspired by the tribulations of his teacher.

21. Tejero's storming of Madrid's Congress of Deputies (the lower parliament) was part of an attempted coup on 23 February 1981 that saw tanks appear on the streets of Valencia. Only prompt action by loyal troops acting under the command of King Juan Carlos ensured that order was restored in the country.

22. Miró's films include *Gary Cooper, que estás en los cielos* (Gary Cooper, Who Art in Heaven, 1980), which deals with an independent woman's brush with death and was based on her own medical trauma, and *El pajaro de la felicidad* (The Bird of Happiness, 1992) in which the characters reflect upon the director's most intimate concerns. Miró died in 1997, shortly after achieving an astounding popular success with the production – in verse-form no less – of a film of Lope de Vega's *El perro del hortelano* (The Dog in the Manger, 1995).

23. Miró also oversaw the legalisation of cinemas that screened films in the 'X' classification (i.e. pornographic films). Twenty-two such cinemas opened in March 1984.

24. The term *movida* comes from the slang phrase to score drugs: *tener una movida* is to have a business-thing happening.

25. Unless otherwise stated, all quotes from Pedro Almodóvar are from the transcript of an interview conducted by Tom Charity and generously ceded to the author for inclusion in this chapter.

26. Actually, it turns out that it's not Luci's husband but his identical twin.

27. Interview with Pedro Almodóvar in *Dirigido por*, No.111, January 1984, p.13.

28. Nevertheless the final credits to *¡Qué he hecho yo para merecer ésto!* play over a series of dissolves that reveal a panorama of high-rise flats on the outskirts of Madrid – clearly this is just one of many similar stories in the naked city.

29. There were two heroin addicts per thousand inhabitants in Spain in 1990 – twice the estimated level in Holland. More than 40 per cent of heroin users were thought to be HIV positive (Hooper, 1995, pp.196–207).

30. The films and career of Almodóvar are analysed further in Chapter 9.

CHAPTER SEVEN

An independent style

Basque cinema and Imanol Uribe

Euskal Herria, País Vasco and the Basque Country are three nations in one. *Euskal Herria* – the land of the Euskera speakers – is a mythic place, hidden deep inside the impenetrable and ancient language from which it takes its name: a world of warriors, whalers and woodsmen. *País Vasco* is the Spanish equivalent and seems much smaller, a primitive rural area of northern Spain: a land of cow-farmers, great sportsmen and vociferous, violent nationalists. And the Basque Country is the new, autonomous, industrialised nation as seen from abroad. Any analysis of Basque cinema must therefore deal with this three-way split personality in relation to language, politics and a history of almost total censure during the dictatorship; for it is also the linguistic, aesthetic and thematic obsession of Basque film-makers. The director Imanol Uribe, for instance, has exposed the tensions that exist between myths and propaganda by developing the form of the documentary as both a political and a narrative device, often deliberately confusing the two. Even fictional Basque films, whose narratives commonly explore the prevailing themes of rural introspection and urban degradation, have mostly concealed a multiplicity of political intent. More recently the vast investment in film-making by the new Basque government, keen to promote its singular voice in both national and international markets, has produced film-makers whose treatment of these themes reveals a fresh, often subversive approach to questions of Basque identity.

Conflicting definitions of the Basque Country have been the subject of Basque cinema since its inception in 1896 with Lumière's filming of the single reel *Llegada de la Corte en San Sebastian* (The Arrival of the Royal Court at San Sebastian). San Sebastian was the Basque vacation resort of the Spanish royal family and, at a time of accelerated industrialisation, rampant socialism and the politicisation of the nationalist cause, this record of their arrival purposefully celebrated the subservience of the region to the centralist and royalist government in Madrid: the Basques were merely subjects of king and camera. Shortly thereafter, as in the rest of Spain, filmshows appeared at funfairs and as occasional entertainment in cafés and churches, though it was the travelling showmen known as *barracas* that introduced the new invention to the Basque Country's mainly rural population with their moonlit shows in remote village squares. Meanwhile entrepeneurs exploited the appeal of the cinematograph by hiring camera-owners to film religious festivals or sporting occasions and then charging the populace for the chance of seeing themselves in the flickering images of crowds.

Early fiction films, mostly imported from the United States, became rapidly popular and several cafés in San Sebastian began offering two filmshows per day, mostly comedies and occasionally 'naturist', with the added attraction of in-house narrators or *explicas*, who explained the plots for barely literate audiences and often became greater attractions in themselves than the films they narrated. Theatre-owners took to showing short, silent films and travelogues in between their comedians and boxing matches. Such films as those made by Fructuoso Gelabert (*San Sebastián en Tranvía*, San Sebastian by Tram; *Viaje de Bilbao a San Sebastián*, Voyage from Bibao to San Sebastian) were designed to flatter their audience with ideas of a devout, expansive country that was heir to a unique cultural heritage, and they prompted an awareness that film could serve as a political weapon in the causes of Basque nationalism and the kindred socialist movement. This, in turn, led to the establishment of a workers' cinema in Vizcaya in 1915 and the first Congress of Basque Studies in Oñate in 1918, which proposed the filming of traditional Basque dances and folklore as a means of preserving a national identity that was being actively suppressed. Manuel Inchausti, a typically enterprising individual, duly set about a series of documentaries entitled *Euzko Ikusgayak* (1923) that made up in ethnographic value what they lacked in the way of technique. These and other short films communicated a sense of disappearing nationhood at a time of economic hardship; but it was still the imported comedies and melodramas that formed the basis of an evening's escapism for an audience that would be further enthralled by live orchestras, celebrity *explicas*, and amateur, in-house smoke and fire effects that only added to the hazard created by the projection of flammable film – a risk which led to several blazes and one false alarm in the Teatro Circo de Bilbao in 1912, when forty-six people, mostly children, died in the panic.

The indigenous production of fictional shorts began in 1923 with the appearance of Hispania Films in Bilbao, which produced both the first fictional short film, *Un drama en Bilbao* (A Drama in Bilbao), and the first full-length feature made entirely in the Basque Country with Basque actors, *Edurne, modista de Bilbao* (Edurne, Dressmaker of Bilbao, 1923). Because of their popularity, fictional films displayed an even greater potential for propaganda than documentaries, though any exploitation of this fact was rapidly suppressed, when the dominant Catholic clergy branded the cinema a corrupting force and invoked the centralist government's censorship of films such as *El mayorazgo de Basterretxe* in 1928, in which, with knowing incitement to nationalism, directors Victor and Mauro Azkona had featured the outlawed *ikurriña* (the Basque flag). Nevertheless the invention of sound film in the 1930s allowed the first words in the Basque language of Euskera to be spoken onscreen in a French documentary entitled *Le Pays des Basques*, and in 1933 the first entirely propagandist documentary feature was produced by a leader of the Basque Nationalist Party (PNV), Teodoro Ernandorena, whose *Euskadi* expounded upon the ideology of Basque nationalism that had been set down in the nineteenth century by Sabino Arana. Arana's writings established many of the precepts of modern Basque nationalism and quickly acquired the status of a biblical text, thereby conferring a certain sainthood on its creator and elevating his cause to that of a religious crusade. The burgeoning nationalist movement of the twentieth century was thus presented as a legacy of a divine, illustrious past and Ernandorena's film, which would be deliberately sought out and destroyed by Franco's army during the Civil War, firmly established this purposeful fusion of myth with social realism that would prove itself the dominant theme in Basque cinema.

Nevertheless the production of sound films required a massive investment on the part of production companies and distributors that was clearly inadvisable during a period of grave economic crisis and political uncertainty. The Civil War split the Basque Country and Basque film-makers in two: right-wing propagandist documentaries such as *Bilbao para España* (Bilbao for Spain) stressed the deeply ingrained Catholicism of the people as a reason for solidarity with the Francoist armies while, on the other side, newsreels that featured the bombing of the Basque town of Gernika were smuggled out of the country for fund-raising screenings in France and Britain.

The beginning of Franco's dictatorship brought an even fiercer censorship to bear on the indigenous film industry, with the result that the Euskera language was outlawed from schools, songs and cinema screens. Many film-makers went into forced or voluntary exile, the industry ground to a halt, and there would be nothing in the way of Basque cinema beyond innocuous travelogues until the 1950s, when private film societies called *zine-klubs* provided a meeting place for amateur film-makers to screen their efforts and collaborate on projects with a Basque theme. Thanks to their efforts the San Sebastian Film Festival was founded in 1953 and would be followed by festivals of documentary films that commonly served as a forum for the expression of the nationalist tendencies of film-makers such as Gotzón Elorza, whose amateur 16 mm documentaries, *Ereagatik Matxitxakora, Erria* and *Elburna Gernika* were filmed and defiantly titled in the Vizcayan dialect of Euskera.

In addition to vindicating their mother tongue, documentarists and avant-garde film-makers sought to create a Basque language in the art and techniques of film-making that would dialectically oppose the creaky, moralist narratives of the propagandist historical melodramas and musicals that were churned out by the Francoist CIFESA studios. Nestor Basterretxea and Fernando Larruquert's *Pelotari* (1964), for instance, displayed an aggressive montage in its expression of the Basque sport that it documented, thereby approximating the clatter of consonants and hard edges of Euskera. Documentarists thus moved closer to the notion of avant-garde cinema with its use of symbolism, abstraction and directorial sleight of hand, and it is from this moment that modern Basque cinema may be said to have emerged, with Basterretxea and Larruquert's *Ama Lur* (Motherland), a full-length documentary that premiered in the 1968 San Sebastian Film Festival after two years of filming and much meddling from the censor.

Ama Lur was made without a script but with the collaboration of over 900 business partners and shareholders, all inspired by the nationalist fervour of its makers. The film sports commentary in both Castilian (the standard dialect of European Spanish) and Euskera, and its accumulating images of traditional Basque culture effect a display of rebellion and defiance. Moreover, the editing of *Ama Lur* purposefully imitates the *bertsolari* (the traditional improvising Basque poet) in a free association of images that allows for a series of dissolves between, for example, a carnival, a religious procession and battling rams. The flow of Basque motifs appears experimental but it obeys an internal logic of national pride that is tantamount to jingoism. The official censor retaliated with demands that the word *España* should be heard three times during the film and that the image of Picasso's *Guernica*, which commemorated the bombing of the town, be excised. In addition the makers were ordered to film again a wintry image of the emblematic Tree of Guernica (a traditional meeting place for Basque leaders and the inspiration for their anthem of militancy *Gernikako Arbola*), so that the political connotations of the tree's bareness would be reversed by a new shot of it in full bloom on a sunny spring day. *Ama Lur* was a sensation in the Basque Country and inspired many, both politically and artistically, though Franco had closed universities in fractious provinces of Spain, and Basques with an urge to make their own short films and documentaries were obliged to move to Madrid to study at the Official Film School.[1] Amongst them were Imanol Uribe, and Víctor Erice, whose *El espíritu de la colmena* (The Spirit of the Beehive, 1973) would earn worldwide recognition for its director and the new Spanish cinema.

At the end of the 1960s the Basque Academy established a common written language called Batua, which unified the various dialects of the Basque Country, and countless demonstrations, strikes and cultural events became a movement for the dissemination of a reclaimed linguistic identity. The 1970s brought an escalation in the Marxist tendency and terrorist activities of the ETA organisation; yet it was also at this time that the leaders of ETA made a pragmatic decision to define Basqueness in terms of sensibility rather than language. Thus a *Euskaldunberri* or 'new Basque speaker', who took classes or was otherwise commitedly auto didactic, was deemed equal to an *Euskaldun* whose Euskera was his or her mother tongue. In contrast with the linguistic dogmatism of Catalans therefore, and the consequences of such imperiousness on the limited dissemination of Catalan cinema, the Basque language was supported as an ideal, but not a vital characteristic of Basqueness. The political differences over the importance of the Basque language as a cultural signifier would gradually widen, but this tolerant, pragmatic response to the problem of massive state-sanctioned immigration to the Basque Country would allow young film-makers with no knowledge of the language, such as El Salvador-born Imanol Uribe, to begin making short documentaries on Basque themes.[2]

As in any description of Spanish cultural history there is a before and after that hinges on the death of Franco in 1975. One year later ETA killed eighteen people and split itself into military and political wings. The year 1976 also saw the first Festival of Documentary Film celebrated in Bilbao, in which many film-makers pooled their political extremism towards a vindication of the role of the cinema in the cause of Basque separatism. The incipient Basque film industry thus fragmented into factions that demanded either the development of film as political discourse or the abandonment of the overbearing rural introspection of most documentaries in favour of a more commercial approach to the representation of Basque culture in film – an approach that necessarily denied the prerogative of Euskera as the defining factor in Basque cinema. The *zine-klubs* were polarised within themselves and against each other. There were those termed *nacionalistas*, which demanded that Basque cinema should be made by *Euskaldunes* in Euskera and in *Euskadi* – the nationalist term for the Basque Country, which unites the provinces of Álava, Guipúzcoa and Vizcaya but excludes Navarre and those in France. And there were just as many *zine-klubs españolistas* protesting that such a restrictive definition could not possibly exist with a limited infrastructure and a maximum audience of only two and a half million Euskera-speakers. Differences of opinion escalated into vibrant discussions in the press and at film festivals, with even leaders of the PNV speaking out on the issue: did '*Hecha* (Made) *en Euskadi*' presuppose '*Hecha en Euskera*'?

The controversy brought the most reactionary film-makers to the forefront of the cultural reappraisal of Basqueness that had become imperative since August 1976, when the Civil Guard had laid siege to a folk festival in Gernika that had dressed itself up in *ikurriñas*. New production companies emerged, including Bertan Filmeak and Araba Films, whose *Estado de excepción* (State of

Emergency, 1977) described the torture and execution of a Basque soldier and was seen as an encouragement to terrorism by the Spanish Civil Guard, who promptly arrested many of those involved in its making, including its director Iñaki Núñez. Yet the infrastructure of new Basque cinema was established in a series of documentaries produced by Bertan Filmeak under the umbrella title of *Ikuska* and the supervision of Antxon Eceiza, who remained in exile in Biarritz. *Ikuska* provided apprenticeships for film technicians and a training ground for directors, including Montxo Armendáriz and Imanol Uribe. The common themes of *Ikuska* were the condition of Euskera and the increasing urbanisation of the population, though there was also Uribe's episode on new Basque folk song and another on the survivors of the bombing of Gernika. The series lasted from 1979 until 1985, when its twentieth and last episode presented a retrospective of the entire series, by which time many of its contributors had graduated to full-length features.

Imanol Uribe was born in San Salvador in 1950 to Basque parents, but was soon sent back to Spain to attend boarding school: 'From the age of seven I was separated from my family. I was always a lonely kid and that loneliness made me seek refuge in the cinema. I'd see three or more films a day.'[3] He spent most of his youth outside Euskadi, except for the summer holidays, which he passed with his grandmother in a house near Gernika.[4] Hers was a staunchly nationalist household, though the young Imanol remained relatively unaware of the reality of Euskadi, preferring instead the evasion that a diet of American genre films afforded him. His father wanted him to be a doctor but, as Uribe recalls,

I was obsessed with film. At that time the only place to study film was Madrid, so I studied one year of medicine, got excellent grades to show my father, then left and came to Madrid. It was the final year of entry for the Official Film School.

He studied under Pilar Miró, who became a close friend, and made a western for his final film project, following the rules of a genre that he knew so well. Thanks largely to the influence and political passion of Miró, Uribe developed a more personal commitment to the process of film-making that collided with a growing awareness of his rootlessness. 'I was a kind of exiled Basque,' he remembers. 'I was searching for something that I'd lost but didn't know what. Basqueness was a mythic thing, of longing, of melancholy. Film-making for me was a means of getting to know the real Euskadi.' Such was the genesis of his first full-length documentary, *El proceso de Burgos* (The Burgos Trial, 1979), a film that would precede (and endanger) the declaration of autonomy for the Basque Country in 1979.

The trial of Burgos was the culmination of a series of tit-for-tat killings that had begun with ETA's assassination of a police captain in 1968 and had seen thousands of Basques arrested and tortured. In December 1970 sixteen alleged members of ETA (including two priests and three women) were sent to trial on charges of military rebellion, banditry and terrorism. Proceedings were disrupted by the accused singing Basque anthems and shouting slogans in court, while public protests extended to other European cities and resulted in considerable international pressure being brought to bear on the Spanish government. The inevitable death sentences were commuted to life imprisonment following a request for clemency from the Vatican and in 1977 they were revoked in the general declaration of amnesty. *El proceso de Burgos* is a record of the remembrances and testimony of those involved, interspersed with footage of Basque landscapes and overlaid with folk songs, thereby establishing an historical, near-mythic context for the remembered events.[5] However, as Uribe has stated,

It was a personal project rather than a political one. The subject of ETA and the anti-Franco battle was the most interesting subject available. For those of us who lived through the political transition, ETA symbolised the fight against fascism. Now that's changed, but back then they were almost mythic, they were heroes fighting against Franco.

The film itself was structured in the editing booth and the final print left the laboratory only two days before it was due to open the San Sebastian Film Festival. However, as Uribe recalls:

On the morning of the premiere, Field Marshal Milans del Bosch[6] woke up in Valencia to read in ABC *that there was this film called* El proceso de Burgos. *So he got on the phone and tried to stop it. I was with the editor, heading for San Sebastian with the film in the boot of my car. We knew that the film might be confiscated or banned – the editor was so nervous that I had to take him to hospital because he was urinating blood. But we got to San Sebastian and hid the film in a broom cupboard, then took it reel by reel to the projection room so that if the police came for us they'd only get one reel and not the whole film. Then we lost the key to the cupboard.*

In fact Milans del Bosch had phoned Marcelino Oreja, the minister for foreign affairs, who quickly relayed the order to his nephew Jaime Mayor Oreja (then leader of the UCD;[7] later home secretary in the government of José María Aznar), who, in turn, asked for a private meeting with Uribe. As Uribe recalls:

He asked me how much it would cost to get the film withdrawn from the festival. I told him it'd be the first time in the history of the cinema that a director had withdrawn his own film! But, if he wanted to confiscate it, to go ahead!

In the event *El proceso de Burgos* won that year's top prize at the festival and was a commercial success due partly to the controversial fact that, with the exception of the hard-liner Julen Kalzada, all of the participants had agreed to abandon Euskera and conduct their interviews, not without humour, in Castilian. However Uribe was threatened by a radical faction of ETA that had rejected the moderate policy of its own leadership and taken offence at what they perceived as the film's similar lack of conviction.[8] 'I've never been a militant in any political party,' avers Uribe:

Indeed, El proceso de Burgos *would have been an impossible project without that distance. All of the accused were now in different political factions and facing off against each other with me in the middle, negotiating with them all, with the innocence of someone who was outside it all. They saw me as a Martian and thanks to that I could make the film.*

Despite (or because of) the film's success, national Spanish television was forbidden from mentioning the film's title, with the result that it became known as *la película de Imanol Uribe* (Imanol Uribe's film), thereby transforming this first-time director into the figurehead of a new Basque cinema that was relevant, committed and determinedly provocative. The approval by referendum of the Statute of Autonomy for the Basque Country in December 1979 had led directly to the first autonomous Basque government in 1980, which saw the ruling PNV reform and revitalise the indigenous film industry by dedicating 5 per cent of its budget to the task as part of its fierce promotion of Basque culture. At first the rather informal attitude of the new administration appeared to consist of rewarding any enquiring film-makers with subsidies that they were not required to repay, though a policy soon evolved which limited the awards to those directors and producers who promised to make 35 mm films in the Basque Country with at least 75 per cent of Basques in the cast and crew and an introductory credit for the government. The only other condition was that a single copy of the film should be made available dubbed into Euskera: the linguistic debate appeared over.

The first film to receive such a subsidy was Uribe's second feature on an ETA theme, *La fuga de Segovia* (The Segovia Breakout, 1981), a curious hybrid of documentary reconstruction and flat-out thriller that recounts the escape from Segovia prison in 1976 of political prisoners, most of them members of ETA, who were shortly thereafter recaptured.[9] It was, says Uribe, 'a great way to move from documentary to fiction with the aid of a safety net, little by little, taking up positions. It was a way to control the story, basing it all on the details of the truth.' Indeed the prison scenes are realistic and the escape itself is every bit as involving as that of Don Siegel's inspirational *Escape From Alcatraz* (1979), but what distinguishes this fusion of the generic conventions of the prison feature with the agitprop of a political documentary is the fact that eight of the actors are the actual protagonists of the fateful escape (since amnestied), including Patxi Bisquert, who would become a respected actor, and that the script is by Ángel Amigo, who collaborated with Uribe on adapting his own memoirs for the screen. 'We started using the actual people as extras,' remembers Uribe, 'most of them wanted to play members of the Civil Guard. Then when shooting started I realised that these people were better as themselves than the actors.' Entertaining and provocative in equal measure, the film won several major international festival prizes and proved that Basque films could function beyond the territorial limits of the autonomy, earning healthy dividends in the national and international market for the private investors who had added to the 10 million peseta government subsidy. 'The idea,' says Uribe,

> was to make a genre film. The choice of theme was obviously political but, more than that, we wanted to prove that in the Basque Country you could make films like you could anywhere else. That was the challenge that inspired so many.

The subsidies provided financing for many new film-makers and a warm welcome for those Basques directors who returned home from Madrid. A massive surge in production resulted in a glut of Basque films, ranging from expensive historical adventures such as Alfonso Hungría's fourteenth-century *La conquista de Albania* (The Conquest of Albania 1983) and Pedro Olea's sixteenth-century *Akelarre* (1983) to more personal, idiosyncratic films from artists who took clear advantage of the no-risk, no-payback nature of their budgets. Film became the flagship of Basque culture in a blatant attempt at nation-building by the ruling PNV. In the words of Uribe:

> It was a time of great optimism. It felt like the long night of Francoism had finished and there were all these fresh hopes and I was part of it. We were going to launch a whole system of Basque film-making, but little by little we were disillusioned. The Basque government realised that film could be a weapon, they began organising things and the subsidies became political – it was the perfect way to ruin it all.

Franco's dictatorship had indeed proven that film was an ideal medium for rewriting history and thereby influencing present-day notions of national identity at home and abroad; perhaps the PNV believed that generous subsidies and absolute creative liberty would find its recompense in film-makers who would return the favour by making ennobling, exportable films about the Basque condition. But such blithe ideas would soon be challenged by directors such as Montxo Armendáriz, whose *Tasio* (1984) displayed an understanding of Basqueness and the Basque Country that was based on the director's own experiences of hardship and injustice – experiences that could only countenance a more rational, less romantic approach to the nationalist crusade.

The infant Montxo was the last hope for his parents, who had already lost three baby sons. But Navarre in 1949 was a miserable piece of Spain all round, having been the centre of much conflict and consequently punished by poverty for its resistance to Francoist troops during the Civil War. Since Roman times several periods of conflict and restructuring had separated Navarre from the rest of the Basque Country, with the result that notions of Basqueness were perhaps more polemical in this region than in any other. Armendáriz's father was a farmhand and blacksmith at a time of deep recession and it is from these childhood years that *Tasio*'s themes of landscape and the interdependence of its human inhabitants clearly originate. Armendáriz spent his youth on typical activities that would feature in *Tasio*, including robbing nests and *pelota*, in which a small, hard ball is smacked around two high walls by men wielding nothing more than clenched fists. Euskera was outlawed and there was little formal education beyond the tales of the local schoolteacher, whose imaginative storytelling awakened Armendáriz's fascination with history and myth. In 1955 his parents aban-doned the rural way of life and, like many thousands of others, moved to the burgeoning provincial capital of Pamplona in search of work. Armendáriz lost his open spaces and found himself sharing benches with privileged middle-class children in religious schools, where the priests censored books and cut full-length films down to twenty minutes or less (though at least the local cinema did repeat these versions three times to give their audiences value for money).

Aged eighteen Armendáriz discovered existentialism in the works of foreign authors, carried out his obligatory miltitary service and took to teaching in a Salesian college, where his particular brand of dialogue-based lectures and general interaction with students was anathema to his disciplinarian col-leagues. Then in 1968 the Europe-wide air of rebellion prompted vague ideas of Basque nationhood that were brought into focus by his first viewing of *Ama Lur*. Armendáriz joined *zine-klubs*, studied folklore, wrote and performed protest songs and bought a Super-8 cine-camera to make his own short films. His creativity coincided with the melting pot of ideas that accompanied the end of the dictatorship and in 1975 he was arrested for protesting the killing of a Basque activist and faced trial on charges of conspiracy; then Franco died and the amnesty was declared. He joined *Euskal Zinegille Elkartea*, a new association of Basque film-makers, and made short films that expressed his con-flictive relationship with the Basque Country, including *Ikusmena* (Landscape, 1980), in which the frame narrative of a ten-year-old girl winning a prize in a school painting competition is disrupted by flashbacks that reveal how her creative expression has been stifled by censorship and social pressures. Thus, for example, a priest, viewing her work in progress of males and females dancing around a spilt jug of wine, is prompted to warn her of hell and to redo the work, which she does, separating the dancers and painting out the wine. The prize is for spontaneity; the girl is apathetic: the political meaning is clear.

Ikusmena was a success at festivals, but it suffered the inevitably limited distribution of short films. Armendáriz turned towards the more socially relevant documentary genre and made the eleventh episode in the *Ikuska* series: *La ribera de Navarra* (The Riverbanks of Navarre, 1981). This he followed with *Nafarrako Ikazkinak* in 1981: a portrait of the charcoal burners who still practised their archaic trade, and it was here that he met Tasio Ochoa, who would inspire his first full-length feature. *Tasio* is a naturalistic portrait of a charcoal burner in the Urbasa mountains, whose threatened way

Patxi Bisquert in *Tasio* (Montxo Armendáriz, 1984)

of life is detailed in a series of elliptical sequences. Scenes of courtship, *pelota* and nest-robbing betray the autobiographical nature of several early scenes, while the detailed observation of the adult Tasio at work on his bonfire-like charcoal kiln alternates with tense, involving sequences that follow his exploits as poacher and his consequent encounters with a corrupt and vengeful Spanish Civil Guard. Despite the magnificent landscapes and emerging consideration of man's place in nature, *Tasio* is distinguished by a lack of sentiment and romanticism. Instead Armendáriz's own script accumulates a catalogue of bleak, dramatic, often silent images of rural subsistence that speak of the hardship and injustices involved in this disappearing trade – an example being the disturbing sequence of Tasio's near-suicidal rescue of a young boy from a charcoal kiln. The character of Tasio is played by three actors at different ages, though the transitions are deliberately abrupt and unforgiving of an audience that might expect narrative dissolves or visual clues to soften the effect of what amounts to a relentless exposition of the consequences of one man's decision to detach himself from the emerging Basque nation of the 1970s. *Tasio*'s realism demanded a three-month shoot that involved the actors living and working in primitive conditions, and it is therefore of note that the adult Tasio is played by the same Patxi Bisquert who had begun acting in Uribe's *La fuga de Segovia*.

Tasio ends with the next generation, including Tasio's own daughter, heading to the city in search of gainful employment and economic independence, thereby abandoning an ageing and obstinate Tasio, who remains in the mountains, clinging to his own singular sense of dignity and personal freedom. In its honouring of a character marginalised by progress, therefore, *Tasio* may have betrayed the generous subsidy that its producer, Elías Querejeta, drew from the Basque government with all their proud ideas of industrialisation and urban prosperity. Moreover, Armendáriz's next film *27 horas* (27 Hours, 1986) would display an even more severe social criticism in its austere depiction of youth problems and drug abuse in a grim and perpetually overcast San Sebastian. Armendáriz subsequently moved away from the Basque Country to depict the harsh reality of Senegalese immigrants to Spain in *Las cartas de Alou* (Alou's Letters, 1990), and in 1994 he relocated his interest in youth and drug culture to Madrid with the huge commercial success and nascent cult of *Historias del Kronen* (Stories from the Kronen). *Historias del Kronen* chronicles the reprobate antics of the spoilt rich kids who populate Madrid's club culture; yet the film clearly stems from the same staunch directorial perspective as begat *27 horas*. Armendáriz presents these disaffected youths as both the creators and products of their hostile environment and, just as Tasio and the immutable mountain landscape of Navarre create a truce of interdependence that is essential for their survival (witness, for example, his trapping and release of a magnificent wild boar), so too do these causeless rebels exacerbate the urban and moral decay that has led to their disenchantment. Drug abuse, casual sex and thoughtless violence are merely stages in their initiation into the urban culture of the 1990s that affords such meaningful contrast with Tasio's parallel apprenticeship in his rural trade and the dedicated process of raising a family. *Historias del Kronen* ignited tremendous debate in the Spanish press, not just for inspiring the copycat antics of malcontent youths but for reawakening the controversy over the definition of Basque cinema. Was this an example of the new Basque cinema or did the nationality of its director not determine that of the film? Didn't the film's critical exposé of Madrid's urban alienation and aimless youth constitute a propagandist version of the evils of centralist Spain from a separatist, Basque perspective? Certainly the sensitivity, humour and lyricism of Armendáriz's subsequent *Secretos del corazón* (Secrets of the Heart, 1997) reinforced that perspective with its newly nostalgic view of childhood in Navarre.

Nevertheless the journey towards international recognition for Basque film-makers had been hindered by pessimism about the commitment of the government that subsidised them. In 1988 the film subsidy had increased from 20 to 40 million pesetas, but by 1990 the Basque government had begun channelling this money through Euskal Media, a new limited company with a remit to invest wisely and a subsequent reputation for expediency. Even so, in 1991 the company put 80 million pesetas into the production of seven films and saw a fair return on its investment; but with the commercial intentions of the government now denuded the possibility of obtaining financing for a film in Euskera became even more remote. Consequently the curtailing of funding cut short the careers of young, politically committed film-makers such as Ana Díez, whose Euskera-speaking *Ander eta Yul* (Ander and Yul, 1988) was a complex examination of the reunion between two friends since transformed into drug dealer and ETA terrorist.[10] The quality of Basque films inevitably suffered as second-guessing, budget-watching and artistic compromise squeezed out inspiration, commitment and ambition, and there were a number of notable failures. Too many cheap, opportunist films were produced and few of them were even released.

On the brighter side, many of the directors and producers who emerged in the 1970s had already used the profits from their films to set up their own production companies in the 1980s and independent film-making in the Basque country had flourished as a result. The most notable independent producer was Elías Querejeta, who had already contributed decisively to the professional trajectories of Carlos Saura, Víctor Erice and Montxo Armendáriz. Imanol Uribe, meanwhile, had used the profits from his first two features to set up Aiete Films and make *La muerte de Mikel* (Mikel's Death, 1983). In common with Armendáriz, Uribe anchors his protagonists to their

Imanol Arias as Mikel leads the demonstration in *La muerte de Mikel* (Imanol Uribe, 1983)

environment both visually and dramatically, though his characters are often framed in doorways and windows as if caught between commitments in opposing worlds: the moral tightrope that his characters walk is a narrative thread which he unravels with skill and tension. In *La muerte de Mikel* Uribe employed a minimalist aesthetic in his portrait of a character who is marginalised within an already marginal culture. Mikel, an activist in the cause of Basque separatism, has marital problems as a consequence of his latent homosexuality, and his 'coming-out' provokes the disgust of his supposedly progressive comrades, who exclude him from standing in local elections. But, in death, Mikel is celebrated as a martyr to the separatist cause and the variously hypocritical responses of his family and friends accumulate into a vivid, unflattering portrait of contemporary Euskadi.

La muerte de Mikel is unravelled in flashbacks and the jigsaw-puzzle narrative recalls *Citizen Kane* in its musings on the meanings and interpretations of the deceased. The film marked Uribe's 'definitive leap into fiction', though his documentarist zeal for capturing the image which encapsulates a drama remained evident in such shots as that of Mikel draped in the *ikurriña* like an icon of liberty and standing his ground in a cloud of tear gas. The shot approximates the purity and directness of newsreel such as that of the Chinese student in front of a column of tanks; yet the overtly symbolic function of this and similar scenes also mythicises a narrative that depends upon Mikel's interaction with such similarly emblematic characters as his devout and dominating mother and the hard-line nationalists who snub him. Like the *ikurriña*, then, Mikel is a potent symbol of liberty and self-determination and is consequently destabilising. The flashback structure allows Uribe to reflect on the events with objectivity, though the emergent whodunnit of Mikel's murder leads to an implied accusation of his mother that is less effective as immediate social criticism than it is redolent of Lorquian concepts of matriarchal honour and vengeance, while the film's commitment to the gayness of Mikel (movingly played by Imanol Arias and based on a real person[11]) is moderated for a Spanish audience by his romantic involvement with a simpering transvestite rather than a macho homosexual male. Nevertheless *La muerte de Mikel* was a serious and even-handed attempt at exploring the Basque situation in a fictional narrative that was both critically acclaimed and commercially successful.[12] The overall effect of this brief, fragmentary film remains, as with all the best documentaries, one of deliberate, filmic shorthand.

However, rather than continuing to explore the potent themes of Basque separatism and ETA, Uribe next moved into the genres of noirish thriller (*Adios, pequeña*, 1986) and horror (*La luna negra*, 1989) in an effort to break the thematic stranglehold that ETA and Basque separatism had on Basque film-makers:

I felt trapped by what I'd created. I was in crisis and I needed to separate myself from Euskadi. I tried to make films that didn't have any reference to the political situation, but they were so decaffeinated that they just didn't work.[13]

Uribe needed a commercial success that would assure his independence at the same time as he found himself in the curious position of having to make a film in a hurry in order to take up a subsidy that would otherwise be shortly rescinded: 'I went straight to an all-night shop and picked up a book.' The resultant *El rey pasmado* (The Dumbfounded King, 1991) was a playful satire that faithfully recreated the novelist Gonzalo Torrente Ballester's Velásquez-inspired vision of the baroque Spanish court of Felipe IV in a tale of libertarians versus dogmatic puritans. Several inspired performances from an able and attractive cast, who clearly enjoyed themselves as much as the audiences, made of this project a popular success. Beneath the period costumes and sumptuous set design lay another tale of intolerance that clearly reflected the main thematic obsession of its director, but it was not until *Días contados* (Running Out of Time, 1994) that Uribe's ambition and technique fused this inspiring theme with a passionate tale that combined social realism with political relevance in one of the finest Spanish films of the 1990s.

Días contados – the title comes from the Spanish way of saying that someone or something's days are numbered – has a strong Basque background and sensibility, but is set firmly in the social realism of present-day Madrid. It equates sexual violence and urban alienation with repression at the same time as it aspires to grandeur and myth. More specifically it replays the myth of *Carmen* as a fateful affair between a maverick ETA terrorist and a junkie prostitute and, as its title suggests, it's a film in a hurry. It starts on a drumbeat and a helicopter shot of a speeding car. Cut to a close-up of Carmelo Gómez at the wheel, a volatile fusion in looks and manner of the conviction and grace of Gregory Peck and the pent-up angst of Robert De Niro.[14] His character, Antonio, is part of an ETA commando unit heading towards Madrid, which is introduced in a superb panorama shot of dawn breaking over the city and the superimposed title of the film. (Why is the title superimposed over Madrid and not Antonio? Whose days are numbered: those of Antonio or Madrid? Those of ETA or the state?) *Días contados* is about a terrorist campaign against Madrid, but it is also a thriller in which the political reason for the attack is hardly referenced; instead Antonio's acts of violence seem more personal, more driven by his private demons. Political repression provokes violent repercussions but Antonio's ruthless acts of brutality also provide an outlet for his frustration with Charo (Ruth Gabriel), the seductive child-woman adrift in the underworld of drugs, prostitution and casual violence that Antonio pulls around him in his quest for anonymity.

Uribe adapted the novel by Juan Madrid with an enthusiasm for the female characters that did not extend to the author's invention of Antonio as a press photographer. Instead he toyed with the notion of making Antonio a traumatised medic, recently returned from the tribal wars of Ruanda, until the idea of making him a terrorist took over and, as Uribe describes, 'the part became bigger than the whole. I didn't want to make a film about terrorism. I was using the character of a terrorist to make a film about the society of the time.' In the event, *Días contados* won eight Goyas (Spanish Oscars) in 1995 and was awarded the Golden Shell for best film in the forty-second International Film Festival in San Sebastian. Uribe's reminiscence is of a ceremony that took place in a theatre full of politicians:

> *we were close to elections in the Basque Country. So they were all there like always. And nobody liked the film, not the PNV nor the Popular Party nor the Communist Party nor the PSOE. So I knew then it was good.*

Nevertheless, the film's critical and commercial success did not exempt Uribe from a vicious backlash in the press and media, who accused him of glorifying terrorists at a time of increased ETA activity in Madrid.[15] The powerfully charismatic performance of Carmelo Gómez was deemed an unacceptable portrait of a terrorist. Why, he was even allowed a sympathetic scene in which his own lost innocence is emphasised when he coughs and splutters after his first ever toke on Charo's joint! It's an attack that Uribe is quick to counter:

> *Antonio is a character of flesh and blood. I know people from ETA, just ordinary people with a strong political commitment, maybe it's wrong, but they go home and kiss their kids goodnight. It's not incompatible and that's what people don't understand.*

Being only flesh and blood, Antonio is trapped from the moment he sets eyes on Charo (Uribe even frames him through the bars of the elevator cage). Thereafter, it is with Charo that both Antonio and the film ascend to the myth of *Carmen* that serves as model for the central relationship of the film; for Charo, like Carmen, is a gypsy girl whose tragic destiny lies in seducing a soldier. Only here the soldier is Antonio, a member of ETA: a soldier of the Basque nation. The allusion arose from Uribe's fascination with Bizet's opera:

> *The first time in my life that music moved me was with* Carmen. *There was a time when I was obsessed with it, it was as if I had discovered music. And it showed me how a love story can take place in the most terrible, most sordid conditions.*

149

Carmelo Gómez and Ruth Gabriel: Antonio meets Charo in *Días contados* (Imanol Uribe, 1994)

In the film, Charo makes her way into Antonio's supposedly safe apartment and heads into his bathroom. When she does not reappear, Antonio enters and finds her in a heroin daze. Thus, though Antonio has been identified as a character living on the edge, he comes up against a character who is so beyond the limits of common morality that the political conviction which determines his own marginalisation from contemporary Spanish society is thrown off balance. The scene continues with Charo posing pornographically for Antonio, who, like Felipe IV in *El rey pasmado*, is dumbfounded by the sight of a naked woman.[16] Having assumed the guise of photographer, Antonio snaps away and moves to touch her, but, to his amazement, she rejects him. Unlike Antonio, this junkie prostitute appears to have a moral limit.

Thus, though Uribe may allow the political context of *Días contados* to be absorbed into the machinations of a sharp, effective thriller, he also explores evolving notions of marginalisation and prevailing morality that are fundamental to any discussion of national, regional and individual identity. Consequently, the supposed injustices in the Basque Country appear so abstract in comparison with the day-to-day misery that surrounds Charo and the other low-life characters in Madrid that the actions of ETA resemble little more than the posturings of a privileged few. As Antonio will discover, there is a subterranean world of misery and degradation that lies beneath the society he is aiming to destroy and there will occur a certain affinity between himself and the various low-lifes that is based upon their mutual antagonism towards the norm. But which of these two marginalised cultures conceals a morality? Is it the political cause of terrorists such as Antonio or the survival instinct of junkies like Charo? Uribe's point of view is clear:

> *What always attracted me was the innocence inside so much immorality. It's a gallery of freaks but all of them have a certain humanity, some degree of innocence. They're all predestined to be what they are, but they all maintain dignity inside so much brutality.*

Consequently, both Charo and Antonio appear as symbols of lost innocence that connect with a subversive tradition in American films such as Ford's *The Searchers* (1956) and Scorsese's *Taxi Driver* (1976), in which the main character is a dangerous, near-psychotic male whose violent life is killing him, but whose battle to save a young woman offers him a chance of redemption. If he can save the girl, he might just save himself.

Although it lacks an explicit discussion of the Basque situation, *Días contados* does reveal the tension in Uribe's work between the political context of his plots and the entertaining effect of their style. The subterfuge and artistry that is involved in this retelling of the myth of Carmen is even signalled explicitly when Antonio uses a street performance of Bizet's famous aria as an excuse for photographing the police station that he plans to destroy, just as Uribe uses the covering of the myth to hide his own intent. *Días contados* is essentially a nihilist film that reveals the moral bankruptcy and madness of all its characters except Charo, but including Antonio, the ETA leadership that he disparages in conversation, and Rafa (Karra Elejalde), the policeman whose clothes and bearing render him purposefully indistinguishable from the junkie pimp Lisardo (Javier Bardem). Yet Uribe also insists upon the dreadful effects of real terrorism in his inclusion of authentic television newsreel of ETA bomb attacks, while Antonio's shooting of a policeman in the back of the head is clearly signalled as a cold-blooded execution (the film would have been very different if Antonio had shot him from a distance or if the policeman had shot back). *Días contados* therefore appears to undo the fusion of myth and reality that was so central to Uribe's early films at the same time as it reverses the polemic of *La muerte de Mikel*, because here Uribe uses the topic of Basque separatism to make a film about a tortured sexuality – and not the other way round. It's a cinematic retort too, for Uribe, who has the authority to denounce the linguistic and thematic dogmatism that obliged film-makers to create films that treated the Basque Country as a fantastically noble, rural, progressive nation, has made a defiantly urban, sordid film about moral degeneracy. Indeed this divide between myth and reality gapes widest when Antonio tells Charo that he wants to sleep with her in quite crude terms and she replies *'tiene que ser en la Alhambra'* (It has to be in the Alhambra). She's right, of course: if *Días contados* is to aspire to the level of myth, they have to make love in the magnificent Moorish palace in Granada that symbolises the fabulously mythic past of Spain.

Antonio accepts the challenge and they journey through the night to be greeted by a stunning panoramic shot of Granada at dawn that contrasts so meaningfully with the urban smog in the film's title shot of Madrid. Indeed, far from the city of sunshine and glossy colours made famous by the films of Almodóvar, *Días contados* expresses a sordid, dehumanising side to Madrid that was a primary aim of Uribe and his cinematographer, Javier Aguirresarobe:

> Our idea was to show a Madrid made of cement, not the typical Madrid, nor the naturalist one. We based the film on the colour of blue steel and even chose the cars that you see parked in the streets according to this narrow range of colours. All except the scenes in Granada, which have the colour of caramel.

Thus, in what Uribe calls 'an island of warmth and warm colours in the middle of the film', Antonio and Charo check into the Alhambra Palace hotel and make love in a scene that is sexually explicit but subject to the visual distortions of being shot through steam and the blur of a Moorish grille. Clearly the mythic state which is occasioned by the sex is a delusion that Uribe purposefully brackets inside crystal-clear images of Antonio staring at his own reflection and seeing the cold-blooded terrorist within. Moreover, in the post-coital shot it is apparent that he is still wearing his watch: this is a man against the clock in everything he does and, as the film's title insists, his time is running out. They shower hurriedly and the fantasy is further destroyed by the interruption of the television news that confronts them with Antonio's true identity. Charo knows Antonio must kill her, but she locks herself in the bathroom and Antonio, drained and tortured, waits until the Spanish national anthem accompanies images of the Spanish royal family on the television at closedown, thus inciting his hatred and awakening his urge to kill in this most explicit reference to his terrorist cause. The drumming soundtrack and increasing speed of the remaining scenes creates a tangible sense of fate that is linked to the death wish of Antonio. The final act is set in motion with Antonio setting and releasing the car bomb, only to see Charo step out of a police car and be herded into his target. He reacts by sprinting suicidally after the car but the explosion that billows over the end credits of *Días contados* creates a hell on earth for its characters that is richly symbolic and thoroughly appropriate.

Since *Días contados*, Uribe has made the anti-racist parable *Bwana* (1996) and the experimental *Extraños* (Strangers, 1998) again with Carmelo Gómez.

Plenilunio (2000) is an adaptation of the bestseller by Andalusian writer Antonio Muñoz Molina, whose protagonist (Miguel Ángel Solá) is a policeman who spent ten years fighting ETA and now finds himself embroiled in the murder of a little girl. Uribe doesn't rule out adapting one of the novels about ETA from Basque novelist Bernardo Atxaga, or even collaborating on a script together.[17] Indeed his interest in the subject of ETA and Basque separatism is unabated, with recent developments concerning the attempted ceasefire, the government-backed hit squads known as GAL and the frequent public rallies all clearly on his mind: 'All these years of killings and brutalities. It's all inside and hasn't yet come to the surface. One day they must emerge.' Meanwhile the subject of ETA emerges sporadically in films such as Juan Miñón's *La blanca paloma* (The White Dove, 1989), Mario Camus' *Sombras en una batalla* (Shadows in a Battle, 1993) and Helena Taberna's *Yoyes* (2000). The last-named is a biopic of the eponymous ETA leader who was murdered by her own ex-comrades after seeking *reinserción* (government-sponsored assimilation into society). It features an intense but grim central performance from Ana Torrent and its structure owes a self-conscious debt to Uribe's *La muerte de Mikel*, but the climactic murder of Yoyes in front of her own daughter carries little of the resonance of Mikel's offscreen death. Moreover, these are isolated examples of a once flourishing political cinema in Spain that appears to have all but disappeared. According to Uribe, 'we're all disappointed in politics since Franco. In the past it was something that thrilled us, but there've been too many disappointments.' And therewith, the end of *Días contados*. 'It was always meant as an apocalyptic film,' says Uribe, 'an end of the millennium chronicle that ends with an explosion that destroys everything and allows us to start again from zero.'

Apocalypse in downtown Madrid also formed the climax to Álex De La Iglesia's *El día de la bestia* (The Day of the Beast, 1995), in which a bumbling Basque priest sets about thwarting the Anti-Christ in an uproarious black comedy that is distinguished by intelligent satire and superbly engaged performances from its cast. Born in Bilbao in 1965, De La Iglesia was a philosophy student at Bilbao's Jesuit university, whose inspiration and style of film-making comes from the lurid underground comics that he used to write and draw. A huge commercial success in Spain and abroad, *El día de la bestia* was an elaborate satire of the more fascist elements of Spanish society in the 1990s, in which the meaning of Christmas was inverted along with the moral righteousness of Spain's new right-wing government.[18] Sensational set pieces made full use of elaborate and costly special effects, while De La Iglesia's twisted perspective on the architectural contrasts of Madrid resulted in the poignant juxtaposition of an underworld of crumbling slums with the high-rise chrome and neon of capitalist excess. The final scene sees our heroes as down-and-outs on a bench in Madrid's Retiro Park, ignored by the happy middle classes whose lifestyle has been safeguarded by their sacrifice. It is a begrudging reconciliation with centralist Spain that De La Iglesia still conspires to undermine with a final shot of the statue *of El ángel caído* (The Fallen Angel) that stands in the heart of the Retiro, probably the only public monument to the Devil in existence.

De La Iglesia's subsequent *Perdita Durango* (1997) was a vicious, surprisingly humourless, American-made quasi-sequel to David Lynch's *Wild at Heart* (1990) that paid affectionate homage to Peckinpah but alienated many with its violence and gore, while *Muertos de risa* (Dying from Laughter, 1999) was heavily promoted as a day-glo lampoon of Spanish television in the 1970s only to reveal itself as a nasty exposé of the darker side of fame.[19] De la Iglesia is typical of most contemporary Basque film-makers who have long since relocated to Madrid and are often quoted in the popular press as shrugging off the notion of a collective identity for Euskadi-born film-makers. They produce work that is often self-consciously idiosyncratic and the creative freedom which they take for granted is only exacerbated by the cult of the celebrity *auteur* that thrives in contemporary Spain. They avoid overt political subjects and disdain a literary basis for their films, revelling instead in the audio-visual stimuli of comics, cartoons, video games and the Internet, redefining ideas of Spanish film-making with the help of new technologies and an eye on the international market.

This enthusiasm for comic-book culture revealed itself in the films of Juanma Bajo Ulloa, for instance, who was so impressed by *Star Wars* (1977) that he began making short films and by 1984, aged twenty-three, had set up his own production company. In 1991 he wrote, produced and directed *Alas de mariposa* (Butterfly Wings), a powerful but derivative drama of female psychological trauma and male violence that he would rework two years later for *La madre muerta* (The Dead Mother, 1993), in which a burglar kidnaps the mentally ill young woman whose mother he had murdered many years before. Both films are visually inventive, even disturbing, and their extended silences provoke scenes of suffocating tension, but they would be more satisfying at half their lengths. *Alas de mariposa* blurs the intensity of its focus by following the traumatised girl into adolescence and melodrama, while *La madre muerta* is needlessly padded with a sub-plot about an investigative nurse that is of little consequence. Bajo Ulloa's wild, laddish comedy *Airbag* was a massive hit in 1997, though its female caricatures and sniggering machismo suggested that, in retrospect, the treatment of female trauma and male violence in his first two features was rather more exploitative than thoughtful.

In the nominally Basque cinema of the new millennium De La Iglesia and Bajo Ulloa are typical of a generation that makes films for pleasure instead of political commitment or militancy. Both are talented film-makers with unusual visual flair; yet, in disregarding their roots in Basque cinema, they might be risking anonymity. Of the emergent Basque directors of the 1990s only Julio Medem and Daniel Calparsoro have demonstrated any commitment to the evolution of common themes in Basque cinema. Medem's intricate and tortured but delightful films have earned him worldwide recognition: *Vacas* (1991) subverts the rural genre so beloved of Basque nationalists by appropriating the godly gaze of cows to observe a society that is suffocating under the weight of tradition and endogamy, while *La ardilla roja* (The Red Squirrel, 1993) parodies the sacred myth of origins in its tangled tale of convenient amnesia, false identities and lies. Calparsoro, meanwhile, has provided the heartless, urban flipside to Medem's rural emotionalism. His *Salto al vacío* (Jump into the Void, 1995) was a raw, punkish début that dealt with the survival of a fragile young woman in the industrial wastelands of Bilbao. Powered by an aggressive soundtrack and an intense lead performance from Najwa Nimri, *Salto al vacío* revitalised the theme of marginalisation and urban alienation with a ferocious energy that was indicative of the recent growth in economic discontent and concomitant political activism amongst young Basques. Calparsoro had begun by making imaginary films with his schoolmates and, when a student, skipped lectures to ingratiate himself with the crew of Ana Díez's *Ander eta Yul*. He studied film-making in New York and made his first short films on video. *Salto al vacío* played in the Berlin Film Festival and his subsequent films, *Pasajes* (1996) and *A ciegas* (1997), display similarly brutal, feverish imagery in long takes that encapsulate the worlds and imaginations of characters whose feelings of alienation are rooted in the post-industrial landscape of the Basque Country.[20]

'*¿Qué hago yo entre tanta mierda?*' wonders Álex, the unloved heroine of *Salto al vacío* (What am I doing in so much shit?); but despite her expression of existential despair, the Basque country is in many ways booming. It now has two national television channels, one of which transmits only in Euskera, thereby fulfilling the Law of Linguistic Normalisation – an edict of bilingualism that was approved by the Basque parliament in 1989 – and films in Euskera are once more possible with the financial backing and guaranteed transmission outlet of the Euskal Telebista 1 channel. Eneko Olasagasti and Carlos Zabala's *Maité* (1995), for instance, was a warm-hearted comedy that was made in collaboration with Cuba and gave rise to a popular television series, while *Hirkuntza eta Kirolak* (Days of Smoke, 1989) allowed Antxon Eceiza, the veteran producer of the *Ikuska* documentaries, to look back over the previous twenty years of Basque history from a defiantly separatist perspective and conclude that Franco's aim of eradicating cultural difference had clearly failed.

However, independence and autonomy have also brought new problems and hardship. Franco transformed the isolation of Spain into an ideal of self-sufficiency by supporting archaic Basque industries to serve the Spanish market but, post-Franco, the abandoning of government protection to industry was a precondition for Spain's entry into the EEC and Basque industries collapsed, leading to massive youth unemployment and a fresh upsurge in support for the policies of Herri Batasuna, the political wing of ETA. In film-making too, Basques found themselves battling distribution companies that would rather play American blockbusters with supposedly more than merely regional appeal. Thus marginalisation and repression are the themes that continue to resonate through Basque cinema and the language prerogative is once more coming to the fore. Euskera was once the denigrated language of rural people who emigrated to the big cities: it is now the dominant language in primary schools and an essential quality of a Basque politician that he be, if not an *Euskaldun*, at least an *Euskaldunberri*. Bernardo Atxaga's superb 1998 novel *Obabakoak* has sold 45,000 copies in his native Euskera and won Spain's national literary prize for its author. Euskera on film is still rare, but surely amongst the youth of Bilbao, San Sebastian and Vitoria there are those who have already taken to the task with video and digital cameras, with commitment and style; for the Basque language of film-making is theirs to inherit. Somewhere between documentary and fiction, between myth and reality, there is a vision of their nation as a hard land and a heartland that will find its expression on film.

Notes

1. Most of these film-makers who moved to Madrid would not produce their best work until a decade or two later: Iván Zulueta (*Arrebato*, 1979); Eloy de la Iglesia (*El Pico*, 1983); Antonio Mercero (*Espérame en el cielo*, Wait for Me in Heaven, 1987); Pedro Olea (*El maestro de esgrima*, The Fencing Master, 1992).
2. Uribe:

   My father spoke Euskera but never taught me more than a few songs. It wasn't a problem; maybe once in the making of El proceso de Burgos, when Julen Kalzada refused to participate unless it was in Euskera. So then I needed an interpreter, but I never felt the need to learn.

3. All quotes from Imanol Uribe are from an interview with the author conducted in Madrid, April 2000.
4. This 'powerful, terrible' grandmother would be the inspiration for the character of the murderous mother in *La muerte de Mikel*.
5. Uribe first used this technique in his thirteen-minute documentary *Ez* (No, 1977) which contrasted the rural utopia so beloved of radical nationalists with stark images of the polemical Lemóniz nuclear plant that had become a focus for dissent and the target of over two hundred and fifty terrorist attacks.

6. Field Marshal Milans del Bosch would later achieve infamy as one of the co-conspirators with General Tejero of the attempted coup of 23 February 1981, when he gave the order for tanks to take over the streets of Valencia.
7. The UCD had been formed to fight the general election of 1977. It combined supporters and opponents of the Franco regime, but quickly degenerated into factions.
8. One cinema in Oviedo had twenty-two bomb warnings in a single day.
9. The second subsidy went to Juan Ortuaste and Javier Rebollo, who received 1 million pesetas towards a budget of 20 million for *Siete calles* (Seven Streets). The film includes dialogue in Castilian and Euskera in its ambitious seven-strand narrative of urban life.
10. Díez moved to Madrid to work as a teaching assistant in the Complutense university and would not return to directing until 1996 with the murder mystery *Todo está oscuro* (Everything is Dark).
11. The real character was a chemist embroiled in drug dealing and himself an addict, who was celebrated as a martyr after dying following a period in police custody. What fascinated Uribe, however, was, 'the manipulation of the corpse.'
12. Uribe's investment in his own production therefore safeguarded his company Aiete, which continues to produce his own and others' films to this day. It was, however, a risky venture: 'We really didn't have any money. We'd finish shooting and I'd get straight on the phone to find some.'
13. Indeed, by Uribe's own admission, both films are fairly anonymous, though more commercial exercises in genre would be attempted by Enrique Urbizu, whose screwball comedy *Tu novia está loca* (Your Girlfriend is Mad, 1987) and violent thriller *Todo por la pasta* (Everything for the Cash, 1991) managed to suggest that Basque cinema was not all about terrorism.
14. Uribe: 'Don't laugh, but Antonio was going to be played by Antonio Banderas and Charo was going to be Penélope Cruz. It would have been an absurd blunder [*un disparate*].'
15. A year later the attacks continued when the film premiered on the pay-tv channel Canal Plus the day before an ETA bomb attack in Euskadi. The journalist Vicente Verdú wrote an article in *El País* that Uribe describes as 'practically accusing me of the attack.' Verdú wrote: 'Any other wholly democratic country would have persecuted this film that is so clearly intended to teach meticulously how to love a terrorist.'
16. Carmen was a wilful, sexually independent woman, but Charo is, in truth, a fragile near-infant, which is why she's naked for most of the film: Uribe doesn't so much present her as a sexual temptress as he does a new-born.
17. The rights to Bernardo Atxaga's novels *Esos cielos* (The Lone Woman) and *El hombre solo* (The Lone Man) are currently held by Enrique Urbizu (see note 13).
18. Prior to *El día de la bestia*, De La Iglesia's exuberant but tiresome science-fiction farce *Acción Mutante* (Action Mutant, 1992) was produced by Pedro Almodóvar's El Deseo production company.
19. Unable to convince potential investors of the viability of his long-mooted epic version of *The Return of Fu Manchu*, De La Iglesia made *La comunidad* (2000), a raucous comedy starring Carmen Maura that was a massive commercial success.
20. Calparsoro's fourth film *Asfalto* (Asphalt, 2000) also starred Najwa Nimri, but was set in Madrid.

CHAPTER EIGHT

Projections of desire

Julio Medem

Cow-eyes, eyes that entangle, blue-flecked lamb's eyes and the dilating pupils of dead eyes. It's all there in Julio Medem's eyes: a much darker creative sensibility than the texture of his films might suggest. *Vacas* (1992), *La ardilla roja* (The Red Squirrel, 1993), *Tierra* (1996) and *Los amantes del círculo polar* (Lovers of the Arctic Circle, 1998) have amassed awards and effusive praise in international festivals and markets for their striking images and ideas, establishing their creator as the leading light of contemporary Spanish film-makers. Yet Medem is less Basque or Spanish than universal in his themes. He uses the camera to focus on dilemmas of duality, chance encounters, fateful symmetry and a body-and-soul divide, while incest, amnesia, schizophrenia and death are just a few aspects of the human condition that he treats with a sensuality that is expressed in the responsiveness of his colours, camera-work and editing. For desire is the driving force of Medem's films and their metaphorical complexity, both visually and structurally, is invariably traversed by characters in search of love and a little enlightenment. Medem, too, is after a little clarity in his vision, criss-crossing the border between post-modernism and metaphysics in his search for images that express emotional truths.

Born in 1958 in the Basque resort of San Sebastian, Julio Medem was the eldest son of a Basque-French designer mother and a German-born draughtsman father. His infancy was meticulously documented on Super-8 film by his father, who had spent his own childhood as a member of the Hitler Youth until, aged twelve, his Valencian mother had brought him to Spain. This strict and distant patriarch would remain commitedly right wing for the rest of his life and the natural rebelliousness of the teenage Julio would consequently escalate into a political stance that required him to reject the middle-class social group to which his family belonged after moving to Madrid. As with many film-makers, Medem's childhood desire to transcend timidity and loneliness found its release in the cinema, which only further stimulated the hyperactive imagination that he struggled to exorcise in writing stories.

Frustrated by the stasis of his written words, Medem took to raiding his father's Super-8 equipment at night and making films with his sister Ana – a vague but curious presentiment of the nocturnal subterfuge of the half-siblings in *Los amantes del círculo polar*. By day Medem was a model student at Madrid's upper-class Colegio del Pilar – a school that educated Spain's president José María Aznar and a number of the most notorious yuppies of the 1990s, who would gradually reinstate the influence of the political right on democratic Spain. Barely eighteen at the time of the political transition, Medem was one of Spain's first ever teenagers, a few decades behind James Dean and even too late for punk. And then, like so many of his characters, Medem's life found meaning and lost all hope when he fell madly in love with a woman, a neighbour, who didn't love him back. Tortuously intro-verted, he spent hours tending his obsession:

> *I invented everything so it was how I wished it had been. The mannerisms, for example, I interpreted them to fit in with the fantasy. I thought I would always be in love with her, even though she would never take any notice of me. I would have been hurt if I hadn't acknowledged that eternal love didn't exist, despite the pain it caused me.*[1]

The outpouring of this frustration and desire became a secret novel titled *Mi primer día* (My First Day) about a boy who dreams that he returns to the moment of falling in love and manages to stay there, never to wake or be disillusioned by reality. Already, therefore, we may identify themes that will dominate his films: the conflict between desire and reality, the wilful self-delusion of characters, the alternative worlds of the imagination and the gullibility of the physical self to flattering tricks of the mind. Simultaneously, in some sort of physical exorcism of desire, Medem threw himself into a punishing sports regime and soon held Spain's national record for hurdles and a grant to represent his country in the Olympics, only to realise the therapeutic nature of his endeavour and abandon athletics to dedicate himself to the study of psychiatry. Seeking to improve and define himself, he enrolled in university in Soria in north-east Spain, entering into a hippy student lifestyle that obliged him to confront his father. Alone but empowered, Medem, like Sofía in *La ardilla roja*, chose to assume a new identity by consciously favouring his Basque extraction from the equal parts of Basque, German, French and Valencian blood that he'd inherited. Indeed, his choice of Basqueness is a personal illustration of the fabricated myth of origins that both frees and ultimately confounds so many of his characters.

Thus, aged twenty-one, Medem returned to his birthplace of San Sebastian and would subsequently graduate from the University of the Basque Country with a degree in medicine and general surgery, though by then he had once again been distracted from an obvious career path, this time by his increasing enthusiasm for the cinema. His first, belated viewing of Victor Erice's *El espíritu de la colmena* (The Spirit of the Beehive, 1973) was a revelation. Here was the world of his imaginings made real through the paraphernalia of film-making, for Erice's masterpiece explores the same confusion of harsh reality with fantasy that defines the films of Medem, shifting between scenes of innocence and guilt as its characters move from wide open landscapes to dark interiors. Medem's desire to achieve the same prompted his absorption in the theory and craft of the cinema. He made short films on Super-8 and began contributing somewhat idiosyncratic film reviews for the Basque newspaper *La voz de Euskadi* at a time of increasing separatist fervour and tremendous ebullience for Basque cinema.[2] He criticised the previous generation of film-makers for placing political intent above artistic considerations, while rejecting the need of directors such as Saura and Berlanga to revisit or revise recent history – there were enough problems in the present.[3] His was a generation for whom even Pedro Almodóvar, with all his early camp excess, was a rather embarrassing father figure.

However, his own attempts at combining story-writing with film-making were hindered by the distinction he pursued between narrative construction and visual impact – still the most common complaint of his critics. Storylines either enslaved his visual dexterity and weakened his ability to manipulate and surprise the viewer, or were subordinate to framing and editing, only serving to contextualise those images that might deliver emotional impact. His last film in Super-8, *Teatro en Soria* (Theatre in Soria, 1982), for instance, details the obsession of a man who spends years looking through the window of his apartment; one day he steps outside and is immediately aware that he is being watched from his own window. Again, the timid individual who ventures beyond the enclosed world of the imagination and is destroyed by contact with reality.[4] Unlike, say, Spielberg, his childhood fantasies were not about wish-fulfilment but an attempt to exorcise those fantasies that hindered his functioning in the real world. No cute aliens here, only an alter ego – a boy suffering in make-believe.

The year 1985 saw him graduate to 35 mm film stock and a budget of 3 million pesetas (thanks to the generous subsidies that the Basque government was throwing out to film-makers) that he used to found Grupo Delfilm with Luis Campoy and make *Patas en la cabeza* (1986), which won the prize for best short film in the International Documentary and Short Film Competition in Bilbao. Clearly predating *Los amantes del círculo polar* in its geometric structure, *Patas en la cabeza* evokes the symmetrical fantasies of a boy and girl who invent a mutual friend as a means for them to be together. The following year he won the prestigious Telenorte prize with *Las seis en punto* (Six o'Clock Sharp, 1987), a surreal tale of a boy who invents a nightmare to trap a girl and finds he cannot control it (thus clearly predating the plot of *La ardilla roja*). The prizes brought him to the attention of legendary producer Elías Querejeta, while professional contacts appeared amongst the many friends who were similarly caught up in the surge of Basque film-making in the 1980s.[5] Medem worked as editor and assistant director on José María Tuduri's *Crónica de la segunda guerra Carlista* (Chronicle of the Second Carlist War, 1987), edited the full-length film *La espalda del cielo* (The Back of the Sky, 1988), made an educational film for novice journalists called *El diario vasco* (1989) and edited *El puente* (The Bridge, 1990). Then, nothing. Changes in the administration of government subsidies saw funding dry up for new, commercially unproven film-makers and Medem was back to being an unemployed doctor. Worse, economically compelled to abandon the expensive resort of San Sebastian, Medem moved to the mountain village of Amasa, where he would live for the next three years, supported by his wife, who worked as a medical intern, while he kept house and brought up their son. It is tempting to ascribe some of the sensuality and delicacy of Medem's films to this period of role reversal in which he assumed the traditional maternal duties in a country where machismo rules. Indeed the situation also suggests something of the notion of assuming another's identity that is a primary theme of his films. But Medem was not annulled by the experience; rather, he wrote obsessively – short stories that each turned on the notion of a lie, and a strange, complex script for an epic, rural saga entitled *Vacas* that sprang from the experience and knowledge gained from his time working on the film about the Second Carlist War.[6]

Vacas

In Medem's mind *Vacas* began with an *aizkolari* – a Basque woodsman – hurling his axe into a forest. The scene is still there, and even though it appears in the middle of the film it is still the beginning, for Medem's films have a habit of spiralling out from their centres rather than following a linear path. Thus the impact of this axe sends out shock waves like ripples on a pond, each wave representing past and future generations of the two Basque families, the Irigibel and the Mendiluze, that are doomed to suffer, cyclically, the self-destruction of an oppressive, incestuous society. *Vacas* is divided into four chapters that cover a period from the end of the Second Carlist War in 1885 to the beginning of the Spanish Civil War in 1936. Yet, rather than imitate the pious introspection of the rural genre that had been such a mainstay of Spanish and Basque cinema and literature, Medem subverts the conventions of the family saga by replacing the human subjectivity of conventional melodrama and historical epics with a diffidence about life and death that is expressed through the disinterested gaze of three generations of cows. Human strife is thereby dwarfed by the grand, sensorial interior of the natural world which is represented by these cows, whose points of view are frequently appropriated by Medem for shots that provide the viewer with a detached, ironic perspective on all the incest, adultery and rivalry that occurs and recurs in the bleak, human drama.

The film actually opens on an *aizkolari* standing barefoot on a log, hacking out chunks with reckless force. Schwok-schwok-schwok: Medem matches each stroke of his axe with a fresh edit, cutting film in the same way, chopping and changing shots from all angles so that the scene becomes an abstract representation of human aggression against the natural world. However, rather than celebrate the masculinity and strength of the *aizkolari*, this paragon of Basque mythology is quickly undermined by a freeze-frame and a cut to the first chapter heading – I: The Cowardly *Aizkolari* – an oxymoron that subverts the traditionally mythic status of the archetype. Instead of a warrior woodsman we have Manuel Irigibel (Carmelo Gómez), who stands trembling with fear in the trenches at the Carlist Front near Vizcaya in 1875. Terrified by the battle, Manuel drops his rifle, screaming as if shot, and stumbles backwards into the accumulating mound of corpses. Lying still in the aftermath of a resounding defeat, he swipes blood from the pumping jugular of a dying Carmelo Mendiluze (Kandido Uranga) and daubs his own face to escape detection amongst the dead. His ignominious escape will be from a cartload of corpses, pulling himself out of the jumble of limbs and dropping to the forest floor unseen by all except the cow that emerges from the undergrowth to observe him with a minimally curious consideration of his condition. It is a look that Medem seizes for his camera in a point of view shot that encourages his audience to reflect on the irony of such a shameful and pathetic image in an epic of the Carlist War. For all its historical detail, therefore, *Vacas* exhibits a post-modernist sensibility in its parodic recycling of the conventions of the rural saga. Indeed the customary introspection of the genre is literally turned in on itself when Manuel/Medem returns the cow's gaze and the camera journeys into the cow's iris to emerge thirty years later in the spring of 1905, through the eye of another cow, who observes with similar forbearance the efforts of an aged Manuel to paint her.

Although *Vacas* exhibits a strong cultural identity in the detail of life in the Basque valley,[7] Medem is clearly aware of the constructed nature of Basqueness as it relates to the conventions of the rural genre, the contemporary nationalist cause and the quasi-biblical writings of the founder of Basque nationalism, Sabino Arana.[8] Instead of a society that is traditionally presented

Duelling aizkolaris. Carmelo Gómez and Kandido Uranga in *Vacas* (Julio Medem, 1992)

as oppressed and belittled by exterior forces, *Vacas* presents the Basque people as a race that, in petty rivalries, civil war and incest, has consumed itself from within. In order to illustrate these malignant desires and traumas Medem conjures a brooding, mysterious and sensual atmosphere from numerous travelling shots through dank and mossy undergrowth. These shots accumulate into a metaphor for the subconscious that extends, for example, to the scene of Ignacio, son of Manuel (Gómez again), chasing an unseen observer through the wood and assailed by rapid and sexually charged female breathing that dissipates on his exit. The revelation that his prey has been his rival's sister, Catalina Mendiluze (Ana Torrent), not only sparks his adulterous sexual attraction for her but also establishes the complicity between females and nature that is a dominant motif of Medem's films. 'Don't worry, we're going to win,' whispers Ignacio's daugher to Pupille, the cow, when it is used as the wager in the wood-chopping contest between the families. But the cow isn't worried: as always, bovine passivity suggests a far greater wisdom about the cycle of fateful incidents than that of their human subjects. After all, the film is called cows, not bulls, and it is only fitting that a more natural, fluid and feminine perspective on the action should be substituted for the intransigent macho posturing and steadfast chauvinism of traditional Spanish society and film.

The second chapter – II: The Axes – brings a shift in the focus of the unfolding drama from Manuel to his son Ignacio. The abruptness is probably due to Medem filming only two-thirds of the scenes in his script, the rest having been cut for reasons of budget and length.[9] The consequently sequential narrative is an often shaky prop for the striking imagery in such scenes as the wood-chopping contest, though any criticism of sensationalism is countered by the skilful pacing and editing of a scene that, nevertheless, displays a certain impudence in the shot of a flying slice of wood from Ignacio's axe landing pat in the apron of Catalina, the future mother of his illegitimate son (a chip off the old block, indeed!). However, the abundance of striking imagery never seems superfluous or pretentious; rather, such images are a visual shorthand that links the world of the subconscious with that of reality. It is, for example, the rapidly consummated attraction between Ignacio and Catalina that, as Catalina's widowed mother insists, will resuscitate the enmity between their families: 'Stop looking at that old coward's son or your brother's lost. Your father will die again and I'll be killed for the first time.' Another fine example of Medem's dense and ominous imagery is the sinister scarecrow that Manuel constructs: a man of twig-bones and moss-flesh, topped off with a red Carlist beret, bearing a hefty scythe and turning in the wind like a Basque grim reaper. It's more of a soldier than Manuel ever was, and thus a monument to the shameful cowardice that endures in his son and grandson.

As always in the films of Medem, characters take refuge in the worlds of make-believe, and it is only when reality intrudes upon the fantasy that the delicate balance between the conscious and subconscious worlds is destroyed. So it is that the third chapter – III: The Burning Hole – centres on a wizened tree hollow, deep in the forest, which acts as some sort of unstable portal to the alternative world of the subconscious. 'What's on the other side of the hole?' asks Peru, bastard son of Ignacio and Catalina and already ten years old. 'The same as here or similar,' replies Manuel, 'You are on the other side.' Thus the 'lighting' of the hole (with the sacrifice of a live mouse) is followed by the brutal birthing of a calf, torn from its mother's uterus by a rope tied around its legs and a tug-of-war between foolhardy humans on the outside and the warm, pre-perceptual calm of the womb – an interior world that has already been illustrated in a scene where Manuel squints into the eyes of the pregnant cow as Medem cuts to a shot that is accompanied by a hefty heartbeat and can only be understood as looking back at Manuel from inside the cow, until a fall away into blackness dissolves into a panorama of an other-worldly, peaceful, misty landscape.[10]

Following this rupture of the subconscious come scenes of incestuous tension and violence between Juan Mendiluze and his sister Catalina[11] as well as the more innocent but no less incestuous longing felt by Peru for his half-sister Catalina (Emma Suárez) who, in a psychologically complex image, he follows around the forest with a camera on his head. Incest, like civil war, is yet another indication that the enemy lives within; war between brothers is as immoral and self-destructive as sex with sisters. Medem therefore appears to suggest that the Basque pride in racial purity as enshrined in the writings of Sabino Arana was the primary cause of the wars and intermarriage that seeded their own stagnation. Precepts of Basque nationalism are therefore subverted in *Vacas*: most characters wish for nothing more than to escape the supposed idyll of the Basque Country, though those who do are fated to return and suffer the consequences of inescapable roots and blood ties.

Instead of typifying the beauty of the land, the mists of this Basque valley create a malignant atmosphere that enshrouds the protagonists of *Vacas*, stimulating and manifesting their latent desires and urges. At first this occurs in minor details: shots of phallic and poisonous mushrooms, close-ups of insects and animals oozing sensuality and menace that are accompanied by the mantra of Manuel, *'esto es importante, muy importante, importantísimo...'* Then the subconscious emerges in more direct ways, with Manuel painting boar's tusks on his portrait of a footless Pupille, the hollow, howling tree that devours the meat of the slaughtered cow, and the increasingly intrusive role of the camera in Medem's representation of this world as it turns itself inside out, with fish-eye lenses, distorted perspectives and self-conscious zooms all attesting to the perverse artificiality of the rural idyll so beloved of Basque nationalists.

It may be that Manuel's increasing derangement signifies a logical response to the growing surrealism of the world. Chopping the hooves off Pupille, for instance, makes reality conform to the illusion of his painting. In addition, the movement from the real world to that of the subconscious is explicitly referenced in the shot of Cristina's terrified reaction to Peru being taken from her by Ignacio, the father they both share, who is, of course, exhibiting the same cowardice as his father by simultaneously abandoning Cristina and her mother to their fate. In a technique utilised to great effect by Hitchcock in *Vertigo* and by Spielberg in *Jaws*,[12] Medem situated Emma Suárez at the end of a long dolly track, along which the camera was pulled backwards at great speed while the operator zoomed in, with the result that Suárez remains the same size in the frame while the changing depth of field makes the background drop away suddenly behind her. The technically complicated shot is a fine example of Medem's mission to transmit emotions and sensations visually; it has the effect of amplifying her reaction and transporting the viewer into her shocked state of mind. We surge into her subconscious and abandon any sense that might reside in the notion of the pure, hard-working family unit as a paragon of the Basque nation. And so it is that the Spanish Civil War erupts as if it were a violent but necessary reaction against the stagnating society, once more pitting Basque against Basque in order to disperse their genes.

The tearing apart of the Basque Country in the film's final chapter – IV: War in the Woods – creates a fissure in reality through which subconscious conflicts and desires come to the surface like bubbling lava. Medem keeps his camera low in the undergrowth, tracking Cristina's feet as if she were wading through water, and only rises to repeat the fast dolly out and zoom in when she meets Peru, now grown and returned to cover the war as a press photographer (again played by Carmelo Gómez, here completing his generational triptych). The adult Peru is, of course, the spitting image of the father they share and the spark of attraction between them is all the more disturbing for its Oedipal overtone. Silently, Cristina shows him paintings by their mutual grandfather that reveal the long-gestating malignancy of the old man's subconscious: a cow riddled with bulletholes; themselves as children astride a two-headed cow like a pushmi-pullyu, showing how they were always bound together by fate; and dead cows in trenches, one with a gaping neck wound and the other, the artist as an emasculated young bull, gazing black-eyed into the inescapable trauma of his cowardice.

The grim reality of war constitutes an assault on the subconscious and its more obvious symbolism. Boy soldiers use Manuel's scarecrow for target practice while, as always with Medem, the assailed take refuge in the mind. Cristina falls into what appears to be a self-induced coma and Peru leaves her there, safe and hidden in dreams and undergrowth, as he surrenders to the enemy forces, thereby exhibiting the same cowardice as his progenitors by denying his true identity and attempting to hide behind the neutrality that might be afforded an American journalist.[13] Yet he is saved from a firing squad by the intercession of Juan Mendiluze, now old, bearded and probably mad, but still capable of recognising Peru as his nephew and, in relation to Juan's incestuous desire for his own sister, as the son he never had. Peru stumbles away from the carnage and finds Cristina waking from a deep and restful sleep, watched over, as ever, by a cow. 'All my life I've been waiting to love you,' she tells him, and they ride away on the horse of a slain soldier. It is a ludicrous, fairy-tale ending to a film that so consistently undermines stereotypes and genre conventions. But it is also one last assault on logic from a director who aims to parody definitions and those who would impose them; for its romanticism is unexpected, illogical even, and therefore par for the workings of the subconscious.

In one way or another the reunion of mismatched lovers forms the conclusion to all of Medem's films. Here one must consider the irony that Cristina and Peru are heading for France and will surely be caught up in the greater conflagration of the Second World War. Moreover, as befits their escape from a world gone mad with civil war, their journey promises to be more psychological than physical, especially as the terrain covered by Medem's protagonists most often functions as a metaphor for their inward voyage.[14] This inward search, as Medem has admitted, also explains his relationship with his films:

> *I compare film-making to making a very intense journey; having completed the journey, I never go back. A part of me remains there and I have to move on to something else. I can never be the same again after making a film, so the person who made* Vacas *is someone else.*

What is curious, however, is that his films display certain connections in narrative and character that are often sharpened by his repeated use of actors. Between *Vacas* and *La ardilla roja*, for instance, it is tempting to connect the union of Suárez with Gómez in the first with the violent breakup of their marriage that occasions the plot of the second.

La ardilla roja

Like *Vacas*, *La ardilla roja* is a parody of mythic origins that deals with constructed notions of self. It begins on the seafront of Medem's home town of San Sebastian with yet another coward, Jota (Nancho Novo), plucking up the courage to kill himself, when a young woman falls out of the night sky and crashes on to the beach. Though her motorbike accident has been set up in an establishing shot, Medem insists on the notion that she has fallen to Earth from outer space by staging an impossible stunt: she falls straight down, thereby suggesting that men and women hail from different planets. Jota rushes to help her across the beach, which is lit and filmed like a lunar landscape, and finds a stunned, amnesiac Sofía (Emma Suárez). It's only boy meets girl but Medem shoots it as if it were science fiction. We see Sofia from Jota's viewpoint (she's upside down with her helmet on and looks just like an astronaut); then a reverse point of view makes the viewer privy to her view of him, with Medem actually placing the camera inside Sofía's helmet. It's a shot through the eye-slot that will be repeated several times during the film, thereby changing the frame to cinemascope and emphasising the subjectivity that sees in such a cinematic way. The scene is all about establishing alternative points of view in the battle between the sexes, and the fact that Medem engineers a balance between them immediately contradicts the fact that cinema traditionally addresses the male spectator. As Laura Mulvey suggests, women on film are commonly rendered as passive objects of a male voyeuristic gaze that converts them into objects of desire and obliges the female spectator to either identify with the masculine point of view or with the feminine objectified position (1992, pp.746–57). Thus, as with hearing and accepting one person's version of events, it's the male psychology that is privileged, whereas *La ardilla roja* immediately sets about challenging the autocracy of the male because it shows the female returning the look. It's a film where, for once, we see the male through female eyes, whereby Medem's reverse objectification of the male challenges both the status of the male protagonists and the conditioning of the male spectator.[15]

Now Jota's an attractive character, but he's also a kind of moral rapist, who kidnaps and imposes a new identity on Sofía, even changing the colour of her eyes to suit his idea of a woman. 'Blue eyes that entangle,' he lies in answer to brown-eyed Sofía's question, though there's a warning here too. Eyes that entangle? It's the beginning of the web that Sofia weaves around him, for at the end we learn Sofía got her memory back in the ambulance, but decided to play along with this new identity because it suited her. *La ardilla roja* therefore presents itself as the story of a perverse, freewheeling courtship between two fabulists that mirrors Medem's own method of film-making:

> I like to be free at first to explore blindly. If I didn't allow myself that freedom I'd be forewarned of how everything ends up. That's common in love as well: that you invent a space to share with the other person. A film-maker too makes these secret, private places, these projections of desire.

La ardilla roja grew out of one of the short stories based on lying that Medem wrote during his three years of unemployment and housekeeping. He wrote the script from Jota's point of view in only ten days, doubtlessly improvising as wildly as his character, yet the character of Sofía remained vague until he met Suárez while making *Vacas*. Her melancholic sensuality in that film provided evidence of her potential to embody contradictory emotions in a role, thus inspiring Medem to base the complex and contrary Sofía on his actress/muse. Smart, cocky and independent, troubled, sad and fragile, Sofía will harness her contradictory nature to the task of filling out her new persona, thereby typifying the struggle of many independent women in contemporary Spain. Moreover, *La ardilla roja* effects a keen parody of the myth of Spanish women that was propagated by Francoist ideology (a system of beliefs which maintained Spanish woman was a servant to her man) in the sense that Jota, who has doubtlessly been preconditioned in his attitudes towards women, attempts to create a female whose perfection will, by contrast to real women, flatter his superior sense and sensibility.

Romantic invention or despicable lie? Sofia goes along with Jota's imposition of the name Elisa and accepts her new identity because it erases her conditioning as masochistic victim in past relationships; but she is never passive, never just a willing pawn in Jota's game. Just watch her choose the details that she likes about her new persona (apartment at the beach? 'Great!') and reject the details that she doesn't: 'Shoes!?' – she doesn't work in a crummy shoe shop. 'You used to, it closed,' says Jota, reacting with desperate aplomb. But, more than verbal sparring, it's the frequent shots of Jota from Sofía's point of view that reveal him as he truly is: a guileful, jilted boyfriend, terrified by autonomous females and striking back at women by making himself a girlfriend who adores him ('You're crazy about me, everyone knows it'), who looks to him for everything, even her name.[16]

In the larger context Sofía's travail may also be seen in relation to the post-Franco rise of feminism and in parallel with the struggle for autonomy of regions such as the Basque Country. A sense of identity is based on memories of ourselves, but memories change with time, becoming, in effect, an edited version of events that shows us in a better light – a 'director's cut' that lets us all be *auteurs* in the new, improved version of our lives. Lies have this useful habit of turning into truths, with the result that fabricated memories do not necessarily result in a false sense of identity. Indeed it might not be any different for a place, such as the Basque Country, where separatists mytholo-gise its historical identity in the service of jingoistic definitions of Basqueness. In terms of structure, *La ardilla roja* is shaped by the process of remembering that forms its plot, but the whole film is a jigsaw puzzle of a woman's identity which builds into a picture of female independence and, by inference, Basque autonomy. However, rather than stage a metaphorical battle between the

Sofía's nightmare. Carmelo Gómez, Emma Suárez and Nancho Novo in *La ardilla roja* (Julio Medem, 1993)

sexes, Medem and Suárez conspire to make Lisa a romantic and generous character, who actually has the power to redeem Jota. All Jota has to do is shed the weight of his same patriarchal past (which Medem parodies in a flashback to a cheesy pop video in which Jota appears as a prehistoric man with, no doubt, a matching attitude to women) and both he and Sofía will be liberated from the specious stereotyping of men and women.

Jota accompanies Sofia to hospital, play-acting her boyfriend and thereby assuming an identity that is every bit as false as hers. Meanwhile a doctor, who will later be revealed as Sofía's brother, is also involved in identity games with a petrol station attendant. This is the first of the film's two happy homosexual couples, suggesting how successful relationships might be founded on the exclusion of the stereotypical, chauvinist male that is typified by Sofía's vindictive husband Félix (Carmelo Gómez). But what is worrying is that Medem also makes us see the world from Félix's point of view, like that of some maniac in a slasher film, thereby suggesting that this vengeful, murderous male can still claim control of the narrative. Indeed he dramatically emerges from Sofía's subconscious when a psychologist shows her a photo of the back of a black-clad man as an aid to recovering her memory, and the photo springs to life in her hands. It's a neat visual trick, a vibrant image that Medem employs to prioritise an emotional response over reasoning.[17] In addition, this intrusion of the subconscious into the real world, which is so typical of Medem's films, is further illustrated by the following scene, where the commentary from a television documentary on squirrels invades Jota's dreams, linking thoughts of Sofía with a description of the squirrels as 'crafty, humble, nimble as flies, elusive, but strategically so, sinuous and able to carry out their plans behind the backs of men.'[18]

In common with many of Medem's characters, Jota and Sofía escape the reality of the city and head for a country campsite where everything is false and fantastic: the trees, the lake, the 'mediterranean atmosphere' and their own relationship. It's as if they have wandered into a fairy tale, where even the laws of time and space no longer apply – a rewriting of the rules which affords Medem, the playful post-modernist, various opportunities to indulge in visual flourishes that integrate blatant artifice within the drama without ever upsetting the emotional core. Jota, for example, stages his own slow-mo action replay of catching a biker's helmet, thereby delivering a cock-eyed parody of a cinematic technique that is customarily employed to glorify the act of a macho male – a goal, perhaps, or a particularly well-aimed punch. Except the film also darkens considerably when Sofia signs into the campsite with her own name and, though both she and Jota notice it, neither makes any comment. It is a shot like that of hurling the axe into the forest at the centre of *Vacas*, from which the action spirals outwards and towards a conclusion that will force the viewer to reconsider the film's beginning. It is also a shot that Medem follows with a leering gaze at her shapely bottom – one of the few times that the point of view in the film is so stereotypical in the way it regards the female, except that this is from the lesbian site-worker's point of view and thus a strikingly original challenge to the traditional way of looking at women in films from the perspective of the male.

For all its artifice, the reduced space of the campsite is a microcosm of Spanish society in which various family units are represented. In addition to the 'newlyweds' of Jota and Sofía there is the traditional, chauvinist household which boasts arrogant Antón (Karra Elejalde) as its head, as well as the incestuous make-believe that is maintained by the 'mothers and fathers' role-play of his son and daughter. When they all come together for an evening meal it is fittingly observed from the point of view of the squirrel, high up in a tree and watching the over-complicated humans with wry and knowing amusement, just like its soulmates, the cows in *Vacas*. Sofia drops a glass, testing Jota's capacity for redemption by virtue of his prodigious reflexes (in other words, his ability to change) and so it is that Jota will subsequently edge one step further towards reconstructing himself as a new man by not insisting on sex with Sofía, but by going off quietly to sleep on his own. It's a disconcerting act, which is probably why Sofia makes a mistake in recounting details of her relationship to Carmen (María Barranco), confusing the present (her and Jota) with the past (her and Félix). It's a glimpse under the skin of the real Sofia that Medem matches with the visual metaphor of creeping below the surface of the lake (already revealed in the opening credits as teeming with bone-like trees and veiny plants). Such imagery is an example of the film's ample visual evidence of collusion between females and the natural world, but it is also part of a sequence of related shots, which includes a close-up of the hairs on Sofía's arm standing on end, that reveals how, despite the freedom afforded by her new identity, Sofía cannot deny the truth of her own instincts, namely fear.[19] Unlike Jota, she recognises the danger in all their deceit and lying: 'Jota, you and I, are we good people?' It's a question that goes right to the heart of the morality play that we are watching – and it goes without an answer.

Rather than the casual sexual encounters that punctuate most commercial films, sex in the films of Julio Medem constitutes a profound, moral commitment that is the primary spur to characters' actions. As part of their romantic charade Jota and Sofia take turns detailing their sexual preferences in a scene in which female desire is presented as equal to that of the male. In truth, however, Jota's fantasy is rather more homely than erotic – 'What I want is to cook for you, care for you all the time' – with the result that traditional sex roles are reversed: it is Sofia who has the erotic fantasy and the power to express it and it is Jota who wants to settle down and, importantly, has the power to express that too. Medem thus engineers a transfer in the subjectivity of desire, with the result that Jota becomes contemptuous of the fantasy that he has created and will try to destroy its artificiality: 'Everything here is a lie,' he tells her. Nevertheless, his admission (and the fact that they *do* make love) suggests that Jota's course of redemption may lie in his bourgeoning femininity. 'I've no balls either,' he replies to Antón's criticism of women, whereupon Sofía puts the brakes on his emasculation by challenging the limits of his masculinity: a challenge that he ably surpasses by unsubtly 'erecting' the motorbike.

Subsequently, Sofía will actively build on the fantasy of her relationship with Jota by accepting, repeating and adding to his lies (she even wears his T-shirt with his face on it – a sign that she's wholeheartedly accepted his point of view). Why? Because it's empowering, because she reclaims the identity that she had lost in her marriage (she even encourages Carmen to leave her husband as well), and because, well, isn't it obvious? She's fallen in love with the guy. Feminists might well criticise the cliché of Sofía's falling for her kidnapper, but this is a Julio Medem film, where truth is based on the emotional resonances that unite the characters and reason has little to say.[20] Emotions are the bridge between fantasy and reality and lies are an acceptable means to a happy ending because, ultimately, *La ardilla roja* contends that if the emotions are true it doesn't matter what they're based on. Indeed, in reference to the larger context once more, it may be argued that it was an emotional response to the nationalist mythology of Sabino Arana that inspired the formation of ETA.

On the other hand the narrative does walk a tightrope between the emotional fantasy of Sofía's fulfilment and the psychological reality of her condition as traumatised victim of a violent marriage and kidnapping. For a resolution we might look at the scene where the taxi-driver's son slaps her bottom and Sofía dares him to follow through on such a feeble and clichéd male gesture. When he hesitates she grabs his wrist and pushes his hand down the back of her jeans until, in a visual pun on Freud's concept of *vagina dentata*, she 'bites' him with her labia. The stunned reaction shots of all the males, including Jota, prove that Sofía is clearly in control of the male perspective on her actions, and therefore suggests that her awareness of her constructed myth of origins affords her the opportunity to use that knowledge to her own advantage. Except the strain of pretending provokes a psychological crisis that is illustrated in her dream of a bizarre sexual triangle between Jota, herself and Félix, in which Félix ridicules Jota's masculinity and climaxes with an important question for her: 'Who are you?'

The final, violent confrontation will see Félix appear like a character from Sofía's nightmare – 'I'm her angel!' – whereupon Medem emphasises this eruption of the subconscious with a furious mix of strange angles, distorting lenses and low-level shots that suggest fear and retribution on a mythic scale. Sofía escapes and the men race after her, only to drown in the reservoir that has become a metaphor for her mystery. In the end, however, this is an ingenuous and romantic film that sees Jota survive because his love for Sofía is based on real memories now of the short time they actually spent together. His reward is the photo which springs to life in his apartment, disclosing visual clues by means of the outrageous visual trick that Medem pulls off with tremendous assurance, cross-cutting between past and present, between reality and fantasy, and emerging, amazingly, with an emotional truth. Jota tracks Sofía down to Madrid's zoo and his final point of view shot is through branches and foliage – an effective simile for the web of lies that *he* has had to wade through during the film. 'We're two unknowns,' he tells her as they embrace in the luscious garden like some modern day Adam and Eve; only, instead of a snake, there's a squirrel.

Tierra

La ardilla roja is a chaotic film, both visually and narratively, so it's hardly surprising that the protagonist of Medem's next film, *Tierra*, seeks a little simplicity. 'Another mystery: Me!' he declares as he drives into the red lands of Cariñena on a mission to eradicate the plague of beetles that is spoiling the taste of the wine. This is Ángel (Carmelo Gómez), who might be, as his name suggests, a fallen angel.[21] 'Half-alive and half-dead, halfway between the stars and the atoms', he's like Christ amongst us humans, on a mission to make some sense of the world and revealing himself in the opening scene by his recovery of a lost lamb and his resuscitation of a shepherd hit by lightning. But he is also tortured by a hyperactive imagination and an excess of conscience that speaks to him through his alter ego, a troublesome Jiminy Cricket type who testifies to the essential duality of man by being also played by Gómez: 'I'm that part of you that died and I'm speaking to you from the cosmos.' Then again, he might just be nuts.

    Tierra, like *La ardilla roja*, *Taxi Driver* and *Apocalypse Now*, filters reality through the subconscious of its protagonist and shares with its audience an absurd world that Ángel traverses with wry humour and dedication to a task. Though working towards simplicity, his journey is complicated by the women he meets. On the other hand, they might also provide him with the opportunity to resolve his own personality split in choosing between them. Trusting Ángela (Emma Suárez) or lusting Mari (Silke)? By dividing Ángel's character in two Medem creates a comparative subjectivity in his appreciation of these two females that often results in violent arguments inside Ángel's head; for this is a story of options, doubts and choices that are hopelessly complicated by a protagonist who battles his own subconscious for the right to decide for himself.

The spiritual landscape of the adventure is revealed through the storm clouds that rage behind the credits, a red and hollow patch of Earth, one hour from the Basque town of Vitoria. It is a land teeming with beetles and boars that, like all men, go crazy over the sex-smell of Mari, thereby serving the function of all animals in Medem's films by codifying or reflecting the impulses of humans (literally so in the moment when Ángela diverts her flattery of Ángel on to a lamb: 'Those blue flecks in your eyes . . . I was so struck by them that I lied and told you that I saw them in the eyes of the dead lamb that you gave us'). Ángel is bewildered by his own Christlike dichotomy between God and man, but his confusion remains strangely unresolved by the knowledge of life after death that he imparts with grace to the shepherd hit by lightning ('Death is just a voyage through the world'), Ángela's daughter ('Your father's okay. He just doesn't want you to see him dead') and Ángela's father, who is also half the man he used to be since the death of his soulmate wife. For all his spiritual calm, therefore, Ángel still exudes an existential angst – 'Can't you see I'm all alone?' – that is derided by his Gypsy workers, whose honesty and down-to-earthness renders them closer to the natural world and therefore typically scornful of his tangled pysche: 'Your're mad, that's your problem. We all know it!' Ángel is, after all, out to exterminate the natural phenomenon of the beetles, and even if he does grow to like the mysteriously earthy taste of the wine that is somehow a result of the beetles, he remains a waged and mercenary adversary of such a miracle of nature. Ángel's 'what ifs' are as numerous as the beetles he has come to conquer and his choices only become clear when the infinite possibilities of his existence are polarised around the opposite female characters. Indeed he will literally find himself caught between them during his first fumigation of a vineyard, when Medem frames a shot with Gómez, in close-up, turning his head from Ángela to Mari as they stand on the hill behind him, thereby resembling *his* good and bad angels on either shoulder.

Ángel is on a sensual voyage through the cosmos, but the real cosmos, the infinite, resides in his imagination: 'Imagine a beetle – if you can imagine the smallest thing, you can imagine the greatest.' Correlatively, *Tierra* boasts a number of Medem's most striking images: the lambs hit by lightning, the holocaustic advance of the fumigators and the animalistic but non-orgasmic sex scene of Ángel and Mari: 'Have you come?' 'No.' 'Brilliant, me neither!' Yet these accomplishments also show up the conflict that can occur in the films of Medem between imagery and atmosphere on the one hand and narrative logic and depth of character on the other. He cuts extraordinarily well between scenes that take place at different times and in different places, merging disparate conversations and even juggling simultaneous appearances of Ángel and his angel, but the film's resolution disappoints because it is based upon the objectionable male fantasy of dividing the compliant female

Carmelo Gómez as Ángel primes his army of Gypsy fumigators in *Tierra* (Julio Medem, 1996)

into angel and whore. The fluid movements of the steadicam suggest that Ángel is continually followed by his other half, whose point of view this represents, and, ultimately, it is this subjective foreshortening of the females that reduces the cosmic probabilities that so enthuse Ángel to a simplistic choice of archetype. Furthermore, the revelation that Ángel is an ex-mental patient brings the flight of fantasy crashing down with the result that the polarised representations of the women become, when taken at face value, crude and atavistic.

On the other hand, as Medem has argued, 'there are strong contradictions in each of them. The spiritual woman isn't as spiritual as she appears, she wants to become more sexual, and the sexual woman wants to fall in love.' Nevertherless, Ángela, as her name and a whole series of incidents suggest, should be Ángel's rightful other half. Like him, she's 'alone in the world', but she also loves him, shares his taste for the earthy wine, and is clearly tolerant and welcoming of his angel. It's even suggested by a whole series of déjà vu and coincidences that Cristina, the older woman who assists Ángel (and, incidentally, the name of Suárez's character in *Vacas*, with whom Gómez similarly unites) is actually a premonition of Ángela grown old by his side.[22] But in the end it is Mari who enters the hospital room where Ángel is recovering from a blow to the head; it's her overexcited libido that matches up to Ángel and his immense imagination. Ángel does not so much assuage his conscience as he does split from it definitively, leaving his angel guarding Ángela, while he takes off with Mari for the coast.[23]

There is a caveat that, as with the eradication of the beetles, Ángel's detachment from his angel may be a temporary solution to his dilemma, that a sexual adventure with Mari is a short-term distraction from the family values that are established in Ángela. Nevertheless it's a dubious sort of hero that triumphs by jettisoning his conscience. Medem had only recently separated from his wife after eighteen years of marriage and his enthusiasm for the character of Mari was such that he planned on producing a parallel film from her point of view that would be shot in black and white with handheld cameras.[24] The producers baulked at the expense and the story of 'Mari en la tierra' was published later, offering, in diary form, Mari's version of the events in the film. It reveals, for example, that both Ángela and Mari were outside Ángel's hospital room in the penultimate scene, but that it was Ángela who convinced Mari to enter, saying, 'Mari, it's so clear to me. There's no one better for Ángel than you!' (Medem, 1997, p.149). As ever though, with Medem, it's a wonder whether to take him seriously or not: 'Tierra is about absurdity,' he admits. 'And it's a game. I like to see Tierra laughing.'

Los amantes del circulo polar

Medem took Tierra to the 1996 Cannes Film Festival but his disappointment would only add to the personal crisis that was compounded by the death of his father only a week earlier and the recent breakup of his marriage.[25] Steven Spielberg had asked him to direct the blockbuster version of The Mask of Zorro that was to star Antonio Banderas and, possibly, Emma Suárez,[26] but, as usual, Medem took refuge in fantasy by hiding himself away in his brother's apartment in Paris and writing two scripts.[27] The first was based on hate, a Basque story, 'strong and hard', and the second was Los amantes del círculo polar, a fragile, tender love story that centred on reconciliation. Expounding upon a very personal interpretation of the themes of desire, lies and duality, Medem began Los amantes del círculo polar by dividing his own, recent traumas between the characters:

> It starts with two families breaking up, one due to death, one due to separation. Later, through a spontaneous situation, a new family is created, but this new family is based on a situation where they can't be honest and truthful.

Although written in strict chronological order, Medem shot his film backwards starting with the end, with his lovers reflected in each other's eyes at the moment of one's death. It was, by all accounts, a heartfelt and emotional shoot for Medem, who employed his own son Peru as the adolescent Otto. A double narrative resurrected the technique that Medem had employed in *Patas en la cabeza*, in which characters take it in turns to recount their version of events. Here, however, the concept broke out of the hidden world of the imagination to become a geographical phenomenon of symmetry and chance, with the tribulations of his young lovers interacting with a cyclical series of familial coincidences and a natural metaphor that functions on a global scale.

It starts with an image gleaned from a short story by post-modernist writer Ray Loriga, in which a boy chases a girl because she likes being chased as much as he likes chasing her. Schoolboy Otto, who remarks in voiceover that he knows nothing of girls, runs after a football and finds himself, quite by chance, in the position of chasing Ana, who runs ahead of him. Frantic, handheld camerawork establishes the subjectivity that we expect of Medem's characters: Ana slips and falls and the reverse cutting between the two establishes a balance between the characters that, in Medem's films, most often signifies love, or at least its potential. It also confirms *Los amantes del círculo polar* as a film based on faces, that will find its central image in the eyes of Najwa Nimri, who plays Ana as an adult, and whose intense, fragile, Basque-Arabian features reminded Medem of a girl he had known when young. Through a chain of coincidences that seem to controvert the multiple possibilities of chaos theory, Otto's recently divorced father (Nancho Novo) marries Ana's widowed mother (Maru Valdivielso), with the result that Otto and Ana find themselves forced to assume the roles of brother and sister. The false but insistently incestuous overtones of their romance are thus heightened by the subterfuge which they employ in their nocturnal trysts and the pretence of incompatibility that they maintain in front of their parents. (Perhaps coincidentally Medem had since confessed to the woman with whom he had been so infatuated as a boy, subsequently learning that 'her grandmother was the daughter of my grandfather, who had a lover in Zaragoza.')

Part of the geometric logic of *Los amantes del círculo polar* comes from the fact that Otto and Ana are palindromes (like Medem, whose own sister, with whom he made secret Super-8 films, is also named Ana) and the reversibility of their names is expressed in visual terms by the succession of sequences that repeat the events from each other's point of view. Their names serve as alternating chapter headings, thereby attesting to the alternate perspectives and subjective reality of the events that are developed in the addition of voiceovers. The first chapter is from the point of view of Otto; the second is from that of Ana, who begins her chapter as an adult, on the shores of an arctic lake: 'I'm waiting for the coincidence of my life.' Her memories of the events of her childhood that Otto has already recounted are then repeated with a fresh perspective that reveals, for example, that she believed Otto to be the reincarnation of her dead father (thereby adding the Electra complex to the Freudian kerfuffle): 'Otto speaking on the outside, my father on the inside.' Their tentative, childish romance is ripened by Ana's telepathic communication with the father within Otto, though the pressures of pretence cause an inevitable crisis in the adult Otto (Fele Martínez), who leaves home to train as a messenger pilot. However, his flight is a futile attempt at escaping the chain of coincidence: firstly, because his trade is a clear extension of his childhood attempt to send Ana a message via paper planes; secondly, because his grandfather had rescued a German pilot named Otto (who had been shot down after the bombing of the Basque town of Gernika and whose own son is Ana's second stepfather[28]); and lastly, because it rhymes – 'Otto *el piloto*, of course!' – a fact that Ana and any imaginative child would recognise as profound.

Los amantes del círculo polar is a love story that Medem constructs with the delicate symmetry of the snowflakes that blow over the opening credits. In common with his previous films, it uses its natural setting as a spiritual landscape that inhibits the characters in the same way as they are themselves dwarfed by coincidence and an overwhelming sense of repeating the (mistakes of the) past. Medem had discovered the natural metaphor of the arctic circle when he took *Vacas* to the Festival of the Midnight Sun in Lapland, where the midsummer sun moves horizontally across the sky, causing Medem to stay awake for three nights watching it. 'I went up on a small hill,' he recalls,

> *and there was a small lake there. And I had the sensation that my entire life was very far away from me, that it was behind me, in a sense. It was as if I couldn't move forward from there, from where I was, towards the sun. That was a space I couldn't enter. Almost as if being there with the midnight sun evaporated all sense of time.*

Like Ángel in *Tierra* and Ana in *Los amantes del círculo polar*, therefore, Medem found himself at the very centre of the universe, in the place that would be occupied by Ana, a tiny black hole into which time and space might bend, which is why Ana keeps so still as she sits all night by the side of the lake, waiting for Otto's crashlanding, the coincidence that she knows will come.

'The whole story follows a very thin and limited trajectory,' says Medem, 'walking between reality and desire.' Indeed the balancing act between the alternate subjectivities of Otto and Ana was the result of only nine weeks of filming but *seven months* of editing. Filming back to front, Medem returned to Madrid from Finland to find that twenty-five-year-old Otto and Ana had regressed into their eight-year old selves for the sequences set in 1980. It entailed, of course, a recreation of Spanish society post-Franco in order to introduce his lovers as characters who are as innocent of the dictatorship as they are of the darker desires they have inherited. It is therefore important to remember that Medem too is part of a generation of film-makers that has little memory of the dictatorship, but which certainly shared in the emotional fallout of their parents' suffering. Tellingly, some of the dominant themes of their films are absent mothers, obscure paternal figures and a lack of communication between the sexes and between the generations, together with urban alienation and the emerging disillusionment with the new democracy. In response, many of the youthful characters in their films exhibited a reproachful morality towards tired, cowardly, shameful or adulterous parental figures. The children of *Los amantes del círculo polar* are therefore typical of their generation in their involvement in a process of immunisation against reality, where sex signifies a profound act of commitment that they have rescued from the profligacy of their parents.[29] Indeed, as Medem has described, *Los amantes del círculo polar* is 'filmed in such a way that the kids practically turn their backs on their parents, filming them either from in front or behind. If the parents are there, they're out of focus.'

The visual language that Medem expresses in *Los amantes del círculo polar* is clearly in the service of atmosphere and emotional effect. The chill whites and blues create an almost sterile texture to the exterior world that counterbalances the internal passions of his characters (indeed, the only instance of

Najwa Nimri and Fele Martínez as Ana and Otto in *Los amantes del círculo polar* (Julio Medem, 1998)

colour in the entire film appears to be the blood-red, pin cushion heart that Otto buys for Ana as a token of his love). Nature, meanwhile, is employed as the source of intimacy and isolation that his characters crave, though its somewhat threatening sensuality is conveyed in scenes which suggest a certain masochistic overtone to the adolescent desires. A naked Otto, for instance, dwarfed by trees and masturbating in the stormy night, stepping back into bed and finding a naked Ana already there (as Ana says of him, 'his guilt was so great that it included me too'). Yet, as the film piles coincidence upon chance encounters that purposefully strain credibility, the film becomes more lyrical as it focuses on the emotions of the couple. Moreover Medem employs a number of tricks in the editing and camerawork to create a kind of shorthand storytelling that only intensifies the tension in the tale: the jump cuts detailing Otto's disaffected one-night stands, for example, or the masterful edit with which he engineers the passage of time, with the prepubescent children thrown forward by the sudden braking of the car and Otto and Ana as adolescents falling back into their seats.

In the final chapter – 'Otto in the eyes of Ana' – Medem engineers a logical conclusion to the parallel subjective realities of his protagonists by offering his audience two separate endings. In the first, Ana finds and embraces Otto; in the second, he arrives too late for anything but the split second reconciliation of seeing himself reflected in her rapidly dilating pupils. There is, however, a final reconciliatory act in the dedication which appears out of the blizzard that returns over the end credits: a dedication to Medem's father. It is a touching epilogue to the series of reconciliations which occur in the film, including that of Otto with his father and that between Germany and the Basque Country that is shown in the newsreel of the German president's official apology for the bombing of Gernika.[30] It is, however, a belief in reconciliation that still seems ingenuous in the current fractious situation of the Basque Country and it has occasioned a ready criticism in Spain of the wilful fantasy of Medem's films. In response, he admits, 'It's hard to ground myself in the current political situation. I don't know if I'm mature enough yet to tackle that with the necessary depth. Perhaps some time has to pass.' Nevertheless, such criticisms ignore the darkness that exists at the core of each of Medem's films, testament indeed to his willingness to explore more universal themes than the localised dramas and comedies of many of his contemporaries. Playful and idealistic though his films may appear at first, their visual and narrative dexterity is anchored to an emotional and thematic density that is, respectively, the result of his dutiful apprenticeship to the craft and a number of personal demons. Which is not to say they're not a lot of fun. 'When I present a film, I suggest people leave their minds open,' he says. 'To let yourself be moved. Let the ideas be born of the emotional movement and not the other way round.'

Notes

1. All quotes attributed to Julio Medem are from the transcript of an interview conducted by Tom Charity and generously ceded to the author for inclusion in this chapter.
2. Medem's short films on Super-8: *El ciego* (The Blind Man, 1976), an adaptation of a Hitchcock short story entitled *El jueves pasado* (Last Thursday, 1977), *Fideos* (1979) and *Si yo fuera un poeta* (If I were a Poet, 1981).
3. *Vacas is* an historical film but it ends at the beginning of the Civil War. Medem's films have yet to include a reference to Franco or the dictatorship.
4. Perhaps, therefore, it's also worth noting that Medem graduated in general surgery instead of the major in psychology that he intended: flesh and blood thwarting the subconscious yet again.
5. Querejeta was at that time setting up a series of mid-length films under the umbrella title of *Siete huellas* (Seven Imprints). Their resultant *Martín* (1988) was the product of compromise and an unsatisfactory experience for both.
6. As its name suggests, the Second Carlist War was a sequel of sorts to a civil war that had raged from 1833 to 1839 between right-wing monarchists (made up of clergy, peasants and aristocrats), who had wanted Carlos, son of Ferdinand VII, to be king of Spain (hence the name Carlists) and the liberal middle classes who wanted his daughter, the three-year-old Isabella. In 1869 a freedom of religion act infuriated the staunchly Catholic Basques and provoked another Carlist rebellion. The Second Carlist War raged from 1872 to 1876 and resulted in defeat for the Carlists. The other Carlist legacy, of course, has been their distinctive red beret.
7. *Vacas* was actually filmed in the Valle del Baztán in Navarre.
8. Sabino Arana is often called the founding father of Basque nationalism. His fury at the Carlist defeat manifested itself in his dogmatic and nationalist writings that, in turn, gave rise to a mythologically charged concept of Basqueness that inspired a fresh rallying to the cause of nation-building that endures to this day. Arana died in 1903, aged 38.
9. Medem's original concept was for the film to finish in Brasilia in the present day with Peru, Ignacio's son, now a grandfather looking at his photographs of cows.
10. The cow's name is Pupille, which suggests the pupil of the eye.
11. The atmosphere and tensions are especially redolent of José Luis Borau's *Furtivos* (Poachers, 1975), a key film of the transition.
12. In *Vertigo* (1958) the technique is used to express the vertigo of James Stewart's character. In *Jaws* (1975) it is used in a shot of Roy Scheider's reaction to a shark attack.
13. The other-worldly atmosphere and the character's fear are strangely exacerbated by the poor dubbing of Gómez's English dialogue in this scene.
14. Note the lake of *La ardilla roja*, the scorched earth of *Tierra* and the placidity of Finland in *Los amantes del círculo polar*, where Ana, like Cristina in *Vacas*, sits waiting for the love that she knows will come.
15. The point of view shot is just one of the techniques for privileging the female psyche that Medem uses in *La ardilla roja*, including dream sequences, voiceover (even if it's only deep breathing), sympathetic framing, close-ups and a montage of image and sound that suggests a magical complicity between Sofia and the squirrel.

16. Jota even gives her the name Elisa, like that of another Pygmalionic creation, Eliza Doolittle.
17. An identical effect appears in a shot of Deckard (Harrison Ford) flicking through photos of Rachael and her mother in Ridley Scott's *Blade Runner* (1982), a film that shares with *La ardilla roja* a need to challenge the reality of memories.
18. The curious simile of squirrels and flies also suggests a double bluff: if Sofía's a squirrel, then Jota's a fly (it was the name of his old pop group and they're all over his t-shirt). Perhaps he and Sofía are equally matched in this surrealist game?
19. Another key factor here and in all of Medem's films is the brooding, neurotic soundtrack by Alberto Iglesias.
20. Not just feminists, as the film was hammered by the four main newspaper critics in Madrid (two of them rating the film zero). However, the political causes of such a reaction are various and the film itself was a notable success from word of mouth, especially amongst young people, playing for several months on Madrid's art-house circuit.
21. Ángel is also strangely reminiscent of Félix in *La ardilla roja*, not just by casting, but by Félix's appearance in the red landscape of that film's first photo to spring to life, and Félix's prophetic declaration of crazed love for Sofía: 'I'm her angel!'
22. Cristina: 'You look like my son . . . what's your name?' 'Ángel.' 'My husband's called Ángel too.'
23. The character of Mari is based on a Basque myth of a seductive witch. Maybe Ángel is spellbound and just can't help himself.
24. Medem also collaborated on the script for the film *Hola, ¿estás sola?* (Hello, Are You Alone?, 1995) directed by Iciar Bollaín, in which Silke plays a similarly adventurous character.
25. Medem hoped to repeat the success of *La ardilla roja*, which had won both the Public and Youth Prizes in 1993.
26. Spielberg had been turned on to Medem's work by Stanley Kubrick, who admired *La ardilla roja* so much that he bought Medem's own copy of the film. Kubrick also recommended Emma Suárez to Spielberg for a role in *The Mask of Zorro* (eventually played by Catherine Zeta Jones). Banderas, however, was originally due to play Ángel in *Tierra*, but went to the United States to play Zorro.
27. Medem: 'I felt so bad that I started to write. I don't know why a love story came out of that and I don't really want to think why.'
28. Medem also had an uncle named Otto, who was a pilot, who died in a plane crash.
29. It certainly contradicts and revises the decision of Ángel in *Tierra*.
30. We should also remember that Medem's father was German.

CHAPTER NINE

Seeing stars

Banderas, Abril, Bardem, Cruz

According to Brother Ángel Ayala, the founder of the ACNP Catholic pressure group in Spain, the cinema was 'the greatest calamity that has befallen the world since Adam. A greater calamity than the flood, the two world wars and the atomic bomb' (Hooper, 1995, p.153). It was the sexual content of the cinema both real and, worse, imagined that alarmed Franco's doomy clergy into setting up their board of film censors; but they had no one to blame but themselves. The seeds of their distress had been unwittingly sown by the determination of their predecessors to divide man from beasts by the imposition of the missionary position; for this turnaround in sexual relationships had the consequence of prioritising the look in the sexual act and so encouraging voyeurism, a pleasure that would, in time, be explored and exploited by the cinema. Actors that an audience liked looking at became objects of dangerous desire: 'Garbo's flesh gives rise to mystical feelings of perdition', Roland Barthes wrote (1983, p.56). In its crusade against spiritual ruin, film censorship during the dictatorship was infamously puritan; but the liberalism that followed brought an amnesty on taboos and there emerged a discourse on changing attitudes to sex and sexuality in the films of directors who worked repeatedly with new stars such as Antonio Banderas, Victoria Abril, Javier Bardem and Penélope Cruz – sex symbols whose symbolism is specific to Spain's evolution since Franco.

As Rosa Montero has stated: 'The influence of Catholicism, for which sexual difference is divinely ordained, plus the legacy of eight centuries of Arab occupation laid the foundations for a sexism that the Franco period would only aggravate' (2000, p.381). The male was the lawgiver, provider, patriarch and spiritual leader in both his teachings and example, while the female was the subordinate childbearer and homekeeper who concerned herself with the physical well-being of her clean and well-fed brood. Spanish civil law actually stated that 'the husband must protect the wife and the wife must obey the husband' and it forbade married women from opening a bank account, buying a car or applying for a passport or job. There was no divorce and (officially) no abortion or contraception.[1] The outlawing of any alternative didn't just make gay men and lesbians invisible, but also erased from public consciousness the plight of females who suffered from the institutionalised cult of machismo and those males who were burdened with its maintenance. However, the clamour of calls for self-determination from the regions that accompanied the transition to democracy in the late 1970s became a bandwagon that inspired complementary activists in the cause of feminism and gay rights. Freedom had previously been determined by class status, professional standing and financial well-being, but it soon became synonymous with the expression of differences. And, just as freedom for the Basque Country meant a recognition of its difference, so too did liberation for females and gays signify their release from the circumscribed nature of identity as ordained by the Francoist regime.

In the absence of censure, identity and sexuality broke free and became a fluid concept that obeyed instinct instead of doctrine. The aforementioned civil law was changed to 'The husband and the wife must show each other mutual respect and protection', adultery was decriminalised in 1978, contraceptives went on sale and divorce became legal in 1981.[2] Female identity (including sexuality and desire), previously accommodated to that of the man, was thereby empowered to challenge and even objectify the male, aided in this respect by the concurrent celebration of the gay consciousness that had occurred in 1979, when the *Ley de Peligrosidad Social* (literally, the Law of Social Dangerousness) which outlawed homosexuality was repealed, thereby legitimising the gay culture that was increasingly evident in the new consumerism, as well as in the reopened universities, the urban nightlife and beach resorts such as Sitges and Ibiza. This transition promoted a rejection of rigid patriarchy in favour of a modern Spain where familiar cultural artefacts reflected the instability of gender roles. Censorship was revoked by royal decree in November 1977, prompting film and theatre stars to reclaim nudity from a tradition of illegality and sinfulness and use it to celebrate and explore notions of sexuality that challenged the generic objectification of the female form for male pleasure, though this finest of lines was soon erased by the opportunism of *el destape* – literally 'the undressing' – a series of films that exploited the new liberalism for predictable, retrograde ends. The new spirit of consumerism also created a demand for films that reflected the changes in Spanish society. Newly independent women flocked to see Carmen Maura in *Tigres de papel* (Paper Tigers, 1977) and other films where female protagonists reflected and inspired their progress, while men welcomed male characters such as José Sacristán in *Asignatura pendiente* (Subject Pending, 1976), who, if not au fait with emancipation, were at least as confused as they were.[3]

These attempts at reflecting the changes in gender roles were a key part of the process by which, as Peter William Evans has described, 'post-dictatorship cinema in Spain succeeded in repoliticising film language' (1993, p.326). Political oppression had previously been explored through the metaphor of sexual repression in such films as Luis Buñuel's *Viridiana* (1961), Carlos Saura's *La prima Angélica* (1973), José Luis Borau's *Furtivos* (1975) and Ricardo Franco's *Pascual Duarte* (1976); but each of these films had suffered at the hands of the censor, thereby proving the tyranny of the regime that they were intended to expose. In the absence of censorship, however, sex became both currency and commodity. At one extreme this led to a fleeting consumer cult of pornography,[4] but it also allowed for that which Barry Jordan and Rikki Morgan-Tamosunas have described as 'a second-wave sexualisation which swept through both arthouse and mainstream cinema often pro-ducing more reflective or provocative representations of gender and sexuality' (1998, p.113). In foreign markets, the distributors of films such as Pedro Almodóvar's ¡Átame! (Tie Me Up!, Tie Me Down!, 1989), Vicente Aranda's *Amantes* (Lovers, 1991), Juan José Bigas Luna's *Jamón, jamón* (1992) and Alejandro Amenabar's *Abre los ojos* (Open Your Eyes, 1997) utilised the erotic appeal of their stars to provide the hook of subtitled sex that has always been a secret thrill of art-house moviegoing. However, as Richard Dyer argues, stars possess an ambiguity that 'needs to be understood in terms of the relation between the performer and the audience' (1992, p.622). Conse-quently, the stars who have embodied the changing nature of sexual identity in Spain must be analysed in relation to the Spanish audience which desires them.

Antonio Banderas

Banderas was born in Malaga in 1960 and christened José Domínguez. As a student of dramatic arts, he battled his way into independent theatre groups and lived off bit parts on the Madrid stage until Imanol Arias, a friend who had the lead in Pedro Almodóvar's *Laberinto de pasiones* (Labyrinth of Passions, 1982), recommended him to the director for the small part of Sadec, a gay Islamic terrorist with a prodigious sense of smell. Almodóvar gave Domínguez a new name and cast him for the impulsiveness that makes for a credibly passionate encounter with Arias as the exiled son of the Shah of Iran. *Laberinto de pasiones* is a film that revels in kitsch excess, but Banderas' portrayal of gayness is neither camp nor effeminate, rather it seems sincere and set on some more thoughtful, romantic plane. Nevertheless, the role brought Banderas into the heart of the *movida*, the fun and funny seizure of Madrid's nightlife by fervid revellers and those of previously marginalised sexualities, a party powered by drugs, solidarity and a flood of glam rock, disco and punk all pouring into Spain after so many years of prohibition and isolation. Although Banderas also played supporting roles in Saura's *Los zancos* (The Stilts, 1984), Montxo Armendáriz's *27 horas* (27 Hours, 1986) and Vicente Aranda's *Si te dicen que caí* (If They Tell You that I Fell, 1989), it was Almodóvar who saw the potential of the quick-witted and charismatic actor, whose athletic build, clean-cut masculinity and lack of inhibition made him an ideal muse for the director's delve into the ambiguity of machismo. In *Matador* (1985) Banderas was a frustratedly sexless Ángel, trying to prove his heterosexuality through rape, and in *La ley del deseo* (The Law of Desire, 1987) he explored the sadistic and masochistic consequences of a too fluid and somewhat malevolent sexuality. In reflecting the sexuality of its characters *La ley del deseo* was also fluent in its appropriation of genres, swerving between melodrama to film noir with a catch-all camp sensibility that affectionately desecrates traditional icons of catholicism and Spanishness; but this vortex of mischievous degeneracy finds its match in Antonio (Banderas) who is introduced masturbating furiously in the toilets of a cinema after a premiere. Obsessed with the film's director (Eusebio Poncela), Antonio is capable of switching sexualities just to be near him, even romancing his transsexual brother (Carmen Maura), murdering his passive, unimaginative rival for the director's affection (Miguel Molina) and taking the director prisoner in his own flat. Yet Banderas also renders his namesake romantic in the final scene of him cradling the wounded director in a *pietà* that points to an other-worldly passion.[5] As Marsha Kinder describes, Almodóvar's deployment of Banderas' energy and magnetism was so successful that it 'established a mobile sexuality as the new cultural stereotype for a hyperliberated Socialist Spain' (1997, p.3).

Banderas' skill in assimilating his roles meant that he was convincingly bland in *Mujeres al borde de un ataque de nervios* (Women on the Verge of a Nervous Breakdown, 1988), where, unrecognisable in curly hair, suit and glasses, he stutters and fusses ineffectually and is removed from the film's climax by the disinterest of females in solidarity and Pepa's (Carmen Maura) spiked gazpacho. Ironically, therefore, Banderas was only incidental to the film that brought international fame to his mentor, though the audiences who warmed to this flattering portrait of an independent female would be shocked by the violent power-play between the sexes in his next film, ¡*Átame!*. As in *La ley del deseo*, Banderas once again takes a star of the film world prisoner in their own home, only this time it's a woman and Ricky (Banderas) is a heterosexual male, who, coincidentally or not, also happens to be mad. Indeed his character's desires for the trappings of heterosexual bliss appear to be linked to his condition as an ex-mental patient who, as Almodóvar shows in the first shot of him twisting a screwdwriver against his forehead, has clearly got a screw loose. 'I'm twenty-three years old,' he tells Marina (Victoria Abril), 'I have 50,000 pesetas and I'm alone in the world. I'll try to be a good husband to you and a good father for your children.' Thus Almodóvar's bitter twist on gender roles in Spain is that Ricky expresses his madness in terms of a sincere adhesion to patriarchy and heterosexuality that is wholly correlative with the supposedly sane dictum of the Catholic Church.

Perhaps, after being fêted as the director of the glossy, upmarket *Mujeres al borde de un ataque de nervios*, Almodóvar reconsidered his responsibilities to those stars, friends and characters who had appeared in his previous films and were still considered freaks by the society that now embraced him and with *¡Átame!* he took a sideways look at the supposed normality of that same society. Ricky's obsession with Marina dates from their first encounter a year previously, when he snuck out of the mental hospital and picked her up in a bar. Back then she was a drug addict and pornographic film star and he'd promised to return and rescue her from a life on the streets; but a year later she's cleaned up, gone legit and is appearing in a respectable horror film that utilises her as the archetypical female in peril, thereby suggesting a parallel with the professional trajectory of Almodóvar, who, it was supposed, had 'cleaned himself up' after the sordid exploits of his earlier films and turned respectable with the heterosexual, middle-aged and middle-class concerns of *Mujeres al borde de un ataque de nervios*. However, rather than a rejection of roots, *¡Átame!* presents itself as a retort to normality and a parody of respectability, for Ricky, who is pronounced normal on his release from mental hospital, immediately goes in search of Marina, the junkie porn star who he thinks will be the 'good wife and good mother to his children' that is supposedly the common goal of all decent, law-abiding, God-fearing Spanish men.

However, as Paul Julian Smith asks, 'can Almodóvar's abstracted desire escape the gender hierarchies which inform heterosexual relations?' (2000, p.108). Indeed, can an audience condone the existence of desire beyond the limits of respectability and, correlatively, can a film star be anything other than heterosexual? Typically, Almodóvar plays with the sexual coding of Ricky, undermining his adherence to the philosophies of heterosexuality and patriarchy with the 'gay-coded register of [his] all too masculine image' (Smith, 2000, p.117). He also lingers on evidence of his empathy with the feminine sensibility, which has him shopping for softer rope with which to bind Marina, cooking for her and weeping at her rejection of his desire: 'How long will you take to fall in love with me?' Moreover, although Ricky ties Marina to a bed (an aspect that enraged many critics and viewers), the bondage never appears to have sexual connotations. Instead, Ricky is embar-rassed by the untimely intimacy of his kidnapping, turning away while

Marina dresses and refraining from masturbation in case he wakes her. As someone says of the film in which Marina is starring, 'More than a horror story it looks like a love story'. Rather than illustrate the Stockholm Syndrome by which captives come to rely upon and even love their captors, Almodóvar shows that Marina comes to desire Ricky not because he breaks down her resolve but quite the opposite, because he redeems her badly damaged self-esteem and reawakens her faith in romanticism. For all its scandalous reputation, ¡Átame! is the most romantic of features, wholly celebratory in its final union of our beauty and her beast as they motor home to meet the rest of her family with the raucous pop song Resistiré (I Will Resist) playing on the car stereo.

Ricky and Marina are marginalised characters, damaged and labelled as such by a society that also pigeon-holed Almodóvar as a gay or women's film director and, with ¡Átame!, was unsure whether the director's portrait of a perverse but ultimately equal and fulfilling heterosexual relationship was a laugh at their expense. It wasn't just the film's conventional ending that jarred but the sly, dry humour that simmered beneath the straight-faced performances of its stars: Abril, an actress who had become identified with roles of sexual intensity, played a reformed porno actress, while Banderas, who had thrived in roles of sexual ambiguity, was so straight he was (literally) crazy. As

'Look, this reminds me of my parents'. Antonio Banderas and Victoria Abril in ¡Átame! (Pedro Almodóvar, 1989)

188

always with Almodóvar, the precepts of authority and propriety are appropriated and reapplied so that marginalised characters come to seem paragons of that same normalcy, which is why Ricky takes to constantly checking the construction of he and Marina as a respectable couple: 'Look,' he tells her as they prepare to leave the flat in handcuffs, 'we're like a married couple getting ready to go out.' It's a process of subversion that reaches its climax in the sequence where Ricky returns to the flat after being beaten up by the drug dealer's henchmen and Marina slips her bonds to treat his wounds. 'Look, this reminds me of my parents,' he tells her as he stares into the bathroom mirror, whereupon Marina takes to kissing him and the two celebrate prototypical coupledom in a prolonged and explicit sex scene whose realism is a calculated and joyous alternative to prurient fade-outs or censorious cuts.

In addition, this enthusiastic copulation between two of Spain's most desired film stars allows Almodóvar to challenge the religious censure that commonly denies or castigates the fun and *sexy* side of sex.[6] Right from the start of *¡Átame!* there are clues to this subversion of Catholic doctrine in the pictures of the Virgin and Christ that form the Warholian background to the opening credits. The camera focuses on the sacred hearts of these entirely sexless Catholic icons and generic role models for a Spanish audience, while the credits herald the presence of an actor and actress whose scandalous, even profane physicality had made them this same audience's favourite film stars and sex symbols. However, as with the realignment of authority figures alongside marginalised characters that occurs in many of Almodóvar's films, *¡Átame!* does not so much satirise heterosexuality as it does invite those of that persuasion to join in the revolution against the prejudicial standards of decency that prohibit them (as they once forbade gays) from exploring their identities through sexuality, which is why Almodóvar celebrates the couple's orgasm by multiplying it in their reflection in a kaleidoscopic mirror on the ceiling. In effect, *¡Átame!* constitutes a satire of society because it plays happy families with a psychopath and a degenerate and refuses to broker any contradiction; but it's not laughing at Ricky and Marina because sex in the films of Pedro Almodóvar is only funny when eroticism is absent. Whenever true feelings, both physical and emotional, are present there is also eroticism, ably conjured through explicitness and realism in the service of an intimacy that is romantic, not pornographic, and actors such as Banderas and Abril who explore the contradictions of being sex symbols in a society which often condemns what their characters do.

Banderas was due to play the role of the transvestite judge Femme Letal that was subsequently taken by Miguel Bosé in Almodóvar's next film *Tacones lejanos* (High Heels, 1991), but went to Hollywood instead, having been singled out by Madonna as the sexiest man alive in Alex Keshisian's documentary *In Bed with Madonna* (aka Truth or Dare, 1991). Thereafter he appeared as an exiled Cuban trumpeter in *Mambo Kings* (1991) and in a breakthrough role that drew on his iconography in Spanish cinema as Tom Hanks' lover in Jonathan Demme's Aids-drama *Philadelphia* (1993). Thereafter, Hollywood squandered Banderas' talent in roles that required him to conform to the machismo of the comic book in such films as *Desperado* (1995), *Assassins* (1995) and *The Mask of Zorro* (1998). Away from Spain, it seems, Banderas' intensity is diluted, his subtlety is swamped by grander gestures, his ambiguity is erased. It's a disappointment, but it's not beyond repair. 'I'll wait a while,' says Almodóvar, 'till Antonio has a few wrinkles, until he's an interesting forty-something, who's triumphed and also known failure, and then he'll be mine again!' (Rioyo, 1996, p.53).[7]

Victoria Abril

Victoria Abril has a throaty voice, a raucous laugh and a sweet smile. In her own words: 'Other actors intellectualise a lot. But me, I'm at least 80 per cent organic and 20 per cent cerebral' (Rioyo, 1999, p.12). Although not the most physically imposing of actresses, Abril has often represented the flipside to Banderas' ambiguous interpretations of masculinity, with the erotic and psychological intensity of her characters challenging not only men's view of women but women's view of themselves. Born in Madrid in 1959, Abril was a headstrong child who studied classical ballet and married her Chilean agent when aged just fifteen, much against her family's wishes. Her husband pushed her into a singing career that she shored up by appearing as a game show hostess on television; and it was there, dolled-up and sporting outsize glasses on the original Spanish version of '3–2–1', that Abril came to the attention of the Catalan director Vicente Aranda for the part of the transexual teenager in *Cambio de sexo* (Change of Sex, 1977). Her conviction in the role provided ample evidence of a furious talent and lack of inhibition that, nurtured by Aranda, would take her beyond notions of respectability for an actress. She is naked for much of *La muchacha de las bragas de oro* (The Girl in the Golden Panties, 1979), for example, and central to the morass of perversion that is *Si te dicen que caí* (1989), in which, though several months pregnant, Abril plays a character who performs all manner of degenerate acts for the pleasures of a voyeuristic patron.

Her roles for Aranda were often challenging but Abril was never miscast, largely because of her animalistic determination to inhabit each role; though it did almost happen in Aranda's *Amantes*, where she was first considered for the role of Trini instead of Luisa, her finest role and one that earned her the award for best actress at the Berlin Film Festival.[8] *Amantes* was to have been an episode in the second television series of *La huella del crimen* but the series was

190

cancelled and Aranda turned it into a film, updating the true story from 1949 to the mid-1950s and shooting the film in only six weeks. *Amantes* tells the tale of the recently demobbed Paco (Jorge Sanz), who, though engaged to the adoring, virginal Trini (Maribel Verdú), is distracted from a routine and decent life by the palpable wiles of his landlady, the amoral and hell-bent Luisa (Abril).[9] As Luisa, Abril was noticeably maturing from roles that had required her to maintain and project a certain desirable and often vulnerable physicality. 'It was,' she reflected, 'the first time that I didn't feel like the object of desire. It was liberating' (Álvares and Frías, 1991, p.304). Her Luisa is sexual, urban, active and sadistic, and therefore a vivid contrast with the virginal, rural, passive and masochistic Trini.

Amantes begins with Trini praying, clothed in the pastel blues of her idol, the Virgin Mary, while her fiancé Paco stands at the back of the church in full soldier's uniform. Thus Aranda immediately sets out the context of the film's passion and criminality against a background of the strict religious and military regimes that ruled a grim and grubby Madrid (exquisitely rendered by cinematographer José Luis Alcaine), where the only light, colour and excitement comes from Luisa, the landlady who answers the door to Paco like a parody of the sacred virgin, wearing a bright blue, embroidered silk kimono and a shawl of multi-coloured tinsel.[10] Rather than focus on the economically motivated machinations of the original crime, *Amantes* is concerned with the destabilisation of rigid, socially determined gender roles and the way that Luisa's acting on carnal and criminal instincts allows her to play men at their own game by exploiting the currency of sex and the valuelessness of life in the exploitative post-war economy. During the dictatorship the Catholic Church in Spain augmented its responsibility for education and moral discipline, instructing Spaniards that, for example, women who engaged in sex for anything other than procreation were committing a terrible sin. The success of this indoctrination is evident when Trini invites Paco to the empty home of her employers on Christmas Eve and urges him to act out his corresponding role in her fantasy of them as a respectable married couple; but though she pampers him with rich food and a cigar – 'For the man of the house' – she fearfully rejects his sexual advances, like any good Catholic girl would in a society that demanded virgin brides, faithful wives and asexual mothers. Frustrated, Paco hurries back to the less infantile comforts of Luisa, leaving Trini little option but to follow the advice of her employer and confidante (the wife of Paco's army captain no less) and assume the slatternly appearance and disposition of a whore in order to regain Paco's attentions. However, rather than gratifying Paco with her pretence of liberation, Trini's transformation turns him into the object and victim of desire, fought over by Luisa and Trini, emasculated and fetishised as that which Marsha Kinder has described as an allegory for 'the 1950s generation torn between the "two Spains"'

(1993, p.206). Consequently, Trini's switch from the iconography of the virgin to that of the whore is an ambiguous betrayal of social dictum because her threat is not to Paco (the male whose promiscuity is condoned) but to Luisa (the female whose promiscuity is condemned).

Abril, like Aranda and Almodóvar, has often been criticised for the sordid and explicit nature of her films, but sex and the sexuality of her characters have never been incidental or superfluous to their themes. Rather, Abril's performance of sex on film is, like dance for Antonio Gades or violence for Takeshi Kitano, a medium of expression and a means to an emotional end.[11] Typically, the sex scenes in *Amantes* are focused on both the mechanics and emotions of the act, as well as being essential to an understanding of the increasingly desperate power play between the characters. The film is darkly claustrophobic and uncomfortably intimate in its increasing resort to close-ups of characters who cannot see beyond desire, especially during the sex scenes that illustrate how social deprivations have forced these characters together, for, as Abril has stated: 'When there's misery and poverty, the only thing left is sex' (Álvares and Frías, 1991, p.289). Yet in her survival response to the misery and poverty brought on by a patriarchal regime, Luisa's usurpation of the dominant role in seduction and sex threatens the sacred status of machismo and is therefore tantamount to a crime against the state. It is Luisa who controls the sex play with Paco, penetrating him anally with a handkerchief, obliging him to perform cunnilingus on her and subverting the cliché of erotic display by making him caress his own genitalia for her own, voyeuristic female pleasure.[12] Thus, although it is set in the mid-1950s, *Amantes* is analogous of the changing role of women in the years after Franco, when Spain metamorphosed from a patriarchal dictatorship into a democratic nation in which the correspondent liberation of women as evidenced in the roles of Abril was by some perceived as a threat to the sanctity of the family unit and a challenge to the privileged status of the male. Why, Luisa even sanctions murder as a valid response to any threat to the stability of the newly independent female such as herself: 'I killed my husband and I'm still here.'

In attempting to regain Paco, Trini effectively imitates the liberation enjoyed by Luisa but her innate masochism and indoctrinated servility will not allow her to maintain this deviation from the norm and she will suffer the guilt-ridden fallout of her transformation from the cultural paragon of virgin to the social pariah of whore. *Amantes* ends with Trini asking Paco to relieve her from her unconscionable sins by killing her. Paco then runs to the station and bangs his blood-soaked hands against the window of Luisa's departing carriage, whereupon Aranda employs the romantic cliché of freeze-framing their embrace, but counters it with a written epilogue of the prison sentences that the real-life couple served. However, the epilogue has a deliberately

Victoria Abril as Luisa in *Amantes* (Vicente Aranda, 1991)

staged superfluity that suggests the sentencing was handed down by a society that saw the licentiousness of the woman as a greater threat than the murderous crime of the male. Paco killed Trini, but Luisa served an identical sentence for collusion, while, as the epilogue explains: 'Luisa is dead now. Paco lives in Zaragoza and is known to have a considerable fortune.' The question left hanging by Aranda is whether this comparison of fates would be regarded as unjust by contemporary audiences, or if the coda might still find support as an example to females who needed to be dissuaded from their pursuit of freedom and desire.[13]

Correlatively, the grim fate of a libertine such as Luisa points to the moral backlash that took place in the early 1990s, when the political corruption of the socialist years was linked to moral decay and many Spaniards switched their support to the opposition campaign of the right of centre People's Party (*Partido Popular*). The years since Franco had seen all manner of previously marginalised groups escape illegality, ranging from Communists, women who aborted or used the pill, homosexuals, and the members of ETA who were released from prison in the general amnesty of 1977; but by the early 1990s this celebration of liberalism had lost its appeal as Spain suffered general strikes, high abortion rates, a declining birth rate and an escalation in the violence of ETA. As Abril and Almodóvar would discover from the vitriolic response to their *Kika* (1993), those who continued to challenge prudery were in danger from the new cult of nostalgia for the propriety of the Franco years. Aranda, Abril and Almodóvar (who was never taken too seriously in Spain until he won the Oscar for *Todo sobre mi madre* (All About My Mother) in 1999) were criticised for making films with a high sexual content that created an infamous international reputation for Spanish cinema. Perhaps in response, Aranda's films since *Amantes* have met with limited distribution and critical success, while the films of Almodóvar, as Paul Julian Smith argues, 'can be read as a progressive disavowal of homosexuality' (2000, p.2); yet the unabashed sexuality *and* femininity of Abril's performances continued to mock half-measures, leaving tired or mediocre liberals flailing to denigrate her stardom as the result of typecasting and self-serving exhibitionism. Like Madonna, Abril's fame, public persona and performances taunted the validity of conventional models of femininity, becoming, in effect, a challenge to those women who could not compete with a sexual icon that revealed the shortcomings of their own supposed liberation, partly because of an ingrained misogyny and partly because, as Peter William Evans suggests, of their 'addiction to the rougher form of supremacist masculinity' (1993, p.329).

As if responding to censure, Abril went beyond conventional male–female relationships as Becky in Almodóvar's *Tacones lejanos* (High Heels, 1991), where she grows to fend off the emotional demands of a deeply confused male (Letal, played by Miguel Bosé) and achieve an acquittal for what amounts to serial patricide in a deathbed reunion with her mother (Marisa Paredes). Tellingly, Abril even ventured beyond Spain to play Loli, a bored, cuckolded housewife who enjoys a curious and comfortable lesbian relationship in Josianne Balasko's *Gazon Maudit* (French Twist, 1994),[14] though the following year she would return to explore this new-found sanctuary of female solidarity in Agustín Díaz Yanes' *Nadie hablará de nosotras cuando hayamos muerto* (Nobody Will Talk About Us When We're Dead, 1995). Gloria (Abril), the prostitute wife of a comatose bullfighter, returns to Madrid to steal the savings of Mexican gangsters, but instead finds salvation by befriending her mother-in-law (Pilar Bardem) and taking her high school exams, her determination to achieve independence now redirected from violent means to a pursuit of the education that has allowed Spanish women to triumph since the transition. As Abril described it with typical aplomb, it was 'the story of a girl who starts on her knees, giving a blow job, and ends on her feet, slapping an imbecile who beeps his car horn' (Rioyo, 1995, p.24).

In real life too, Abril was a restless, uninhibited individual, divorcing, and raising her children alone, known for her outrageous outfits at awards ceremonies, a coarse-voiced contempt for decorum and a steadfast refusal to parade her relationships for the gossip magazines. It has always seemed that Abril's worst fate might be respectability; though that was exactly what she did suffer in Manuel Gómez Pereira's convoluted *Entre las piernas* (Between the

Legs, 1999), in which she played Miranda, a middle-class housewife and mother, struggling against her addiction to rough, anonymous sex. The Hitchcockian thriller was dark and daft, because fans of Abril knew all along that it wasn't so much the sex that was her problem but the monotony of everything else. Miranda struggles against her addiction but does penance for her sinfulness when she falls for the murderous Javier (Javier Bardem). The denouement sees her banished from the routine enjoyed by her policeman husband, perfect daughter and new puppy; but maybe, for the unconventional actress who played her, that might just pass for a happy ending.

Javier Bardem

The challenge to sexual stereotyping that made stars of Banderas and Abril was a principal theme of Spanish cinema during the socialist years, one that reflected a change in the patterns of education and cultural programming. Catholicism lost ground as the primary definition of Spanishness as Spaniards moved away from a rural, familial sense of roots towards an urban redefinition of identity that was based upon financial well-being and consumerist ambition. Spanish cinema too had largely moved away from rural considerations of sexual identity, with its traumas of incest and blood weddings, to examine sexuality in an urban milieu. Yet, despite the optimism of films such as Emilio Martínez-Lázaro's *Amo tu cama rica* (1991), in which Ariadna Gil's modern miss enjoys both great sex with Javier Bardem and sweet romance with Pere Ponce, there would be fallout from accelerated change in films such as Montxo Armendáriz's *Historias del Kronen* (Stories from the Kronen, 1995), in which casual sex has a numbing effect that begets casual violence. In a country not far along from a dictatorship, the looser urban morality was bound to enter into conflict with traditional sexual stereotyping and inhibitions. Such is the case with Juan José Bigas Luna's *Jamón, jamón* (1992), a delirious comedy which flails so widely at machismo that it clobbers any notion of corrective feminism as well.

Having begun his film-making career with the production of eleven 16 mm soft porn films that were centred (and predicated) on voyeurism and released under the banner title *Historias impúdicas* (Shameless Stories), Bigas Luna may have been an unlikely satirist of machismo.[15] His first full-length films were similarly immodest, with *Bilbao* (1978), *Caniche* (1979) and *Lola* (1985) taking place in the urban hells of lowlife characters whose sordidness made it hard for him to escape the label of pornographer/voyeur. It was the success of *Las edades de Lulú* (The Ages of Lulu, 1990) that brought him into the mainstream of a national cinema that had come close to his equal in terms of sexual explicitness. The film was based on Almudena Grandes' attempt to write an erotic novel from a female perspective that nonetheless fell into the trap of imitating the conventions of male-oriented pornography, and the film was more of the same.[16] No Spanish actress would touch the role of Lulú for its scenes of bondage, rape, sado-masochistic orgies and genital shaving, and it went to the Italian Francesca Neri, who, though dubbed, makes a brave stab at the role of the woman-child who moves from the masochism of male domination to a sadistic addiction to watching gay men fornicate. As one of three male prostitutes that she hires for her viewing pleasure, Javier Bardem made his cinematic debut as the carnal embodiment of Lulú's consumerist desire, choreographing his cohorts in the grim and explicit orgy which drags her down to hell.

Born in Las Palmas, Gran Canaria, in 1969, Bardem is the son of the actress Pilar Bardem and the nephew of the director Juan Antonio Bardem and, like the young Marlon Brando, his strapping physique and bashed-in nose are offset by the intelligence and sadness of his eyes. Bullish in fishnet tights, his performance in Las edades de Lulú is of such astounding physicality that it mocks the film's pretence of respectability. If only he'd winked at the camera he might have saved the film from the hypocrisy of its po-faced derision of porn. However, that wink was not long in coming, for Bigas Luna and the producer Andrés Vicente Gómez hit on the idea of an Iberian trilogy that would become Jamón, jamón, Huevos de oro (Golden Balls, 1993) and La teta y la luna (The Tit and the Moon, 1994), though the notion of a trilogy is far more convincing if the incongruously sweet and nostalgic La teta y la luna is replaced by Las edades de Lulú, not least because all three films now feature Bardem.

Jamón, jamón begins by focusing on a crack in the scrotum of one of the massive billboard-bulls that stands at the side of Spain's motorways, and it continues to hack away at the most blatant symbols of Spanishness and machismo until it uncovers a surrealist undercurrent to their construction that is playfully ironised and celebrated.[17] Bardem plays Raúl, an underwear model and would-be matador who is hired by a possessive mother to seduce her son's pregnant girlfriend, thereby occasioning an Iberian La ronde of such mythic intensity that every character's pretence of sophistication becomes a target for lust in the dust. To wit: Silvia (Penélope Cruz) is pregnant by José Luis (Jordi Mollá), who is a client of her prostitute mother Carmen (Anna Galiena), who's a former lover of Manuel (Juan Diego), who is José Luis' father and therefore married to José Luis' Oedipal-fixated mother Conchita (Stefania Sandrelli), who sleeps with Raúl (Bardem), the guy she hires to charm the pants off Silvia. Like Banderas in ¡Átame!, Bardem in Jamón, jamón adheres to a cult of machismo but undercuts its authority with the homo-erotic narcissism of his character. Even the film's poster acknowledged the displacement of desire in its tag line: 'A film where women eat men and men eat ham', where 'ham' is also the preferred style of acting in a film that is all about showing off. Bardem poses in Samson underpants, bullfights nude in the moonlight and, very much like Brando in *On the Waterfront*, takes a beating that becomes him.

Much of the appeal of *Jamón, jamón* resides in the fact that its stereotyping is not negative; rather it exaggerates clichés of Spanishness to vindicate them, much like the Gay Pride movement celebrates the condition of being gay. The film's narcissism is all-consuming: it aspires to a masturbatory fantasy of Spanishness but rejects all notions of guilt. Unlike the serious debunking of myths and clichés of Spanishness that characterises the cinema of Carlos Saura, Bigas Luna wallows in the fun of Buñuelian dream sequences, Catholic kitsch and Goyaesque pastiche, thereby reflecting the outsize pride in Spanishness that characterised the socialist years and resulted in the renewed and massive popularity of cultural signifiers that were also excuses to party, such as religious festivals, bullfighting and flamenco. In other words *Jamón, jamón* does not laugh at its audience, but with them; whereas Bigas Luna's follow-up *Huevos de oro* (Golden Balls, 1993) simply wasn't laughing. *Huevos de oro* is an incessantly vulgar film in which Bardem plays a thuggish entrepeneur who dreams of putting up a building 'that'll go up like a dick.' Scenes of Bardem bare-chested, strewn with gold and singing karaoke to his beloved Julio Iglesias present a familiar parody of machismo, but Bigas Luna connects this vulgarity with the decline of Spain's ruling Socialist Party in the early 1990s, when its pretence of democracy and socialism collapsed under the weight of scandal, corruption and negative coverage from the big business-backed media. *Huevos de oro* lacks wit, but perhaps the spoiling of the democratic dream had simply vetoed humour. The reverse of *Jamón, jamón*, *Huevos de oro* reveals a shameful sense of Spanishness that Bigas Luna shrugs off by opting for the easier target of the American dream in a redundant epilogue in Miami where, neither tragic nor comic, Bardem ends his days belching in front of the television.

Three films for Bigas Luna and a similar role in Vicente Aranda's *El amante bilingüe* (The Bilingual Lover, 1993) might have typecast Bardem as a dumb but endearing stud, were it not for the actor's determination to explore, rather than exploit his animalism in two films from 1994: Gonzálo Suárez's *El detective y la muerte* (Death and the Detective) and Imanol Uribe's *Días contados* (Running Out of Time), in which he essays the role of Lisardo, a junkie pimp, with conviction. With Manuel Gómez Pereira's *Boca a boca* (Mouth to Mouth, 1995) Bardem increased public and professional perception of his versatility by playing a shy type in a light-hearted comic role and then starred in Almodóvar's *Carne trémula* (Live Flesh, 1997), in which, precisely because he is confined to a wheelchair for most of the film, he gives a performance of such physicality and emotional focus that the film inclines

Javier Bardem as the junkie pimp Lisardo in *Días contados* (Imanol Uribe, 1994)

to that which Paul Julian Smith has described as 'Almodóvar's rediscovery of masculinity' (2000, p.183). Thereafter Bardem starred in Alex de la Iglesia's vicious and humourless *Perdita Durango* (1997), in which the Mexican production's proximity to Hollywood seemed to limit Bardem to the one-dimensionsional machismo that was the fate of Banderas.[18] Nevertheless, Bardem returned to portray sexual ambiguity in Manuel Gómez Pereira's *Entre las piernas* (Between the Legs, 1999) and homosexuality in both Gerardo Vera's semi-autobiographical *Segunda piel* (Second Skin, 1998) and Julian Schnabel's *Before Night Falls* (2000), a bio-pic of the gay Cuban writer Reynaldo Arenas.

In *Segunda piel* Bardem's simpering gay character seduces Alberto (Jordi Mollá) away from his wife Elena (Ariadna Gil), but what might have been a sensitive and insightful examination of latency and contemporary Spanish attitudes to homosexuality turned out to resemble a lurid soap opera. Perhaps that was the point: weren't representations of homosexuality in Spanish cinema as entitled to the sentimental tear-jerker as they were to the reclaimed genres of noir and melodrama in the films of Almodóvar? More importantly, the popular reception given to this and other end of millennium films that dealt with homosexual characters and themes (e.g. Almodóvar's *Todo sobre mi madre*, Albacete, Molina and Menkes' *Más que amor, frenesí* (More than Love, Frenzy) and Juan Luis Iborra and Yolanda García's *Amor de hombre*,

(Man Love) suggested that Spaniards had learnt to relax. Despite the scare-mongering of the socialists, election victory for José María Aznar's People's Party in 1996 had not signified a return to Francoism but an important step forward in Spain's democratic progress, for this swing to right of centre was not a sign of retrograde politics but of stability. Democracy was here to stay and Aznar, if he didn't do what he promised, could simply be voted out in a couple of years. In the event the election victory of the People's Party's was so slim that support from the regions and minorities became a crucial factor in Aznar's survival, thereby cementing the new pluralist identity for Spain and proving that Spaniards had truly broken free from the religious and militarist doctrine that had excluded minority groups such as homosexuals from its society and constitution. When asked to reflect on the dangers of playing another homosexual in Schnabel's *Before Night Falls*, Bardem replied: 'No, it's not any kind of challenge. For me, homosexuality isn't a condition that the character's in. I simply consider it a circumstance, a choice.'[19] It may be a circumstance that Spanish males have only recently been empowered to declare, but for an actor of Bardem's calibre it is a choice that reflects well on the evolution of Spain and the discourse of sexual mobility for the stars of Spanish cinema.

Penélope Cruz

At the dawn of the third millennium Spain is back in the European mainstream and, with Franco consigned to the pre-history of what Spain is today, the concerns of Spaniards are not much different from those of any other western society. Born in Madrid in 1974 and therefore wholly lacking in experience of the dictatorship, Cruz is typical of a generation that grew up in a Spain which placed no limits on their aspirations. She studied classical and Spanish dance and worked as a model and presenter on children's television before playing the eponymous prime cut in *Jamón, jamón* aged just sixteen.[20] Cruz has since admitted that the sex scenes required for her role as the Latin Lolita who creates nympholepsy in everyone around her made the filming an onerous experience and it was a role that she immediately countered as the meek, compliant virgin in Fernando Trueba's *Belle epoque*. At this age Cruz had outsize features (that have harmonised with time) and a squawky voice (that has softened). Her enthusiasm for the lighter comedy of *Belle epoque* led to personable roles in Álvaro Fernández Armero's *Todo es mentira* (Everything's a Lie, 1994) and Fernando Colomo's *Alegre ma non troppo* (1994), before her growing confidence as a dramatic actress won her roles as a prison inmate during the last years of the dictatorship in Azucena Rodríguez's *Entre rojas* (1994),[21] a stab at the classics as one of the lovers crossed by witchcraft in

Penélope Cruz in *Todo sobre mi madre* (Pedro Almodóvar, 1999)

Gerardo Vera's adaptation of Fernando De Rojas' *La Celestina* (The Spanish Bawd, 1996), and the plum role of the young mother who gives birth on a bus in the prologue to Almodóvar's *Carne trémula* (1997). Screaming, sweating, collapsing in happy tears, Cruz turned lack of vanity to her advantage and gave birth to herself as a mature actress, earning herself the admiration and friendship of her director, who clearly cherished her as the serenely pregnant and Aids-ridden nun in *Todo sobre mi madre* (1999). Here she was quietly radiant in her habit and a sensitive team-player in her scenes with the motley group of actresses, but it was still a supporting role and Fernando Trueba's *La niña de tus ojos* (The Girl of Your Dreams, 1999) was an old-fashioned star vehicle; so old-fashioned, in fact, that her role was a combination of Carole Lombard and Imperio Argentina.

La niña de tus ojos is the story of a Spanish film crew at work in Nazi Germany and was clearly inspired by both Ernst Lubitsch's *To Be Or Not To Be* (1942) and the real-life experiences of Argentina, the star of pre-Civil War Spanish cinema.[22] Cruz was radiant in this designer blockbuster, flushed with self-confidence and belting out folk songs with aplomb (partly mimed, partly her own voice). Here was a star not just in the making but stamped 'Made in Spain' and ready to be passed on to Hollywood. With her talent, looks and gutsy femininity, she was the closest Spain had ever dreamt of getting to a post-feminist icon. In her films with Almodóvar and Trueba she'd been dressed up and paraded, but she had also held on to the spotlight for her own ends, going beyond the rigid polarisation of sexual stereotyping that had circumscribed the careers of many during the Franco years and often threatened the same to actresses whose roles in post-Franco cinema associated them with such a dramatic rejection of machismo that it destabilised traditional notions of masculinity: Abril, obviously, but also Carmen Maura in *Mujeres al borde de un ataque de nervios* and *Cómo ser mujer y no morir en el intento* (How To Be A Woman And Not Die In The Attempt, 1991) and Emma Suárez in *La ardilla roja* (The Red Squirrel, 1993) and *Sobreviviré* (I Will Survive, 1999). Cruz, on the other hand, was a model of reconciliation between the sexes that fulfilled both genders' notions of female identity in contemporary Spain. She was nothing less than a reconstituted ideal – a role she played to perfection in Alejandro Amenábar's *Abre los ojos* (1997).

Amenábar is one of the new generation of Spanish film directors whose films, as Barry Jordan has described, 'show little sign of following any prescriptive political or cultural agenda. Indeed [they] appear not to be burdened by the weight of the past or the need to settle any political or ideological scores' (2000, p.75). Instead, Amenábar feeds off Hollywood and MTV, video games and the Internet, but has harnessed this enthusiasm to an astute sense of narrative and an exemplary way with genre.[23] Amenábar also typifies the energy and initiative of Cruz's generation. Born in 1972, he made his first short film at the age of nineteen and by 1995, aged just a Wellesian twenty-three, was at work on *Tesis* (Thesis), his first full-length feature. *Tesis* was an exercise in the thriller genre that pitted the resourceful film student Ángela (Ana Torrent) against a conspiracy of snuff-movie *auteurs* in the University of Madrid; but the potential for in-jokery was dismissed by the brashness of Amenábar's technique, the mastery of his ambition and the scope of his cine-literacy.[24] Finely tuned scenes of menace punctuate a complex essay on voyeurism and female subjectivity that centres upon the brilliant casting and performance of Torrent, once the little, watchful Ana of Erice's *El espíritu de la colmena* and Saura's *Cría cuervos*, now grown and still failing to get a grip on reality by confusing her look with her imagination. *Tesis* was a major commercial success amongst young Spaniards, who responded to the youthful characters as much as to the tricks of the genre, while critics and older viewers enjoyed its respectful intertextuality about the persona of Torrent. This latter quality was a fluke, however, as Amenábar's first choice for the role had been Cruz, for whom (in collaboration with Mateo Gil) he wrote the role of Sofía in *Abre los ojos*, where, in characteristic mode, Cruz offsets the film's obsession with male angst and narcissism with her calm and confident femininity.

Abre los ojos begins with a thrillingly unsettling sequence of César, a handsome rich kid (Eduardo Noriega), driving into the centre of a perpetually frantic Madrid and finding the streets deserted; but then pulls back from science fiction and starts again like a youthful genre film by detailing the fragility of César's friendship with his ordinary mate Pelayo (Fele Martínez).[25] It's a bonding of males that comes unstuck when Pelayo brings Sofía (Cruz) to César's birthday party and the lads find themselves in competition for her affections, with Cruz playing the object of desire who becomes a symbol of life itself in César's struggle to make sense of a terminal case of déjà vu. It's a complex, disturbing film with a bizarre, elliptical narrative and a climax that seems disappointing only because the explanation of a life already lived being revisited through dreams undermines the credible, intense and personable playing of the leads. 'She could be the girl of my dreams,' protests Pelayo; but the central conceit of this hybrid of science fiction with the sexual paranoia of a Hitchcockian thriller is that Sofía is, quite literally, the girl of César's nightmares. Indeed Amenábar made Cruz watch Hitchcock's *Vertigo* (1958) several times in preparation for the role and his script clearly aspires to a tantalising intertextuality: e.g. *Vertigo*: 'If I'm mad, that would explain it'; *Abre los ojos*: 'No, you're not mad, but what if I told you you were dreaming.'[26]

It may be argued that the film is an anonymous exercise in genre, whose Hitchcockian references cannot disguise a lack of substance; but that is missing the point of a film which deals with themes of anonymity and conformity in contemporary Spanish society. César is unable to come to terms with the facial disfigurement resulting from an accident and hides his pain and solitude behind an expressionless plastic face. Sofía, meanwhile, is an actress whose masks (of make-up and the roles she plays) suggest an equivalent lack of identity. Cruz too, though eminently watchable, is a cipher who, by her own admission, 'tried to arrive almost vacant [*vacía*] every morning on the set' (Rioyo, 1997, p.12). Similarly, since she arrived in Hollywood, many photographers have disregarded her Spanishness and rendered her as the 'woman as child, woman as kitten' that Roland Barthes saw in Audrey Hepburn (1983, p.382).[27]

Many Spaniards fear that Spain might also be losing its identity by allowing its cultural differences to be erased by the flood of American culture and subsumed into the concept of a united Europe. They protest against laws and regulations that bring Spain into line with other countries. They resist the impact of the English language on Castilian Spanish and the influence of American culture on their own. But it's a worry that originates with an older generation, for whom thirty years is less than a lifetime and memories of oppression still punctuate their remembrances of youth. Meanwhile younger Spaniards embrace an optimistic, multi-cultural definition of Spanishness that makes them free citizens of their world. Cruz is not just a sex symbol, but a hard-working young woman from Madrid, whose cosmopolitan education and background makes her more at home in Hollywood, perhaps, than

Banderas or Abril. In her first American films Cruz played a Mexican in *All the Pretty Horses*, a Greek in *Captain Correlli's Mandolin* and a Brazilian in *Woman On Top* (all 2001), and then what else but herself in a Hollywood remake of *Abre los ojos* called *Vanilla Sky* (also 2001), a tribute to her stardom that merely required her to repeat the role of Sofía alongside Tom Cruise.

Films need stars because the public needs film stars. Most film stars are just thrilled to be so desired, but the best of them can also reveal contemporary attitudes to sex and sexuality in the way that they choose and play roles which challenge and explore the limits and prejudices of that primal audience response. In Spain the best have done just that, adding to an accumulating discourse on sexual mores that reveals much about the country's social and political evolution since the transition, because what has made them film stars and sex symbols is that they have personified the sexuality of the Zeitgeist, however fleeting or eternal the moment. The ambiguity of Banderas is indelibly linked to the bewilderment brought on by liberalism, while the vengeful femininity of Abril appears like a grudge against decades of repression. The overripe machismo of Bardem suggests a paean to the period of socialist excess and, in its deconstruction, a diatribe against its deceit. And Cruz? Cruz went to Hollywood: a film star in the United States, she was living the Spanish dream. Definitions of gender are limiting, whether they are imposed by political regimes, religious doctrines, film studios or academic thesis alike; but star quality, like pornography, is impossible to define, you only know what it is when you see it. There is, however, a fabulous, enigmatic line in Almodóvar's *Todo sobre mi madre* that comes close to an explanation: 'A woman is authentic only in so far as she resembles her dream of herself.' Banderas, Abril, Bardem and Cruz are surely the dreams against which the Spanish audience has checked its authenticity.

Notes

1. Nevertheless backstreet clinics and markets respectively did a secret trade in both. In 1975 abortions were equivalent to 40 per cent of live births in Spain. Abortion was legalised in Spain in 1985.
2. John Hooper claims of the legalisation of contraceptives in Spain that 'few developments have had as great an impact on the nature of contemporary Spain' (1995, p.156).
3. See Chapter 6 for a contextual analysis of these two films.
4. Spain's first sex shop opened in 1978 and closed five months later.
5. Banderas' obsessive fan happens to be called Antonio and, as this is Almodóvar's most autobiographical film, there appears to be some wish-fulfilment at work.
6. In addition, *¡Átame!* conspires to insult those who blithely adhere to retrograde assumptions of normality with references to Don Siegel's *Invasion of the Body*

Snatchers (1956) (on a poster in the editing suite) and George Romero's *Night of the Living Dead* (1969) (on television); two films that pointedly reveal 'normal' humans to be a brainless, unfeeling mob of zombies.

7. Almodóvar has a script already prepared for the time when he can unite Banderas with Penélope Cruz under his direction.

8. The filming of *Amantes* was in fact delayed while Abril dedicated herself to her new child, and it was her new maturity that attracted her to the role of Luisa. This was a foregone conclusion for Aranda, who had already given the role of Trini to Maribel Verdú.

9. Jorge Sanz, meanwhile, would become associated with similar roles as the clumsy male object of desire, falling prey to predatory older females such as those played by Emma Suárez in *Orquesta Club Virgina* (Virginia Orchestra Club, 1992), Veronica Forqué in *¿Por qué lo llaman amor cuando quieren decir sexo?* (Why Do They Call It Love When They Mean Sex?, 1992) and, most famously, in Fernando Trueba's *Belle epoque* (1992) a film that also features Maribel Verdú in typically lustful mode.

10. However, as Abril has revealed, the model for Luisa was not a contemporary concept of feminine independence but Abril's own grandmother: 'My grandmother is who I play in *Amantes*. That's what she was like, everything or nothing, rich or poor; she was fantastic, a white woman, almost a redhead, beautiful, daughter of Irish folk and Spaniards. She was very strong. Now she must be laughing at what I do' (Rioyo, 1995, p.24).

11. 'I'm in love with the camera,' admits Abril, 'and I can't resist the impulse to touch it and find out what it means, that it has volume, weight, a particular smell' (Álvares and Frías, 1991, p.293).

12. The trick with the handkerchief was improvised on set and was suggested by the actor Jorge Sanz.

13. In addition, the coda appears as if it were imposed by the censor in order to correct the absence of a scene of their capture and as such it carries an echo of censorial interference with the endings of films such as Nieves Conde's *Surcos* (Furrows, 1951) and Buñuel's *Viridiana* (1961).

14. Abril's other, mostly unfortunate, roles abroad included small parts in Richard Lester's *Robin and Marian*, Jean Jacques Beineix's *The Moon in the Gutter*, Nagisa Oshima's *Max, mon amour* and Barry Levinson's *Jimmy Hollywood*.

15. Born in Barcelona in 1946, Luna worked for the Estudi Gris in Barcelona and one of his tables features in the Mae West room of the Salvador Dalí museum in Figueras – a compliment that he returned in *Huevos de oro*, where the protagonist's home includes Dalí's sofa like Mae West's lips.

16. Luna wrote the script in collaboration with Almudena Grandes.

17. The bulls originate with Osborne brandy. They were to be removed in the mid-1990s, until a public outcry ensured their preservation.

18. Not just in geographical terms – *Perdita Durango* was also a semi-sequel to David Lynch's *Wild at Heart* (1990).

19. Interview with Javier Bardem in *El País* (10 September 2000, p.40).

20. Cruz made her acting debut the previous year in a chaste role in an episode of the soft-porn television series *Lady Roxana* that was helmed by Jaime Chávarri.

21. The title is a play on words. 'Entre rejas' means 'behind bars' while 'entre rojas' means 'amongst reds' (i.e. communists).

22. Trueba has denied the inspiration and pointed out that the character of Cruz's besotted fan was Goebbels, not Hitler.

23. Born in Chile in 1972 to a Chilean father and Spanish mother, Amenábar was brought to Spain when his parents fled the coup of Pinochet one year later. By all accounts he was a brilliant student at school and university, while his interest in cinema was nurtured by an American neighbour with a VCR and frequent visits to Madrid's art-house cinemas in the company of his older brother, another gifted student whose linguistic skills had made him a fan of foreign, subtitled films (Sempere, 2000, p.18).

24. Amenábar also writes the music for his films and others, including José Luis Cuerda's *La lengua de las mariposas* (1998).

25. This scene was actually shot a full year before principal photography began as Amenábar took advantage of a public holiday to shoot the exasperatingly single-take scene with Eduardo Noriega, the star of *Tesis*. Lacking contract and budget, Amenábar instructed his friend Noriega not to look behind during the shot in case the producers demanded another actor for the role in the future. Noriega, needless to say, made sure he looked behind a good three or four times and thereby ensured the role was his (Sempere, 2000, p.92).

26. *Abre los ojos* also features various visual references to *Vertigo*, including spiralling camerawork and Sofía stepping out of a doorway glowing green à la Kim Novak.

27. Not the least of these attempts was the 8 May 2000 edition of *Newsweek* that used Cruz to illustrate its cover story on 'The New Faces of Spain.'

FURTHER READING

Amell, S. (ed.) (1990) *Literature, the Arts, and Democracy: Spain in the eighties* (Associated University Presses, London).

A collection of essays that offers an interdisciplinary survey of Spanish culture and society in the 1980s and includes an important essay on Spanish cinema by Pilar Miró.

Aranda, F. (1976) *Luis Buñuel: A critical biography* (Da Capo, New York).

An extensive filmography and an anthology of Buñuel's surrealist and related texts distinguishes this enthusiastic account of the director's life and work.

Arocena, C. (1996) *Víctor Erice* (Cátedra, Madrid).

A valuable addition to the Cátedra series of biographies of film directors. Arocena offers a systematic and exhaustive analysis of Erice's films. Spanish text.

Besas, P. (1985) *Behind the Spanish Lens: Spanish cinema under fascism and democracy* (Arden Press, Denver, COL, USA).

A detailed, often personal account of the history of Spanish cinema from its beginnings until 1985, with numerous interviews with key figures and an informed perspective on events. In addition, Besas offers fascinating accounts of the life and work of Samuel Bronston, useful filmographies and an English translation title index.

Borau, J.L. (ed.) (1998) *Diccionario del cine español de la Academia de las artes y las ciencias cinemtaográficas de España* (Alianza editorial, Madrid).

Indispensable encyclopedia has thousands of informative entries on directors, key films, actors, producers, genres, etc. The product of more than eighty collaborators, three editors and the supervision of José Luis Borau, this thorough and well-illustrated volume includes an index of more than five thousand films. Spanish text.

Buñuel, L. (1983) *My Last Breath* (Flamingo, London).

The master's warm, philosophical dissertation on the vagaries of his life, especially regarding his childhood, formative years and experiences of the Surrealist movement, Spain, France and Hollywood. By turns hilarious and profound, this glorious book is far more than an autobiography; it is, as Salman Rushdie claims, 'pure delight . . . as funny and provocative as the old *chien*'s best movies; than which there is no higher praise.'

Deveny, T. (1993) *Cain On Screen: Contemporary Spanish cinema* (Scarecrow, London).

Deveny's analysis of contemporary Spanish cinema centres on the theme of 'cainism' – the conflict between brothers. Academic and thorough, Deveny offers readings of films by Aranda, Ricardo Franco and Carlos Saura.

D'Lugo, M. (1991) *Carlos Saura: The practice of seeing* (Princeton University Press, Princeton, NJ).

A contextual study of the life and work of Carlos Saura, with a keen sense of political history and close readings of many of the director's films. A model of its kind. D'Lugo focuses on representations of Spanishness and effects a profound analysis of subjectivity and the reinscription of personal and national history as it appears in Saura's films.

Durgnat, R. (1967) *Luis Buñuel* (University of California Press, Los Angeles, CA).

An early, accessible account of the life and films of Luis Buñuel with plot summaries and accounts of the shooting and critical reception of most of his films.

Edwards, G. (1982) *The Discreet Art of Luis Buñuel* (Marion Boyars, London).

A close, thematic analysis of nine of Buñuel's films including *El ángel exterminador*, *Tristana* and *Viridiana*. Includes biographical details and cast and plot information.

Edwards, G. (1995) *Indecent Exposures: Buñuel, Saura, Erice and Almodóvar* (Marion Boyars, London).

Close, accessible readings of key films by four Spanish directors that relate many of these films to Spanish cultural and literary traditions.

Evans, P.W. (1995) *The Films of Luis Buñuel: Subjectivity and desire* (Clarendon, Oxford).

A complex and challenging analysis of the films of Luis Buñuel, including the lesser known *películas alimenticias* (bread-and-butter films) that he made while in exile in Mexico. Exhaustive and compelling, the book includes a detailed filmography.

Evans, P.W. (ed.) (1999) *Spanish Cinema: The auteurist tradition* (Oxford University Press).

A wide-ranging collection of academic essays on key films from 1952 to the present day by the most important Spanish directors. Includes Marsha Kinder on Aranda's *Cambio de sexo*, Peter William Evans on Borau's *Furtivos*, Jo Labanyi on Buñuel's *Tristana* and Paul Julian Smith on Erice's *El espíritu de la colmena*. Mostly accessible critical language and a wealth of valuable insights.

Fiddian, R. and Evans, P.W. (1989) *Challenges to Authority: Fiction and film in contemporary Spain* (Tamesis, London).

Essays on novels and films (Buñuel's *Viridiana*, Saura's *Stress es tres, tres* and *Carmen*) that focus on the social and cultural significance of each.

Graham, H. and Labanyi, J. (eds) (1995) *Spanish Cultural Studies: An introduction* (Oxford University Press).

An interdisciplinary approach to a wide-ranging study of twentieth century culture and society in Spain. Includes essays on Spanish cinema by leading academics, including Peter William Evans on CIFESA and Jo Labanyi on post-modernism and the problem of cultural identity.

Gubern, R. (1999) *Proyector de luna* (Anagrama, Barcelona).

Detailed but clearly structured account of the Generation of 1927 and its relationship with the cinema. Thorough and expertly documented by one of Spain's leading film historians, this invaluable book includes fascinating accounts of the *Cine-club Español* and *La gaceta literaria* along with analysis of key films and literary works. Spanish text.

Gubern, R. *et al.* (1995) *Historia del cine español* (Cátedra, Madrid).

Written and edited by the most prestigious Spanish film historians, this volume attempts a global view of Spanish cinema and follows the socio-historical evolution of the form. Scant on such subjects as regional cinema post-Franco, the book is none the less essential reading on the subject of early Spanish cinema. Includes an exhaustive bibliography. Spanish text.

Heredero, C.F. (1997) *Espejo de miradas: Entrevistas con nuevos directores del cine español de los años noventa* (Festival de cine de Alcalá de Henares).

This weighty tome includes revealing, in-depth interviews with Spanish directors of the 1990s, including Julio Medem, Alejandro Amenábar, Iciar Bollaín, Álex de la Iglesia and Gracia Querejeta. Spanish text.

Higginbotham, V. (1988) *Spanish Film Under Franco* (University of Texas Press, Austin, TX).

An analysis of Spanish cinema under Franco as both art and political discourse. Higginbotham offers incisive readings of the films of Buñuel, Saura, Bardem and Berlanga and includes a description of early Spanish cinema.

Hopewell, J. (1986) *Out of the Past: Spanish cinema after Franco* (British Film Institute, London).

Hopewell analyses Spanish cinema in its relation to the history of Spain and focuses on the oppression of the dictatorship before describing the evolution of Spanish cinema since the transition to the mid-1980s.

Jordan, B. and Morgan-Tamosunas, R. (1998) *Contemporary Spanish Cinema* (Manchester University Press).

A compelling analysis of the main trends and issues in Spanish cinema since the transition to democracy. Includes illuminating essays on popular genres, representations of gender and regional cinema.

Jordan, B. and Morgan-Tamosunas, R. (eds) (2000) *Contemporary Spanish Cultural Studies* (Arnold, London).

An interdisciplinary approach to contemporary Spanish culture and society includes essays on the subject of the cinema by leading scholars including Barry Jordan on cinema and national identity, Rikki Morgan-Tamosunas on nostalgia in contemporary cinema and Núria Triana Toribio on *la movida* in the films of Pedro Almodóvar.

Kinder, M. (1993) *Blood Cinema: The reconstruction of national identity in Spain* (University of California Press, Berkeley, CA).

An investigation into the question of national cinema that synthesises film history with cultural analysis and produces a challenging, provocative and persuasive series of essays on such films as Bardem's *Muerte de un ciclista*, Saura's *Los golfos*, Borau's *Río abajo* and Almodóvar's *Tacones lejanos*. Kinder utilises a variety of contemporary critical theories that include feminist discourse, Marxist theory and psychoanalysis and also conveys a valuable global perspective on Spanish cinema.

Kinder, M. (1997) *Refiguring Spain: Cinema/media/representation* (Duke University Press, Durham, NC).

A collection of academic essays that explores the central role played by film and other media in redefining the national and cultural identity of Spain since the transition to democracy. Includes Paul Julian Smith on Almodóvar's *Matador* and *La ley del deseo*, Marvin D'Lugo on Bigas Luna's *La teta y la luna*, Jaume Martí-Olivella on the films of Pilar Miró and Arantxa Lacano, and Stephen Tropiano on the films of Eloy de la Iglesia.

Smith, P.J. (1992) *Laws of Desire: Questions of homosexuality in Spanish writing and film 1960–1990* (Clarendon, Oxford).

Smith effects close, analytical readings of films and novels that raise questions of homosexuality in Spanish society and history. A fascinating cultural study that includes perceptive and revealing analyses of the films of Eloy de la Iglesia and Pedro Almodóvar.

Smith, P.J. (2000) *Desire Unlimited: The cinema of Pedro Almodóvar*, 2nd edn (Verso, London).

Smith's benchmark study of Pedro Almodóvar effects a detailed analysis of the themes and context of his films while conveying an infectious and compelling enthusiasm for his subject. Smith addresses questions of gender, nostalgia, nationality and sexuality while tracing the evolution of Almodóvar's cinema. The first edition of this work ended with *Tacones lejanos*; the second edition includes articles reprinted from *Sight and Sound* on the director's successive films and includes an interesting interview with the director.

Vernon, K. and Morris, B. (eds) (1995) *Post-Franco, Postmodern: The films of Pedro Almodóvar*, (Greenwood, London).

A collection of essays that traces the evolution of Almodóvar as a post-modernist film-maker. A variety of contextual analyses are offered by Paul Julian Smith, Marsha Kinder, Marvin D'Lugo and many others.

BIBLIOGRAPHY

Alameda, S. (1997) Interview with Carlos Saura in *El País*, 7 September 1997, p.11.
Álvares, R. and Frías, B. (1991) *Vicente Aranda & Victoria Abril: El cine como pasión* (Valladolid 36 semana internacional de cine).
Ángulo, J., Heredero, C.F. and Rebordinos, J.L. (1994) *Entre el documental y la ficción: el cine de Imanol Uribe* (Filmoteca Vasca y Caja Vital Kutxa).
Ángulo, J., Heredero, C.F. and Rebordinos, J.L. (1996) *Elías Querejeta: La producción como discurso* (Filmoteca Vasca).

Barthes, R. (1983) *Mythologies* (Paladin, London).
Besas, P. (1985) *Behind the Spanish Lens: Spanish cinema under fascism and democracy* (Arden Press, Denver, COL, USA).
Boyero, C. (1988) Interview with Carlos Saura in *El Independiente*, 9 April 1988, p.99.
Brandon, R. (2000) *Surreal Lives* (Papermac, London).
Brasó, E. (1974) *Carlos Saura* (Taller de Ediciones Josefina Betantor, Madrid).
Buñuel, L. (1983) *My Last Breath* (Flamingo, London).

Caparrós Lera, J.M. (1998) *Cine español: una historia por autonomías*, Vols I and II (Centro de Investigaciones Film-Historia).
Cerón Gómez, J.F. (1998) *El cine de Juan Antonio Bardem* (Universidad de Murcia – Primavera cinematográfica de Lorca, Spain).
Cinemanía (2000) 'Noticias de España', June, No.57, p.40. No author credited.
Colmena, E. (1996) *Vicente Aranda* (Cátedra, Madrid).

D'Lugo, M. (1991) *Carlos Saura: The practice of seeing* (Princeton University Press, Princeton, NJ).
Dyer, R. (1992) 'Stars' in Mast, G., Cohen, M. and Braudy, L. (eds) *Film Theory and Criticism*, 4th edn (Oxford University Press) pp.622–28.

Evans, P.W. (1993) 'Back to the future: cinema and democracy' in Graham, H. and Labanyi, J. (eds) *Spanish Cultural Studies: An introduction* (Oxford University Press) pp.326–32.
Evans, P.W. (1999) 'Furtivos: my mother, my lover' in Evans, P.W. (ed.) *Spanish Cinema: The auteurist tradition* (Oxford University Press) pp.115–28.

Fernán Gómez, F. (1998) *El tiempo amarillo, memorias 1921–1997* (Editorial Debate, Madrid).

Gubern, R. (1999) *Proyector de luna* (Anagrama, Barcelona).
Gubern, R. *et al.* (1995) *Historia del cine español* (Cátedra, Madrid).

Heredero, C.F. (1999) *20 nuevos directores del cine español* (Alianza Editorial, Madrid).

Higginbotham, V. (1988) *Spanish Film Under Franco* (University of Texas Press, Austin, TX).

Hooper, J. (1995) *The New Spaniards* (Penguin, Harmondsworth).

Hopewell, J. (1986) *Out of the Past: Spanish cinema after Franco* (British Film Institute, London).

Jordan, B. (2000) 'How Spanish is it?: Spanish cinema and national identity' in Jordan, B. and Morgan-Tamosunas, R. (eds) *Contemporary Spanish Cultural Studies* (Arnold, London) pp.68–78.

Jordan, B. and Morgan-Tamosunas, R. (1998) *Contemporary Spanish Cinema* (Manchester University Press).

Kinder, M. (1993) *Blood Cinema: The reconstruction of national identity in Spain* (University of California Press, Berkeley, CA).

Kinder, M. (1997) *Refiguring Spain: Cinema/media/representation* (Duke University Press, Durham, NC).

Kinder, M. (1999) 'Sex change and cultural transformation in Aranda and Abril's "Cambio de sexo"' in Evans, P.W. (ed.) *Spanish Cinema: The auteurist tradition* (Oxford University Press) pp.128–46.

Lorca, F. García (1994) *Obras completas* (Akal Bolsillo, Madrid).

Maeterlinck, M. (1901) *The Life of the Bee*, trans. Alfred Sutro (Dodd, Mead & Company, New York).

Medem, J. (1997) *Tierra/Mari en la tierra* (Planeta, Barcelona).

Medem, J. (1998) *Los amantes del círculo polar* (Alta Films, Madrid).

Molina Foix, V. (1984) Interview with Víctor Erice, *Positif*, 278 (Paris).

Montero, R. (2000) 'The Silent Revolution: The social and cultural advances of women in democratic Spain' in Jordan, B. and Morgan-Tamosunas, R. (eds) *Contemporary Spanish Cultural Studies* (Arnold, London) pp.381–5.

Mulvey, L. (1992) 'Visual pleasure and narrative cinema' in Mast, G., Cohen, M. and Braudy, L. (eds) *Film Theory and Criticism*, 4th edn (Oxford University Press) pp.746–57.

Pablo, S. (1995) *Cien años de cine en el País Vasco 1986–1995* (Diputación Foral de Alava).

Pérez Manrique, J.M. (1993) *Montxo Armendáriz: Imagen y narración de libertad* (Ayuntamiento de Burgos).

Pérez Turrent, T., de la Colina, J. (1993) *Buñuel por Buñuel* (Plot, Madrid).

Preston, P. (1999) *¡Comrades!* (HarperCollins, London).

Rioyo, J. (1995) 'Reina Victoria' in *Cinemanía*, November, No.2, pp.22–9.

Rioyo, J. (1996) 'Almodóvar y el caché de Banderas' in *Cinemanía*, January, No.4, p.53.

Rioyo, J. (1997) 'Los ojos de Amenábar' in *Cinemanía*, December, No.27, pp.10–14.

Rioyo, J. (1999) 'Javier Bardem y Victoria Abril: Obsesos por el sexo' in *Cinemanía*, January, No.40, pp.10–14.

Roldán Larreta, C. (1999) *El cine del País Vasco: de Ama lur (1968) a Airbag (1997)* (Eusko Ikasuntza, San Sebastian).

Roma, P. (1998) 'Un navarro a la conquista de Hollywood' in *El País Semanal*, No.1119, 8 March 1998, p.34.

Sánchez Vidal, A. (1988) *El cine de Carlos Saura* (Caja de Ahorros de la Inmaculada, Zaragoza).
Sempere, A. (2000) *Alejandro Amenábar: Cine en las venas* (Nuer Ediciones, Madrid).
Sharrock, D. (1992) 'Flamenco on Fire' in *The Guardian*, 6 March 1992, p.26.
Smith, P.J. (2000) *Desire Unlimited: The cinema of Pedro Almodóvar*, 2nd edn (Verso, London).

Uribe, I. (1994) *Días contados* – script (Alma Plot, Madrid).

Vernon, K. and Morris, B. (eds) (1995) *Post-Franco, Postmodern: The films of Pedro Almodóvar*, (Greenwood, London).

Web sites

1. The Unofficial Julio Medem Web site: http://socios.las.es/~bravo/inicio.htm
   This excellent site is maintained by Ignacio Bravo Villalba and includes biographical details, photographs, stills and a selection of articles from newspapers and magazines.

2. Cinexos – the Spanish cinema Webring: http://multimania.com/cinecita/webring.htm
   Contains links to many different Web sites dealing with Spanish-speaking cinema, including sites about South American and Cuban cinema.

3. Spanish cinema Web site: www.ciudadfutura.com
   Lively and entertaining Web site about film in general but with links to specific information on Spanish and South American cinema. Frequently updated.

Other resources

1. The Ocho y Medio Bookshop, Calle Martín de los Heros, 23, 28008, Madrid. Tel: 91-5590628; Fax: 91-5412831; E-mail: ochoymedio@arrakis.es Web site: www.ochoymedio.arrakis.es
   This marvellous shop close to Madrid's Plaza de España is run by Jesús Robles and María Silveyro, who sell a massive selection of books on Spanish and world cinema that includes academic texts as well as commercial publications. Possibly the best shop of its kind in Europe and a first-stop resource for fans and researchers of Spanish cinema. International mail order service available.

2. Filmoteca Española, Cetra. de la Dehesa de la Villa, s/n. 28040, Madrid. Tel: 91-5490011; Fax: 91-5497348; Web site: http://www.mcu.es

Spanish film library and viewing facilities, for which there is a waiting list of several months. Also very efficient illustrations service.

3. Basque Filmoteca, Calle Sancho el Sabio, 17, Trasera. 20010, San Sebastián. Tel: 943–468484; Fax: 943–469998.

4. Filmoteca of Catalonia/Filmoteca de la Generalitat de Catalunya, Portal de Santa Madrona, 6–8, 08001, Barcelona. Tel: 93–3162780; Fax: 93–3162781; E-mail: kfgc0001@correu.gencat.es

5. Academia de las Artes y Ciencias Cinematográficas, Calle Sagasta 20, 3° Derecha, 28004, Madrid. Tel: 91–5934648; Fax: 91–5931492; E-mail: acacine@render.es

6. Madrid Film School (Escuela de cinematografía y del audiovisual de la Comunidad de Madrid), Calle Juan de Orduña, 3, Ciudad de la Imagen, Pozuelo de Alarcón, 28223, Madrid. Tel: 91–5121074; Fax: 91–5121070; E-mail: ecam@mail.sendanet.es

   Holds many and varied short, intensive courses as well as longer, vocational courses.

7. San Sebastián Film Festival, Pl. Oquendo, s/n. 20004, San Sebastián, Guipúzcoa. Tel: 943–481212; Fax: 943–481218; E-mail: ssiff@sansebastianfestival.com Web site: http://sansebastianfestival.com

8. Cervantes Institute/Instituto Cervantes Web site: www.cervantes.es

   This is the Spanish portal to all the different Institutes around the world. The Institute holds many and varied cultural events including film screenings and talks by academic specialists in the field of Spanish cinema. Also offers postal rental scheme for Spanish films.

9. Cornerhouse, Greater Manchester Arts Centre, 70 Oxford Street, Manchester M1 5NH, UK. Tel: 0161–2001516; E-mail: viva@cornerhouse.org; Web site: www.cornerhouse.org/cinema/festivals

   Holds ¡VIVA!, the annual Spanish Film Festival around March, with screenings of new films, retrospectives and visiting special guests.

Magazines and journals

1. Cinemanía E-mail: cinemania@progresa.es

   Quality monthly Spanish film magazine with a healthy bias towards Spanish cinema. Contains detailed interviews with Spanish film-makers and actors, shooting reports and reviews as well as retrospective articles and debate. Essential.

2. Fotogramas
   E-mail: fotogramas@hachette.es

   Long-running, monthly Spanish film magazine. Enthusiastic and entertaining.

3. Nickelodeon
   Web site: www.nickel-odeon.com

   Regular academic journal contains articles, memoirs, interviews and scripts of Spanish and world cinema.

INDEX

Numbers in bold indicate illustrations.

215

Misterios de Barcelona, Los, 20
Molina, Ángela, 76, 84fn21
Molina, Miguel, 186
Molina, Paula, 123
Mollá, Jordi, 196, 198
Montero, Rosa, 183
Morán, Manolo, 45
Morena clara, 31–2, **32**
Morente, Enrique, 82
Morgan-Tamosunas, Rikki, 80, 185
movida, la, 132, 125, 126, 127, 185
Muchacha de las bragas de oro, La, 117, 118, 190
Muerte de Mikel, La, 145, 146–7, **146**, 151, 153
Muerte de un ciclista, 5, 47–51, **48**
Muertos de risa, 154
Mujeres al borde de un ataque de nervios, 126, 186, 187, 201
Muñoz, Amparo, 115
Muñoz Fontán, José, 54
Muñoz Molina, Antonio, 153
Muñoz Suay, Ricardo, 44, 113
Munt, Silvia, 105
Murnau, F.W., 25
Murúa, Lautaro, 117

Nacional III, 112
Nadie hablará de nosotras cuando hayamos muerto, 194
Nafarrako Ikazkinak, 143
national interest classification, 7, 40, 63
neo-realism, 5, 40, 46, 48, 51, 52, 62, 63, 114
Neri, Francesca, 196
Neville, Edgar, 26
New Spanish Cinema, 1, 7, 8, 55, 114, 115
New York film festival, 7, 51
Nido, El, 108fn28
Nieves Conde, José Antonio, 40, 62
Nimri, Najwa, 155, 177, 179
Niña de tus ojos, La, 200
Noche oscura, La, 74
NO-DO, 10, 39, 47
Noriega, Eduardo, 201, 205fn25
Noticias y Documentales Cinematográficos, see NO-DO
Nova cançó, La, 113
Novia ensangrentada, La, 114
Novio a la vista, 46
Novo, Nancho, 167, 169, 177
Nuestro cine, 87
Núñez, Iñaki, 138

Obabakoak, 156
Objetivo, 46, 47, 62
Official Film School (EOC), 4, 5, 41, 55, 62, 63, 87, 114, 124, 136, 138
Ojos vendados, Los, 73
Olasagasti, Eneko, 155
Olea, Pedro, 141, 156fn1
Olvidados, Los, 27, 52, 64

100 Days of Sodom, 24, 25
On the Waterfront, 197
Open Your Eyes, see Abre los ojos
Ópera prima, 123–4, **124**, 130, 132fn19
Ordet, 4
Orduña, Juan de, 28, 39
Oreja, Marcelino, 139
Orquesta club Virginia, 204fn9
Ortuaste, Juan, 157fn9
Other Side of the Wind, The, 12
Outrage, see ¡Dispara!

Pablo, Luis de, 13fn6
paella western, 112
Pagés, María, 80
Pajarico, 82, 104
Pájaro de la felicidad, El, 132fn22
Paredes, Marisa, 128, 194
Parisian Committee of Occupations, 68
Partido Popular, 130, 149, 193, 199
Pasajes, 155
Pascual Duarte, 2, 10, 111, 185
Pasión turca, La, 119
Pasolini, Pier Paulo, 66
Patas en la cabeza, 160, 177
Pathé, 16, 18, 19
Patria Films, 29
Patrimonio nacional, 112
Pays des Basques, Le, 135
PCE, see Communist Party
Peckinpah, Sam, 66, 154
Pelotari, 136
Peña, Candela, 129
Peña, Vicky, 105
Penella, Emma, 56
Pepi, Luci, Bom y otras chicas del montón, 125, 126, 127, 129
Peppermint frappé, 8, 66–9
Pequeño ruiseñor, El, 86
Perdita Durango, 154, 198
Perojo, Benito, 3, 28–34
Peromarta, Eduardo Jimeno, 14
Perro andaluz, see Chien andalou, Un
Perro del hortelano, El, 132fn22
Philadelphia, 190
Picasso, Pablo, 69
Pico, El, 156fn1
Piedra, Emiliano, 75
Pinal, Silvia, 53
Pi, Rosario, 36fn23
Pisito, El, 55
Plácido, 55–6
Plaza, José Carlos, 119
Plenilunio, 153
PNV, 135, 137, 140, 141, 142, 149
policíaca, 112, 119
Poncela, Eusebio, 186
Ponce, Pere, 195
¿Por qué lo llaman amor cuando quieren decir sexo?, 120, 204fn9